Between the Lines

Dorian Williams

Between the Lines

Further Reminiscences

Methuen · London

First published 1984
© 1984 Dorian Williams
Printed in Great Britain for
Methuen London Ltd
11 New Fetter Lane, London EC4P 4EE
by Richard Clay (The Chaucer Press) Ltd
Bungay, Suffolk

British Library Cataloguing in Publication Data

Williams, Dorian, *1914*–
   Between the Lines.
   1. Williams, Dorian   2. Horsemen
  and horsewomen—Great Britain—Biography
   I. Title
   798'.092'4   SF284.52.W54

ISBN 0-413-54140-1

Contents

Acknowledgement and thanks for permission to reproduce photographs are due to Jim Meads for plates 7a, 7b, 8a, 8b and 10b; to Stanley Hurwitz for plate 9b; to Hugo M. Czerny for plates 10a and 12b; to Leslie Lane for plates 11a, 11b and 13a; to Keystone for plate 13b; to Charles Torrington for plate 14b; and to the *Field* for plate 15.

Illustrations

Foscote

B, dear,

By the time that you read this I will be seventy! It is incredible – or so it seems to me! I just do not feel any different from the small boy at Hawtreys who used to write to his elder sister at Endcliffe; or the adolescent at Harrow who wrote to the part-time deb travelling around Europe; or the rather pleased with himself young man about town – trying to find a job in the depressing thirties.

This feeling no different is probably commonplace. I remember a line in a television play a year or so ago: 'I feel exactly as I did when I was twenty – even where physical matters are concerned: this is one of the tragedies of old age: underneath the old skin is still the same person as one was when young.' But I rather doubt whether you or I would really regard this so-called old age as a tragedy, despite all that has befallen us since those depressing thirties: not that I recall them as depressing. We left it to the grown-ups to be depressed!

We have always been close, in a singularly close-knit family, and we have been fortunate in that, unlike so many brothers and sisters, we have never become strangers: indeed we have, consistently, been brought closer together, first by the tragic death of our brother, Maurice, when he was only twenty-eight, followed so quickly by our mother's death, from cancer, at fifty-eight; and then, at the great age of eighty-eight, the final release of our dear father, who, in common with anyone who knew him, we so loved. Other sad losses, too, have gradually brought us closer together over the years: David Satow and Betty Hoskin, each almost one of the family, very special friends such as Ewen Macpherson of Greens Norton days and Dick Russell, my earliest and longest-lasting friend.

Your adult life has virtually been confined to the West Country, first bringing up your family, and then because of your comparative immobility due to the wretched stroke you suffered in

1969 – with which you have coped so courageously. How different my life has been, largely due to the fact that I seem always to have tried to pursue at least three different careers at the same time. When I first became a schoolmaster in 1936, little did I think that in a comparatively short time I would have become a commentator for the BBC, founder and Director of the Centre of Adult Education at Pendley Manor, our old family home, a Master of Foxhounds, a pillar of the British Horse Society and – dare I add? – an author.

As a result of all this I find myself still driving about 30,000 miles a year and hunting two days a week – despite the three score years and ten! A further result, unfortunately, of this busy life which I have been lucky enough to enjoy, although I, too, have had a few problems, is that we have not seen as much of each other as we would both have liked: consequently much of what I have been up to has inevitably been something of a closed book, even to you. How much more, then, to others?

Hence this further book of reminiscences, which I hope you will enjoy. Either there was not sufficient room for them in *Master of One*, my earlier book of reminiscences, or I felt, then, that it was more tactful to omit them! I am toying with the idea of a final, and very frank, volume of reminiscences to be entitled *Underneath the Carpet* – to be published posthumously!

My love, as ever,

Chapter 1

Puppy in a Wicker Basket

I was not, of course, brought up at Pendley Manor, the family home at Tring in Hertfordshire. Greens Norton Court in Northampton-shire was my first home, and, indeed, the first real home of my parents. My father being a soldier, they had previously lived in houses near wherever his regiment was stationed. My sister was born at Ardeen in the Curragh. I was born on 1 July 1914 at Spokane, near Aldershot, at 8.10 a.m., according to the revealing diaries kept by my parents during our earliest years, 'a fine figure of a man weighing 8lbs'. During the war the family which now included my brother, Maurice, lived in various houses, in particular Syrencot, also near Aldershot, Holmbury at Westgate-on-Sea, to be near our relatives who ran Hawtreys preparatory school just outside the town, Aldbury Rectory, the home of my maternal grandparents near Tring and, of course, Pendley Manor, also near Tring, which it seems I visited for the very first time in January 1915.

My Uncle Joe and Aunt Katy lived at Pendley, my father with his brothers and sister being brought up there; their own father had died as the result of a hunting accident when they were very young. Their mother, a lady of some character apparently, had recently left my grandfather, having borne him five children, but I doubt if her departure surprised him as he himself as a young subaltern had eloped with her when she was, in fact, married to the Colonel of his regiment. Inevitably, he earned the title of the bravest subaltern in the British Army – a title well deserved in view of the fact that he then bought a house in Leicestershire next door to his Colonel and, being an exceptionally brilliant man across country, proceeded to pound him in the hunting field.

With the old people still living at Pendley, it was obvious that when my father left the army he would have to find a home of his own. This he did, at Greens Norton where the family moved in November 1920.

Greens Norton was in no way pretentious: far from it, since it faced directly on to the road, albeit a not very busy one. Probably it had at one time been two small houses which were joined into one. The rooms, though not big, were practical and homely: upstairs there were six bedrooms, the best ones facing on to a quite simple terraced garden of about five acres which looked across to the south end of the rather straggling village. Maurice and I shared a room facing on to the street. There was also a vegetable garden approximately the same size as the front garden, and a stable yard with about ten boxes.

It may not have been a very imposing residence by standards then prevailing, but it was certainly the happiest home anyone could ever have desired. The background of this great happiness was without doubt the tremendous affection that my mother and father had for each other. Years after her death we discovered amongst her belongings a soft-backed notebook in which she had written of their marriage. It still makes moving reading, giving clear evidence that she almost literally worshipped the ground on which he trod. Apparently at their very first meeting, when he was eleven and she ten, she had decided that there was 'something about him'. As they grew up she writes that 'through all the lively years he had never forsaken or forgotten his small friend of the Eton-collar days, each holidays finding him just as cheery, just as loyal to her. I never remember the stage when he looked on me as only a girl, and through all his holidays and leaves he always came back to me in the old unaffected, unsuperior ways of our first friendship'.

At her first grown-up dance, when she was eighteen, he proposed to her, but interpreting it as his way of giving their relationship a definite status, she refused. Three years later, on the eve of his departure with his regiment for South Africa, he proposed again. This time she accepted. 'The girl he left behind him,' she writes, 'wore a gold watch bracelet up her sleeve in place of the more usual engagement ring – which is less easily hidden!'

After the First World War, during which he had survived a near fatal wound in 1914 and a serious illness in 1917, they seemed to have been as much in love as ever: Greens Norton was, in a sense, a kind of manifestation of this great love. She saw his faults, of course – did not we all? – 'a trifle headstrong, perhaps: quite impossible to drive – and none too easy to lead! a wee-bit self-opiniated: a wee-bit certain that his way is best: a wee-bit apt to seize upon a hobby with tremendous vigour, then tire of it', but she could never cease to admire his bottomless energy, his remarkable organising ability and his wonderful fun-loving sense of humour.

'We want nothing more, we ask nothing altered: just pray that his sons grow up on their father's model.'

What a background for childhood. No wonder those early years were so blissfully happy, with our ponies and picnics and parties, and always there to look after us the adored Flo, the daughter of a farmer, barely out of her 'teens, who had been engaged when our dear old nanny, Nanny Irving, had left at the beginning of 1922. Old? In fact, she only died about ten years ago, though by then she was well over ninety. Obviously this idyllic existence could not last for ever: for little more than a year, to be precise, for at the age of eight I was to be sent away from home to boarding school. This was a prospect which did not fill me with too much anxiety, firstly because the proprietress of Hawtreys, which had recently in honour of her late husband changed its name from St Michaels, was my Aunt Nellie, the sister of my grandmother at whose lovely old rectory at Aldbury I had happily spent so much of my earliest childhood. Her daughter, Beryl, then married to the headmaster, was one of those women who although, or perhaps because, they had no children of their own were, nevertheless, marvellous with other people's.

Secondly, having spent many months during the war at Westgate-on-Sea, where the school was situated, we had often visited it, for football matches, for entertainments, for 'dancing' on Saturday evenings. I had no fears, therefore, that I would be a complete stranger. At this distance I cannot pretend to know just what I anticipated: indeed, does any child going away to school for the first time know what to expect? I suspect that one part of me looked forward to it because it was 'grown-up' and I had frequently been told how much I was going to enjoy it, while another part feared it because, being shy by nature, meeting a lot of strange people was going to be an ordeal; moreover, there would be the wrench of leaving the comfort and security of Greens Norton. But that, of course, is speculation. Whatever my thoughts at that time actually were I could never have foreseen just what the first twenty-four hours were going to be like.

After a more or less tearless departure, with even a touch of pride, perhaps, in my stiff white Eton collar and my bowler hat, clutching my brand new 'attaché case' for my nightwear, my initials stamped boldly in gold on the top, my father took me up to London by train. We had lunch at the Grosvenor Hotel, Victoria, where I felt rather

sick and looked sufficiently pallid for my father, doubtless longing
for the presence of my mother, to ask me if I was all right: it had,
apparently, been considered more manly for me to be seen off by my
father. In due course we found ourselves on the platform waiting to
embark on the special school train – or more accurately the ordinary
Margate train with three special Pullman-type saloons attached: one
for the Upper School, one for the Middle School and one for the
Lower School. The headmaster, six feet four inches of him – most of
the four inches being neck – was waiting there surrounded by parents
and boys. Seeing my father, one of the few people with whom he
ever seemed to be really at ease – my mother, of course, was his
wife's first cousin, and also her best friend – he waved, and we made
our way through the crowd towards him. At this moment a kindly
looking gentleman, with thick glasses and a dog-collar who I learned
later was the chaplain, the Rev. J.V. Hobbins, approached us and
called out: 'New boys, this coach.'

'No!' barked back the headmaster, 'He'll come with *me*' – in the
Upper School coach I was later to discover.

'All aboard!' A whistle blew; brave and tearful farewells; a
scramble on to the train.

'Sit by me, Shaw!'

'This seat's bagged.'

'Shove-up Mackinnon!'

'Silence!'

'Goodbye, ol' man! Enjoy yourself,' from my unfamiliarly
embarrassed father. 'You mustn't forget this.'

The moment that I had dreaded! The moment when my father
handed 'this' over to me, for 'this' was a brand new wicker basket in
which there was a tiny fox terrier puppy that my father had been
carrying ever since we had left home. Now it was my responsibility.
To this day I can recapture the flush of shame and embarrassment at
being saddled with this extraordinary responsibility on such a
fraught occasion. One of the Hawtreys porters, Henry Shrubsole,
was married to Nora, a girl who had been the assistant parlourmaid
at Aldbury Rectory with my grandparents. Being lonely so far from
home, someone had suggested that she should have a dog. Our own
terrier having recently sired some puppies, it was suggested that
Nora should have one of these. How better to get it to her than with
Master Dorian when he went to school? Logical enough, but one
cannot help feeling that it was a little insensitive of my parents. An
eight-year-old new boy, going away to school for the first time, has,

surely, enough to cope with without a puppy dog in a wicker basket. But the ordeal was far from over. My entry into the saloon was greeted, inevitably, with unsuccessfully suppressed giggles.

'Silence!' hissed the headmaster with a withering glance all round: then to me: 'Here, boy, sit by me.'

How much happier I would have been in the Lower School coach. Here not only was my little whimpering companion the object of curiosity, but being the only new boy in the carriage I, too, was a novelty. 'What's your name?', 'Where do you come from?', 'Why have you got a dog?', 'Let me see it,' from time to time punctuated by a 'Shut up!' – rather surprisingly his favourite way of procuring order – or 'Sid'down, boy!' from the headmaster. If the boys did not ask questions then they just stared and made stupid faces. Eventually it was quite impossible to prevent myself weeping, but fortunately, being very emotional by nature, I have usually been able to weep without actually shedding tears. Realising that I just had to cope with my misery as best I could, I hoped that nobody noticed, praying for the moment when we arrived at Westgate-on-Sea where, surely, I would be welcomed with open arms by my Aunt Nellie and Cousin Beryl and be relieved at last of my wicker basket.

It was not to be. As the school disgorged on to the platform we were immediately formed into columns with the senior boys of each group at the front and the master in charge at the back. Automatically, though half the size of all the other boys in the group, I fell in by the side of the headmaster. Over the bridge and into St Mildred's Road we filed until we reached, about 150 yards down the road, a little cross roads: on the right was an un-made-up road on the corner of which was the headmaster's house, looking rather like an outsize doll's house, and the playing field: on the left were the school buildings, divided by Harold Avenue. When the original head-master, the Rev. John Hawtrey, had, impressed by the bracing air, brought the school from Slough to Westgate, he bought four unfinished boarding houses and adapted them for a school. They may have been adequate for the nineteenth century, but were scarcely so, surely, for the twentieth, though I am sure that it appeared to none of us as unsuitable at the time – but then we knew no different. At this juncture the headmaster peeled off to his own house, leaving me on my own at the end of the file which now turned into Harold Avenue and crossed the road to be greeted by old Mrs Hawtrey, who stood outside her own front door to shake each boy by the hand. When eventually it was my turn she greeted me warmly, even bending down to kiss me, which obviously caused a certain amount of sniggering amongst the other boys.

'So, you've brought Nora's puppy,' she remarked. 'Well done!' But as she made no offer to relieve me of it I just followed the others across the road to the house known, as I later learned, as the Office block. Here, high up on an easel, was a large blackboard on which was pinned the plan that informed each boy where he would be sleeping: either in a single, a double room if brothers, or a 'partition' – a single room divided into two by a partition which reached to within about two feet of the ceiling. (The single rooms, a unique feature of Hawtreys, were a legacy from Eton whence the school had derived.) The boys – they were the biggest, of course – all jostled round the board until they found their names: one, as he turned away, called out in my direction, 'You won't find your name here,' but I did not understand what he meant. By this time more boys had come across the road – the Middle School: more jostling and shouting until they all seemed satisfied and departed, leaving me on my own; and here was my problem, the moment of truth which, instinctively I suspect, I had been dreading. I just could not remember my surname, so how could I find which room I was in? I was sure that I really did know it, but my small mind was too numb to remember. I had been told it often enough, even been made to learn how to spell it, but, in mitigation, I can plead that I had only seldom heard it. It was not, so to speak, part of our usual vocabulary. At home my father and mother were 'Major' and 'Madam'. At Pendley it was 'Major and Mrs Vivian'; at Aldbury it was 'Major Vivian' and 'Miss Vi' – still Miss Vi although she was, of course, married. I was simply Master Dorian, as my sister was Miss Barbara, my brother Master Maurice. But here it was only surnames. Every name on the board was a surname. Just occasionally there was an initial if two boys had the same name; brothers were major and minor, and even minimus. But what was the name that I was looking for? It was getting dark too, that September evening, making it difficult to read: and the poor puppy was whimpering with cold! Just before I was completely overcome by despair, to my enormous relief the splendid person of the head porter, Basil, hove in sight. I knew him from my previous visits to the school when staying at Westgate. I could have thrown myself into his arms, and probably would have done so had it not been for the wicker basket and my attaché case.

'Whatever are you doing here, Master Dorian? You'll be in Mrs

Hawtrey's block, for sure. You'd better come with me. And I see you've Henry's puppy. Let me take it. I wondered what had happened to it. What's its name?'

But I was too choked to reply, and too relieved, as Basil led me down the subway which linked the Office block with Mrs Hawtrey's block, where I was greeted, mercifully, by another familiar face, that of old Kate Crawley, the head housemaid who had also had Aldbury connections.

'There you are, Master Dorian,' she greeted me. 'I thought we'd lost you. Come along,' and she took me upstairs to the first floor to a 'partition' which I was sharing with a certain Peter Clarke who, I was later to discover, hailed from Bristol, a very different sort of place from Greens Norton. He had been at the school one term. He was mad about professional football, which was unusual in those days and very far removed from horses and ponies.

'You'll be all right here,' said Kate, unpacking my attaché case. 'Mrs Hawtrey's just through there,' she said, pointing at the wall, 'and I'm not far away. You'll be all right, right as rain: you'll see.' But would I, I wondered? It was all so totally strange, so different from what I had expected: and I was so exhausted. Then, doubtless meaning well, Kate asked after 'dear old Bessie and Miss Blackmore', my grandmother's cook and lady's maid. That was just too much for me. I sat down on the bed and sobbed.

With Kate's cheerful, practical, no-nonsense help, I soon pulled myself together and was taken across to the Matron's room where the other new boys were assembling with members of the Lower School who were handing over their sweets to the under-matron. Knowing the form through my earlier connections with the school, I had brought no 'tuck' with me, so just stood around, waiting. There were a few minutes before tea when, at the sound of the bell, we would all be led down to the Dining Hall to sit at the lowest table presided over at one end by the Matron, the somewhat forbidding Miss Harper, and at the other the 7th Division (bottom form) governess, a cosy type called Miss Sparshot of whom I became very fond and who, unfortunately, became rather too fond of my brother, Maurice, when he came a year later: her 'little ray of sunshine', she called him! (The music mistress was called Miss Rootham, while the secretary was Miss Pitman: my father, of course, had to make the rather feeble joke which everyone at school thought very clever: 'Miss Rootham's pa shot Miss Pitman!' Eventually the headmaster banned the joke.)

During the few minutes before tea the news boys were, inevitably, subjected to endless questioning by the superior old gentlemen who had been there all of two or three terms. Occasionally there was advice too: 'You have to know the names of the first division by heart,' I was told. 'It's easy because they rhyme: Shoolbred, Lambert, Shaw – Dur*ant*, Watson, Ma*gor*.' Advice that I seem to have taken quite effectively.

One of the new boys that term – there were twelve of us – was only seven, but he showed more initiative then the rest of us. Fed up with so frequently being asked his name, he suddenly leapt on to a chair, declaring in a shrill voice:

'Once and for all my name is Waoul Charles Wobin – and let that be an end of it!'

A dark boy standing next to me, a new boy, the same age as myself but a little taller, turned to me and whispered, 'And my name is Wichard Henwy Wussell', and chuckled in a way which over the years I was to know so well, for that was my introduction to Dick Russell and the start of a friendship that lasted until, sadly, he died in 1982.

Raoul Robin, who hailed from Jersey, was later to command the Coldstream in a distinguished army career: but it was a long time before I was to meet him again, and in rather unusual circumstances.

The routine at Hawtreys was certainly strict, but only in the sense that it was totally unvaried. Each day was to all intents and purposes exactly the same. After breakfast, and a quarter of an hour for going to the lavatory, Chapel (fifteen minutes) was followed by what was called scripture, also fifteen minutes, when the whole school assembled in the Dancing Room, as the assembly hall was called, and, seated all round the outside, was taken by the headmaster who sat in state by a table on a low dais. Officially each boy in turn read a verse from a chapter of one of the books of the Old Testament with constant dissertations from the headmaster, whose father had been a parson. Frequently, however, this brief period was the opportunity for a harangue from the headmaster on any subject or topic – or incident – that might be appropriate. This was the moment when offenders were called out to stand in the middle of the room in front of the whole school to receive an oral castigation from the headmaster, at the end of which they were stood on a table at the side of the hall, facing the wall, on which hung a picture of the Delhi Durbar – or was it the Diamond Jubilee?

At the end of scripture the school then filed out to lessons, the first two classes each morning for the Upper School being classics, the first class only for the Middle or Lower Schools. During the half-hour 'break' there would be 'nets' or goal-kicking practice on the playing field. Two more periods were followed by lunch, which was identical every single day of the year – apart from fish on Fridays – with just one exception. It was identical in the sense that the food was exactly the same, though there was always a choice. It was beef, mutton or hash, the latter presumably being the beef and mutton left over from the previous day. The beef might be roast or boiled as, more rarely, might the mutton, but only occasionally, thank goodness, with revolting white caper sauce! The food, including the vegetables, was, in fact, excellently cooked and presented. Mrs Hawtrey served the hash, the joints being carved by the headmaster and his wife. The three porters and three parlour maids were responsible for the serving, apart from the vegetables which were dished out by the member of staff presiding at each table.

The one exception from the beef, mutton or hash was on Michaelmas Day when the menu consisted of goose 'flown specially over from Ireland', as we used to be told each year. Michaelmas Day was one of the only two whole holidays in the year, the other being Ascension Day – both inconveniently near the beginning of term. There would also, with luck, be a half-holiday if a boy had won a scholarship: I remember, too, a half-holiday in honour of Beryl, the headmaster's wife, reaching the finals of the Ladies Amateur Golf Championship, where she was beaten by Joyce Wethered. Otherwise there were just two half-holidays each week, Wednesdays and Saturdays, with a lantern-slide lecture on the Wednesday evening.

Games were played every single afternoon, while on Sundays there was a 'walk', in crocodile, when considerably to our embarrassment we had to wear top hats and, of course, Eton collars. Frequently we were jeered at by the village boys and on one exciting occasion pelted with sticks and stones. Naturally we never broke ranks! For the smallest boys – and not only the smallest – the quarter of an hour that followed games was the worst part of the day, especially in the winter. With frozen fingers one had somehow to do up one's starched Eton collar and tie one's tie. When my brother and I shared a room we used to take it in turns to sit on our fingers until they were warm enough to do up the other's collar. If one was alone it was a nightmare with the bell for 'absence' – call-over – invariably being rung before one was ready.

Half an hour's free time was followed by another work period, then
tea with a final work period before boys retired to bed at staggered
times, the lowest forms at 7 p.m., the oldest boys at 8.30 p.m. Three
days each week we took a hip bath in our room, being washed by one of
the housemaids. (During my last term I remember Amy – probably
about eighteen – getting rather familiar bathing me while she
repeatedly crooned 'Charmaine', then a very popular song. She
disappeared suddenly and was replaced in this particular task by old
Kate, which I rather resented.)

One certainly knew exactly where one was at Hawtreys. Although
people today might be horrified at such a formal, unimaginative
routine, the fact of the matter was that it did make for both security and
happiness. Nor do I believe that such rigidity denies a boy initiative.
Certainly many of my own contemporaries achieved positions of
eminence in every walk of life. More than one has been a successful
explorer; there has been a number of eminent politicians and diplomats;
and many covered themselves with glory in the services, which hardly
suggests a lack of initiative. Perhaps in modern thinking we expect too
much of the young too soon. A period of regular, unthinking,
unvariable routine is required. In other words, self-discipline can never
be achieved unless there has been a period of imposed discipline.

There was certainly discipline at Hawtreys, but it was far from
brutal. The headmaster was no sadist, but he was a very strict
authoritarian. Only he could dispense punishment: indeed, the
assistant masters had little personal authority other than threatening to
send offenders to the headmaster, which was usually enough. Nine
times out of ten an oral castigation from the caustic tongue of the
headmaster was sufficient – either in front of one of the top forms which
would be working in his classroom, or in front of the whole school in
the Dancing Room. Occasionally it was a visit to the 'boxing room'
where three or four whacks with the slipper would be administered – on
the bare bottom. Nor was the headmaster any respector of persons. I
remember the head boy being called out of tea and sent to the 'boxing
room' for fidgeting during the lecture which had just taken place.

Hawtreys, despite its demanding, un-negotiable standards and
spartan rigidity, was certainly a very happy school. I never remember a
boy running away; few enough tears. There was little bullying, for
bullying, together with any suggestion of bad manners, was the most
heinous of offences and inevitably incurred a visit to the 'boxing room'.

Understandably in such a strict routine the occasional relaxation
provided the greatest excitement and was eagerly anticipated. First of

all there were two great holidays, Michaelmas Day and Ascension Day, when work stopped at break – it was never quite a whole holiday – and there was the termly Swallows and Crusaders match. No one quite knows how these two clubs originated. Almost the moment that one arrived one was asked whether one was going to be a Swallow or a Crusader. One pitied the wretched new boys who had no idea what it was all about: most, fortunately, had been advised by an old boy father or friend or elder brother. My uncle had been a Crusader, perhaps because, coming from a clerical family, he appreciated their 'colours', a red Maltese Cross on black; so I became a Crusader. Anyway, the colours were more exciting to my mind than the mauve and white stripes of the Swallows.

After lunch we would board three magnificent red coaches for our outing, each boy receiving 6d from the headmaster's wife as he climbed in, and were driven off to Richborough Castle, Canterbury Cathedral or the twin-spired Reculver Church. On the way home the coaches would stop at Sandwich where we could spend our 6ds – and how much we managed to buy for 6d in those days: sweets, sherbet, bars of chocolate, eclairs, cream buns, cornets of ice cream. The trouble was that everything had to be consumed before we reached the school, sweets being forbidden, so we usually had a few boys sick before the evening, one, I remember, during the performance of a conjurer, the day's invariable climax.

But there were other highlights that were almost as precious: the half-hour or so after tea on half-holidays when one was left to oneself and could, in the winter, either read or play games – in the Library when one was older – or, in the summer, wander round the playing field with one's 'gang' or a special friend; tend one's garden – we were each allotted about six square feet; watch the traffic returning from day trips to Margate along the main road which ran down one side of the field – on no account were we allowed to wave back to the trippers who waved at us; or just indulge in something as simple as French cricket, an occupation frowned upon when serious cricket or a 'net' was possible, or play tennis over an imaginary or make-do net, there being no courts. Being read aloud to on Sunday evening was a very special treat. Beryl Cautley, the headmaster's wife, not only chose marvellous books but was a wonderful reader, which was not surprising, perhaps, in view of the fact that her uncle, Charles Hawtrey, was knighted as an actor, while many considered her father, Edward, an even better actor than his brother. For the older boys Frank Cautley, who also read well, usually chose John Buchan or Conan Doyle.

Acting, however, was completely forbidden at Hawtreys. The only play that I ever remember being performed was a version of *Henry VIII* which Beryl suddenly suggested I should produce with boys who had been left behind with chicken pox at the end of one term. I was, of course, delighted to oblige and not only produced the play but played the leading part and wrote the script! The highlight of the production, however, was when the cushion representing Henry VIII's stomach suddenly slipped down round my ankles. Doubtless this produced as big a laugh as when, at the age of about four I was taken to see old Edward Hawtrey giving a dramatic recitation and interrupted his performance with a piping, 'Why is Uncle Edward talking so much?' Oddly enough, *Henry VIII* was the first play that I ever produced at the Pendley Shakespeare Festival, some twenty-five years later.

Inexplicably athletics were not encouraged either. Edward Hawtrey had been a running blue at Cambridge; his son-in-law, Frank Cautley, was an outstanding athlete with blues for soccer and for cricket, at both of which he was county standard. Games, it could be said, were his religion: he was unquestionably a brilliant coach. For three years during my time at Hawtreys the school teams were never beaten at cricket, soccer or rugger. (But what a day of despair when a team was eventually beaten. The school all but went into mourning! 'Scripture' next morning was memorable, to say the least.) Presumably the headmaster felt that he could not countenance anything that might interfere with the 'official' games. Certainly I found myself in hot water when I tried to introduce my own brand of athletics. It was during that precious half-hour at the end of the day when there were plenty of people with nothing special to do that I first decided to organise a few flat races. Then – possibly with steeplechasing of the equestrian kind as much in mind as anything – hurdling was introduced, school benches being used as the fences. Later there were obstacles, with some very ingenious hazards – perhaps I was foreseeing eventing! – one of which caused the inevitable: a boy cut his leg quite badly. Obviously he had to report it to the matron, so, as I might have suspected, it soon reached the ears of the headmaster. Inevitably next morning at 'scripture' I was called out before the school, harangued and finally stood on the table. Oddly enough I remember his saying sarcastically: 'I suppose that you think you're Harold Abrahams.' Recently, of course, Harold had won an Olympic gold medal in Paris: later he was to become a great friend, as his wife for many years played leading roles in the Pendley Shakespeare Festival. We also used to meet up at most Olympic Games, commentating, as we both did, for the BBC. Today for a boy to get into trouble because he was keen on athletics would be considered very strange.

The other incident which found me standing on the table in the Dancing Room was a very strange affair which cannot easily be explained – or described: it came to be known as 'the rumour'. As a small boy I used to read a great deal and enjoyed writing stories. Looking back I suspect that I went through a period when I might have been described as a loner. I was quite good at games but was not ambitious. I was in the soccer and rugger teams for two years, but could never be regarded as a real enthusiast, a fact possibly resented by the headmaster. As, it seemed to me, it was those keenest on games who had most attention, I often preferred to keep my own company – not easy in that gregarious climate – reading and scribbling rather than attending 'nets' or goal-kicking practice. One day I had seen a funny old woman with a stick hobbling down the road by the playing field. That evening in bed I heard the tap-tap of her stick as she returned along the street. Probably I had been reading about spies in the newspaper or perhaps in a book: at any rate it was enough to send my imagination into action. At first I just told my brother of this suspicious old woman, and found him a most attentive listener. Before long, as I developed my 'suspicions' into a continuing story, he felt unable to resist telling a few of his friends, especially when I elaborated my story to include the sighting of the spy dressed as Kate, the senior housemaid, on the roof. (I had, in fact, seen the resourceful Kate on a ledge retrieving something that had fallen out of a window.) The rumour spread like wildfire: boys started approaching me surreptitiously asking for the latest news and it was soon quite out of hand. My imagination had completely run away with me and now it was beyond my control and I knew not how to stop it without losing face. It is almost true to say that after two or three days the whole school from top to bottom – I was about in the middle – was in a ferment, caught in a kind of paroxism of excited apprehension and anticipation. At first I had enjoyed the importance that I was attracting to myself. Now I only wanted to rid myself of it, it all being too much for me to handle.

I remember Maurice one night asking me whether it really was true; I did not know how to answer. Ever loyal, Maurice said that he thought it had been a jolly exciting story and could really easily have happened: why did I not now go and tell somebody in authority that perhaps I could have imagined it all? It would then, surely, he suggested, be very quickly forgotten. That it seemed a good idea was probably wishful thinking: in any case I had left it too late. As the headmaster came out of breakfast and was passing in front of the boys, all lined up waiting for chapel, he called me out.

'Williams major! follow me!'

My heart sank as he led me to the lobby outside Mrs Hawtrey's study.

'What's this extraordinary rumour I hear? Well, boy?'

There was just nothing that I could possibly say: I was trapped. But to my surprise he was quite affable.

'What's the trouble ol' man? Been reading too much Dornford Yates?' – his favourite author: it was much more likely to have been John Buchan. 'Doesn't do to invent a lot of tosh like that, boy: unsettles people; don't know what to believe, eh? Better forget it.'

'Yes, sir.'

'Get along to the chapel, then.'

'Yes, sir.'

If I then used the occasion to thank the Lord on my knees for getting me off so lightly, it was premature. As soon as he entered the Dancing Room for 'scripture', even before he sat down, he bawled out, 'Where's Williams major? Stand out here,' pointing to the centre of the room. He then really pitched into me, constantly mentioning Ananius.

'Ananius was a liar, boy. You're another Ananius: a liar!' (Who on earth was Ananius?)

So it went on until the inevitable: 'Get on the table: and stay there for the rest of the week,' by the end of which I knew every detail of the Delhi Durbar – or was it the Diamond Jubilee?

As I have mentioned, the assistant masters had little authority, and were probably as much in awe of the headmaster as we were: they certainly called him 'Sir'. But in themselves they were strict, good teachers and friendly: though most of them having joined the staff during the war they were probably not as well qualified as the masters usually were, and are, of course, today. Mention has already been made of the chaplain, the Rev. J.V. Hobbins who, despite the fact that he preached the most puerile sermons, taken straight from the *Children's Encyclopedia*, was universally popular, especially with the lower forms – or divisions as they were called – which were his main sphere of teaching. The senior master, K.P. James, was quite popular, too, although for some reason, when he was angry, which he was fairly frequently, he used to tremble violently. He was responsible, too, for one of my less happy moments at Hawtreys. He always made a great feature of boys' tenth birthdays: double figures. For a few moments in his class on that important day one was made to feel someone, a little different; which means much at that age. On my own tenth birthday, however, he seemed to have forgotten the fact. Despite one or two hints from others in the division, and even myself, it was clear that he was not going to mention it. Eventually I had to take up my exercise book to be corrected. As I handed it to him I said: 'Please sir, I think you've forgotten something special.'

'What?'

'My birthday, sir.'

To my amazement he exploded and went into one of his tantrums when he shook more violently than ever. Whether it was because he really had forgotten my birthday and was annoyed with himself – no one is angrier than a person in the wrong – or whether he had it in for me because I was related to the authorities, I just do not know. At any rate, I burst into tears and was ordered outside the room – the only punishment available to an assistant master, but an effective one in that one could easily be seen by the headmaster, whose own classroom was down the passage. Fortunately, I was not seen – but what a disappointing tenth birthday.

K.P. James's great friend was N.S. Hoare: they could hardly have been more contrasting. Whereas James was elegant, even dandified, with hair *en brosse*, Hoare was somewhat uncouth: stout and florid with thinning hair and a gammy leg. This latter was, one was given to understand, due to a war wound. It was certainly very unattractive, appearing gangrenous and sweating, made even messier by his constantly scratching it – during class, I might add! A special treat was to be allowed to look at it; even, for the less squeamish, to touch it! Yet everyone liked him as he was extremely human, kind and sympathetic. For many of us the most popular master, perhaps because he was the youngest, having just managed to serve in the war, with the RAF, was P.R. Magrath. He was smart, amusing in a slightly cynical way and played the piano extremely well. Every Tuesday afternoon he used to take community singing, which was very popular. He had considerable influence, certainly on me and, I believe, on many others. Happily he has remained a friend right down to the present. The only other master that I can recall was a very dapper Mr Knight, who taught maths, starting every lesson with five minutes of mental arithmetic:

absolutely invaluable, even if one had, like me, no head for figures.

Frank Cautley himself was an outstanding teacher both of classics and games, but he inspired respect rather than affection. The older boys, if they were good at games, eventually got on well with him and liked him, but for the rest he was remote and awe-inspiring, apparently, unlike his wife, having little rapport with boys. The session that I had with him at the end of my last term when supposedly he was teaching me the facts of life was, as far as I was concerned, totally enigmatic and incomprehensible. I remember that throughout the talk he was peeling an orange and removing the pips, though whether this had anything to do with the subject in hand I have not the slightest idea!

Altogether Hawtreys provided a very orderly, regulated, friendly background which was as valuable an influence in my early days at school as that provided by my parents at home.

Chapter 2

The Hill of Everlasting Youth

The difference between one's preparatory school and one's public school, at least in the twenties, was the extraordinary freedom enjoyed in the latter. Necessarily, as it was then thought, there was at a prep school a certain amount of restriction and an inevitable routine from the time that one got up to the time that one went to bed, whereas, in contrast, at a public school – at Harrow in my case – there seemed to be the minimum of control. Obviously there were classes to be attended, though one could even arrange to get 'signed off' these without too much difficulty as long as one was on good terms with one's housemaster and the house matron. I remember getting off a whole morning's school to attend the International Horse Show at Olympia. Nor was it too difficult to get out of compulsory games, which in any event only took place two or three times a week. On the other days one was expected to take 'ekker' – exercise – which could mean playing squash or fives, going for a run or to Ducker – the swimming pool – or the gym, or even watching a school match. Officially there were three half-holidays a week, which I regarded as a remarkable bonus; but it seemed that any excuse was good enough for an extra one: a master's wife giving birth to a child, the engagement of the headmaster's daughter, a particular honour for an old boy, even, in November 1931, to celebrate thirty-three Old Harrovian MPs.

When I first went to Harrow I was quite bewildered by the amount of freedom, especially in the summer term. I had to spend my first term in a 'waiting' house, one of the small houses in which, as a rule, boys only stayed for a term before they went to their proper house. Presumably the house for which I was destined, The Park, was full, which was why I spent one term at Garlands, with a charming housemaster and his wife, Mr and Mrs 'Tubby' Bradshaw. This was probably the reason why I had also stayed a term longer at Hawtreys than was originally intended, though I was somehow given the impression that it was really because I was considered not quite ready for public school, which hardly boosted my morale or improved my self-confidence, rather lacking at that time. Certainly my last term at Hawtreys was my least happy. I seemed to be older than anyone else, to hav∘ been there longer than anyone else, yet not to have any real seniority. Moreover, I had lost all my better friends, in particular Dick Russell, who had left for Harrow the previous term.

Not surprisingly I loved Harrow from the day that I arrived, despite the disadvantage of being in a small house. I was quickly reunited with a number of old friends, including Dick, and soon made new ones. Obviously the very size of a public school is overwhelming after the confined life at a preparatory school, yet I recall few problems in finding my way around. Everyone seemed so friendly that one never hesitated to ask anyone, even a much older boy, for information. During my very first week I was walking alone along the High Street from one class to another when I suddenly heard the screech of a bicycle behind me and turned to find myself, to my astonishment, face to face with the second head of the school, resplendent in his bow tie – a privilege of members of the Philathletic Club, an elite sports club, the equivalent of Eton's 'Pop' – a striped scarf, the privilege of a captain of games, and a speckled straw hat, the privilege, like the bicycle, of a school monitor. His name was Dick Hobson and he lived with his brother and sister and parents at Pattishall, about five miles from Greens Norton. He was very tall and grand, while I, at that time, was very small and shy, but he could not possibly have been more friendly.

'Everything all right, Dorian? Enjoying yourself? Let me know if you want anything. I'm in The Grove, up at the top of the hill, you know. Jolly good!'

And off he went. I was overcome: his bothering to talk to me, recognise me, even, under my enormous straw hat, call me by my Christian name, the more so in view of something very embarrassing which had happened not all that long ago, in the Christmas holidays. A large party of young people had been invited to toboggan at Pattishall. There was a huge sledge which took eight people or a small single, which I preferred. The slope, which was very steep, ran straight down to the main road, the A5 – a somewhat dangerous finish, one might have thought, though I imagine there was not much traffic in those days, especially in wintry conditions. After a buffet lunch, as we were walking back to the slope we passed

1a. Old Aldbury Rectory of happy childhood memories.

1b. Beloved Greens Norton, where we grew up.

2a.
The remarkable
'Aunt Nellie' Hawtrey,
the school's
chatelaine for
fifty years.

2b. Part of
Hawtrey's School
at Westgate-on-Sea.
Mrs Hawtrey's block
is on the left.

a huge cage or kennel with a wooden partition at the back, used either for gun dogs or, possibly, cage birds. Suddenly Dick Hobson announced that if anyone was brave enough to venture into the cage there was something 'jolly exciting right at the back, so who's brave enough?' Then turning to me he said: 'Go on, Dorian, you looked jolly dashing this morning on the single. I dare you.'

So in I went. I really had no option; he was, after all, my host, and was so much older. I even, perhaps, felt rather proud at being singled out. I went in, a little cautiously, then ventured right through to the back, beyond the partition. It was pitch dark; I could see nothing, so after a minute or two I came out. Everyone had disappeared. Worse, I discovered that I was locked in! I had been tricked, had fallen naively for a humiliating practical joke. I felt a complete fool, and not a little sorry for myself. What on earth ought I to do? How long was I going to be left there? How should I behave? Obviously I must not panic, or burst into tears. I did not like to shout for help, but I could not just wait in there, like an animal or cage bird. I began to feel desperate.

To my enormous relief, after a few minutes Dick's younger brother, John – later to become Attorney General – appeared and released me. I hurriedly joined the others, trying to look as if nothing had happened. Now, here was Dick at Harrow a few months later kindness itself, though something of a god, and probably completely unaware of the embarrassment that he had so recently caused me at Pattishall. We would both, I am sure, have been very surprised had we then been told that forty years on he would, at the end of his distinguished career in the Army, be approaching me as Chairman of the British Horse Society in the hope that I might help him to obtain a job in the equestrian world.

I recall particularly vividly another unusual experience. It was disturbing at the time: even more so subsequently. There was a boy in another small house who was immediately friendly towards me, almost possessive, although he himself had been there over a year.

We were walking down to the cricket field one afternoon when, as we crossed the road to the Philathletic ground he suddenly stopped me, gripped my arm, turned towards the sixth form ground, and in a voice quite different from his normal voice said something like: 'All this, you know, is a complete load of rubbish.'

'What do you mean?' I asked, having no idea what he was talking about.

'Everything,' he said, 'the whole school, your hunting.' I had been telling him how my father was a Master of Foxhounds, when he had told me that his father was an MP. 'It won't last, you know, any of it. The sooner we get rid of it all the better – Harrow, Parliament, the lot. It's all effete, balls!' – a novel, and rather shocking, epithet for a new boy! I said nothing, because I really had nothing to say: but when later I mentioned the conversation to another boy in Garlands he told me that he was not surprised: 'Amory is very weird: everybody knows that. I should avoid him'. Yet until this moment I had quite liked this pleasant if rather unconventional Amory.

The boy was John Amory, the son of Leo Amory, a Cabinet Minister. It was a horrible shock when, about twelve years later, I heard on the radio that he had been shot as a traitor, a colleague of William Joyce, Lord Haw-Haw.

Fortunately not all my friends at Harrow were so weird: far from it. Indeed, I am inclined to think that my most valued legacy from Harrow is the friendships that I enjoyed there: in many instances enjoy to this day. It was, I believe, the amount of freedom permitted that enabled one to develop such friendships. At prep school one was invariably part of a herd, but at Harrow there was always time to wander down to the playing fields with a friend, sit in a friend's room and chat, go for a walk round the Park lake, watch a match with two or three cronies, team up with another for squash or fives. One could, too, develop a hobby – stamps or crests or even cigarette cards with another enthusiast. Many paired up to play chess or even bridge; a few congregated to discuss literature or read poetry. Often a 'beak', as the masters were called, would organise play-readings or an expedition which would lead to friendships stemming from similar interests. Inevitably and easily one formed close, satisfying associations.

It was when I first went to Harrow that I started keeping my little Five Year Diaries, with about four lines to each day. Looking through them now I am reminded of so many close friends of those days. There was Dick Russell, from Hawtreys; John Wyld, who first asked me if we could share a room as his father was very keen on hunting and admired my father, and is still one of my greatest friends; Peter Brodie, a distant relative – as I only discovered at Harrow – who, having been Chief Constable of Warwickshire, became Assistant Commissioner of the Metropolitan Police. Nearly forty years later, he was to write to me, when after twenty-five years I finished lecturing to the Metropolitan Police: 'Amongst our 3,000 detective officers there can be few who have not had the privilege of hearing your lecture and I am sure that each and every one of them on hearing of your decision will have profound gratitude, and regret that those who follow will not have the benefit of such a stimulating talk.' At Harrow, incidentally, Peter was known as 'Efficiency' Brodie!

Other close friends were Bill Nichols, for many years Clerk to the Worshipful Company of Salters, and later Master. Anthony Rugge-Price, Michael Denison – more a friend of my brother, Maurice – who in his biography insisted that I was responsible for his going on the stage by bullying him to take part in a house play; Mark Tindall, who was captain of cricket at Harrow, making a century against Eton at Lord's. Later, after a distinguished cricketing career, he became a housemaster at Harrow. Some fifty years after we had left Harrow, since when we had never met, I was invited to give a talk to the Ashridge Circle at Eastbourne. On arriving at Congress Hall I was handed a note. It was from Mark, reminding me that at our last meeting he had marked me in the rugger Cock House match between his house, Moretons, and mine, The Park. My diary tells me that Moretons won in the last minute of the game. After my talk we had a brief but enjoyable reunion. There were many other friends who are, perhaps, best described as those 'who have no memorial, but whose righteousness will not be forgotten and whose name liveth for evermore' – certainly as far as I am concerned.

And there was Julian.

Frequently one sees it stated that an all-male public school is a hotbed of homosexuality. I can only say that I never found this to be so at Harrow. Obviously in any school there are odd cases of perverted sexual behaviour which lead to a scandal, boys expelled and so on, but I can recall only one such incident during my time at public school. That there were emotional relationships cannot be denied, of course, relationships which at the time often totally consumed those involved. Inevitably, the adolescent with his suddenly awakening emotional and sensual feelings is going to find someone who becomes the object of his affection. It may be a male or it may be a female: frequently it is both – at the same time. It could even be preferable that it is someone of the same sex. A deep affection between two boys is less likely to create problems, have serious after-effects, than a passionate relationship between an immature boy and an inexperienced girl, except, of course, on the rare occasion when the youthful and innocent infatuation of one boy for another leads to permanent homosexuality. But this is very much the exception rather than the rule, in my experience, however intense the feelings may be at the time – feelings as intense, indeed, as any experienced during the rest of one's life.

My feelings for Julian were certainly intense. We were both sixteen at the time, in different houses, though we were in certain 'sets' together. I first became aware of him one evening walking back from Ducker, the swimming pool. In those days we bathed *in peuris naturalibus*, but I certainly have no recollection of him in the pool – nor, indeed, of anyone else; one just took it all for granted – but walking back across the playing field and up the hill I was suddenly aware of his attractive personality. He had a soft, husky, rather hesitant voice, with a very slight drawl, and he had shy, dreamy eyes which he used to half close as he talked. Despite the fact that he was already being hailed as one of the most brilliant ball game players the school had known for a long time, he was diffident, modest and, obviously, shy: otherwise, it is unlikely that he would have been walking back from Ducker alone. Our interests were not very similar. He did not ride. I could not take ball games very seriously: yet we seemed content in each other's company. My affection for him grew apace: I believed myself to be in love, at the same time frustrated, uncertain of what his feelings, if any, might be for me. I knew that they could never be as strong as mine for him. After that first walk our only encounters were in our 'sets', or walking from one class to another – anything up to a quarter of a mile apart – when I might be fortunate enough to walk with him. Being in different houses we never met at games or on what one might call social occasions: a concert, a lecture or school play.

Towards the end of one term I was confined to my room with one of the wretched attacks of eczema which plagued the early part of my life: my legs, occasionally my arms, and most frequently my hands used to be raw for weeks at a time. My room looked out over the High Street. Knowing that at certain times each day Julian would be walking from the old music schools half-way down the hill on the north side of the town to the new buildings, right up the other end, I waited each day to catch a sight of him. If he walked on the other side of the road I could see him easily, but if, as was more usual, he walked on the near side it was only possible to get the briefest glimpse of him under his straw hat. I would wait in an agony of suspense hoping that he might look up, catch sight of me and wave: which he never did because, of course, he could not know which was my room.

When I returned to school he seemed, to my delighted surprise, pleased to see me. But the unbelievable was to happen one Sunday about two weeks later. Having done some work in my room for a couple of hours after lunch, I decided to go for a stroll up the High Street. Finding no one else in my house at a loose end, I wandered off on my own. I reached the chapel, turned on to the terrace, stopped at the top of the steps and looked across the playing fields to London in the distance. I was conscious of another boy approaching from the left but, a little embarrassed at being caught on my lonely stroll – one was expected to be gregarious – I did not look round lest whoever it was might be encouraged to talk to me, ask what I was doing, start a conversation, for which I happened to be in no mood. Suddenly, the boy said 'Hullo,' and I knew, stunned with joyous surprise, that it was Julian. 'Hullo,' I replied; but before I could ask him what he was doing he suggested, quite spontaneously, in that shy, husky voice, that we should go for a walk.

For the next two years on almost every Sunday we used to meet on the terrace and go for a walk. My great affection for him never waned though the close friendship which succeeded the agony and ecstasy proved a welcome relief. Only did our Sunday walks become scarcer, eventually to finish altogether, when, as we reached the top of the school, we found ourselves with so many time-consuming responsibilities; but we still remained close friends. The climax of our relationship was when he invited me one Easter holidays to stay at his elegant home in a charming little village in the eastern counties. I was given a beautiful room with chintz curtains, a quilted dressing table, a sofa at the foot of the large double bed and an armchair – all very different from the humble room that I shared with Maurice at Greens Norton.

We played cards after dinner, danced a little to the gramophone – he had two charming young sisters – and went to bed. I had just got into bed when the door opened and in came Julian. Quite spontaneously he jumped into bed beside me, his intentions I am sure being no different from my own. We drowsily talked the night away until, enjoying, as far as I was concerned, an undreamed-of contentment, we fell asleep. The following night I was asleep almost before we had started talking. Julian, knowing my involvement with horses, had suggested that we cycle to a local point-to-point, providing me with his younger sister's bicycle. She was eleven; I was seventeen: it was ten miles each way! By the time we reached home I was completely exhausted.

Love is the only possible word that I could honestly use to describe my feelings at that time for Julian. I have no shame in using it, convinced as I am that it was both innocent and natural. I might just add that our paths have seldom crossed since we left Harrow. On the rare occasions on which we have met – both now being happily married with children – it has been an easy, unembarrassed relationship. There were other relationships which could, of course, have been more dangerous when an older boy became 'keen' – as was the term – on a younger boy. At one time Terry Rattigan obviously had strong feelings for me, I being three years younger than him. I remember he used to come down to the 'toshes' – bathroom – on my bath nights; though until someone drew my attention to it I had been too naive to appreciate the significance of his invariably singing softly, but audibly, either 'Why must you be mean to me?' or 'I'm all for you body and soul'. He also gave me an expensive book, entitled *The Pegasus Book*, edited by my father's old friend, Ted Lyon, inscribed: 'Dorian, with best wishes from T.M.R.', the significance of which was his using my Christian name, normally unthinkable. According to my diary there was, with this book, a letter, but I do not recall its contents nor, sadly, did I keep it: it might have contained evidence of the genius that was to produce *The Deep Blue Sea* and *The Browning Version*. I remember the attention of two other older boys: one who used to invite me to go for walks with him in the evening; the other who used to write me very romantic letters, my prosaic replies to which must have been very frustrating for him. The former became a distinguished figure in the ecclesiastical world; the other a Lord Lieutenant! But neither they, nor Terry Rattigan, nor anyone else, while I was at Harrow, with just one exception – which in any event was fairly harmless – ever made any kind of offensive advances.

It was another close friendship that was to lead to something that gave me particular enjoyment for the rest of my time at Harrow and, indeed, for a number of years afterwards. My great friend of Hawtreys days, Dick Russell, had discovered at Harrow that with his long legs he was an accomplished high jumper – the scissors, of course! He therefore spent a good deal of time on the running track. One afternoon, after I had been at the school about two years, he persuaded me to go down there with him. Obviously I enjoyed running, as was demonstrated by my abortive attempt to introduce sports at Hawtreys, and soon I was to become genuinely enthusiastic, spending all the time that I could on the track. At first I concentrated on the half-mile (800 metres), but the following year, realising that there were already two established half-milers, both older than me, which meant that I would have little chance of getting into the team, I decided to take up the mile. Selected to run for an 'A' team against a German School which was visiting England, I managed to come third with the result that, much to my delight, I was selected to run for the school against the Achilles, a team consisting of past and present Oxford and Cambridge 'blues'. The race is, perhaps, best described by quoting from a letter written to my sister on Good Friday 1932.

> There were four Harrovians running, all of whom I thought were quite capable of beating me, and two Achilles; Lightly, a chap that ran for the School a few years ago and Price, who broke a lot of mile records last year at Cambridge and in the AAA Championships. It was the deuce of a race. The first lap I felt in absolutely terrific form and then the next two I thought I was going to crack. Price was right out in front with one of the Harrovians: but in the last lap I found myself automatically gaining on both. I passed the boy first and then came to Price about 200 yards from the finish. Remembering the tremendous sprint of Price last year when he won in 4 mins 32 secs I never really thought about beating him, but more about beating another boy who I knew must be coming up behind me: so I started into a bit of a sprint and suddenly found myself in front of Price and saw that he wasn't responding as he might, so then I went into a real sprint. I never expected to be able to sprint at all, but honestly I found that I could do a terrific finish, and I gather that I won by about 20 yards. I simply can't tell you how thrilled I was, B darling. There was one thing which I don't think M told you, but as I hadn't told him, that was impossible. After the match I was awarded my Running Scarf.

(I should add that the Achilles representatives had to run some yards further than the boys!) I wonder how many subsequent achievements in the last fifty years have given me as much pleasure?

My other great friend, John Wyld, was a good sprinter and hurdler. One day down at the track with him I was flicking over a few hurdles to help him with some practice starts. The school coach, E.F. Housden – subsequently a coach of national, even international, stature – was down there and, after watching me for a few minutes, asked if I would like some coaching. Naturally I agreed. So effective was he that I not only represented the school at hurdles for the next two years, also representing Harrow in the Public School Sports, but

was later to represent Kent County and the Southern Counties, even
managing to reach national level. I still have the letter from the
Amateur Athletics Association, dated July 1939, inviting me to
represent England against Germany in Berlin on 3 September 1939.
Needless to say, the match never took place. Perhaps it was fortunate
that it had not been arranged for 2 September. I might then have
been interred in Germany for the rest of the war!

Although enjoying so greatly the athletics during my last two
years at Harrow, they certainly did not dominate my life. Re-reading
my diaries, I cannot help being astonished at the incredible amount
of activity packed into my life at that time, especially in my final
year. First there was the rugger which I greatly enjoyed, playing
regularly for the Second XV. Probably, with so much else on, I did
not quite show the dedication – as has been the case so often in my
career – to make the First XV, which was my ambition, though I
think that I might have done had I taken up the position of
scrum-half earlier. Being tall and fast, it was possible for me having
once passed the ball out to my fly-half, John Wyld, to get round the
outside and provide an extra three-quarter: this way we scored many
useful tries, but the school scrum-half was firmly established and had
been awarded his 'lion'.

Another time-absorbing activity in my life at Harrow was acting.
Having been in the chorus of *The Mikado* the previous year when Bill
Nichols was as good a Koko as I have ever seen, I successfully put in
for the part of Don Alhambra in *The Gondoliers*. I was also selected to
play the title part in John Drinkwater's *Abraham Lincoln*, possibly,
thanks to a brilliant producer, Marjorie James, my greatest achievement at Harrow. I also acted in *Cyrano de Bergerac* by Edmund
Rostand, produced by A.G. Elliot-Smith, later to become headmaster of Cheltenham. He is still a friend, now living in retirement
in Eastbourne with his wife, Ruth, the daughter of a housemaster at
Harrow, D.B. Kittermaster, an unusual, unconforming 'beak' who
was to become a great friend of mine, and of Julian's. There were
also house plays, the singing and reading competitions, and election
to the Philathletic Club, which meant certain responsibilities –
mostly social, like visits to concerts and theatres, usually with my
housemaster, E.M. Venables, or with one of the other 'beaks'. I
remember vividly Gielgud's Richard of Bordeaux and a splendid 'all
star' *Julius Caesar* in a production by Oscar Asshe, who played
Casca, with Godfrey Tearle as Antony and Balliol Holloway a
dramatically exciting Cassius. There were visits, too, to concerts and

recitals by such as Schnabel, Smeterlin and Moisevitch with Dr R.S. (Reg) Thatcher, Head of Music.

Improbable as it may sound, as a House Monitor one did a great deal of entertaining. One could have people in to tea on half-holidays or Sunday afternoons while the big 'spread' was Sunday breakfast. These were called 'finds', to which one could invite anyone from the headmaster to a friend or relative, or, of course, boys from other houses. Fags provided the services – quite happily, whatever progressives might think, for they generally managed to benefit indirectly by carrying off the left-overs.

It is not altogether surprising to find in my diary that on at least three occasions I was excused early school because I was exhausted. I was even made to give up my part in *The Gondoliers* and my last school cross-country race, my housemaster considering that I had far too much on my plate. I objected strongly, but I have no doubt that he was right.

Finally came the time to leave. The entry in my diary is simple and terse: 'Said my goodbyes: very sad and horrible.' In my five years at Harrow I had learned to enjoy the benefits of a civilised existence. The standards that I had acquired in my home life and at Hawtreys had been consolidated. I now felt well-equipped to go out into the world.

I was not the first to discover a little later that I was rather less adequately equipped to cope with life than I had imagined.

If life was hectic at Harrow it was certainly no less so at home. With many friends of our own age in the neighbourhood there was endless social activity right through the holidays. In the summer, with a whole stable-full of horses to be exercised, I had invariably ridden at least three horses by eleven o'clock after which we started playing tennis, either at our home or at a friend's. We went to the cinema at least twice a week and scarcely a month went by without visits to the Repertory Theatre at Northampton where our favourite actors were Noel Howlett, Max Adrian and Joan Kemp-Welsh. At another theatre in Northampton we could see plays either on their way to the West End or on tour after a successful run. We swam in the river or the canal – the sun seemed always to be shining in those summers – played squash with friends at Wood Burcote and at least once a week caught the train to London to see a play. Plays which particularly remain in my mind are *The Miracle* with Diana Cooper and the lovely Tilly Losch, *The Green Bay Tree* with Frank Vosper

and Hugh Williams, *The Good Companions* with John Gielgud and
Jessie Matthews, Noel Coward's *Private Lives* – I included the
balcony scene in my 'Desert Island Discs' – and, of course, the Crazy
Gang.

It was a never-ending whirl of social involvement and entertainment: all, one assumes, on a shoestring, for the economic crisis of the
thirties was already beginning to affect my father. He had given up
his Mastership of the Grafton, exchanged his exotic American Stutz
for a more plebeian Austin – much to my dismay – and sold many of
his best horses. Yet, reading my diary, I am amazed at how many
dinner parties we had. They were not, in fact, so much formal dinner
parties as a few friends coming round to dinner. I do not remember
changing for dinner very often, as most people did in those days –
did I even own a dinner jacket at seventeen? Yet we seldom dined
alone, either my parents or we 'children' inviting in friends. Two
guests I particularly remember were Ted Lyon – Colonel W.E.
Lyon, author of *The Pegasus Book* which Terry Rattigan had given
me – and 'Bush' Dubuisson. Ted was one of the most elegant, witty
and talented men I ever met. Any evening on which he was present
was hilarious – and entertaining, for he played the piano brilliantly.
'Bush' was my father's Hunt Secretary. He was a wonderful
character and very courageous, having only one leg, a disability
which did not prevent him from hunting or when visiting us,
playing charades, forfeits and other silly games. As recently as 1982 I
had good reason to be reminded of his visits to Greens Norton. On
the way home from an Animal Health Trust meeting at Lanwades,
just outside Newmarket, I called in at the races. After the second race
I was standing on the forecourt that slopes down to the rails when I
heard behind me a sound which at once rang a bell, very clearly,
though I knew that it came from a very long time ago. But what?
Where? When? Tap: bang! Tap: bang! Tap: bang! A man with a
wooden leg! Of course! The one-legged 'Bush' Dubuisson at Greens
Norton. I could hear him now walking across the parquet floor in
the hall. Tap: bang! Tap: bang! I turned round. To my astonishment
it *was* 'Bush' Dubuisson and looking almost the same as, yes, fifty
years earlier! He passed by me and sat down on a bench, where I
joined him. To my amazement he knew me immediately and seemed
to be as pleased to see me as I was to see him. He told me that he was
over ninety, but that he never missed a Newmarket meeting, driving
himself there and back from his home five or six miles away.
Meeting him certainly brought back vividly those happy Greens

Norton days. Not surprisingly we missed two races, reminiscing in the Jockey Club bar.

'Bush' Dubuisson had succeeded my father as Hunt Secretary of the Grafton in 1928 when my father had become Master. At that time, especially in the winter holidays, hunting very much dominated our lives. After I had outgrown my pony, Tinker, my father gave me a 15.2 h.h. thoroughbred called Toll Gate which he had bought as a two-year-old intending that it should be ready for me as a five-year-old when I was about seventeen. It was a bright bay, very fast, a little hot, but brilliant. I do not ever remember enjoying my hunting more than that first season on Toll Gate. Mounted for the first time on a horse, as opposed to a pony – the most vital step in a horseman's life – one could, of course, be so much more part of it all; not only in keeping up, but also in the newly discovered ability to take one's own line. In the last holidays before I left Harrow, I could not bear to miss a day. In fact, in just four weeks I had fifteen days' hunting, nine of them on Toll Gate. One I recall as clearly as though it were yesterday was the Boxing Day meet at Towcester, only a mile from Greens Norton, which meant that we would be hunting all over the country that I knew best. How very different it was from my first Boxing Day meet ten years earlier when I finished up on the outskirts of Northampton and thought that I was lost. Now I felt one of the swells. After a gallop all round Easton Neston, the beautiful park which ever since the First World War has been the venue for Towcester Races, we moved to our home covert, Kingthorne. Hounds were quickly away across the Bradden road with Toll Gate right at the head of the field. I remember my father, as Master, calling across to me, 'You're enjoying yourself, aren't you?', then adding with a laugh, 'but don't you dare get in front of me!' Most people kept to the right, expecting the fox to go to Tites Copse, but hounds suddenly swung left, which again gave me an advantage. We raced across the five or six fields which I knew so well at the back of the village, jumping the fences as they came, anywhere; it was like a point-to-point. Turning right for Bucknells, we hit a more difficult line of country, but Toll Gate never put a foot wrong: again and again I found myself following Will Pope, our brilliant huntsman, on his famous dun horse, Drummer, and my father on a grand short-legged horse called The Judge. But it was as we approached Bucknells that I had my moment of glory. We came to a seemingly impenetrable bullfinch but, by luck, where I met it there was a slightly thinner patch. I put Toll Gate at it. Bold as ever,

he never hesitated. We were through, and over, and away –
followed by Will Pope and my father! Unbelievably hounds ran
straight through this huge woodland, Bucknells, and on to Crown
Lands, straight through this and right-handed to Wappenham and
Weedon Bushes – the covert made famous both by Cecil Aldin and
Lionel Edwards in their pictures – and finally to Abthorpe where
they were stopped in the dusk. What a Christmas Hunt for a
seventeen-year-old on the first horse that he had ever owned!
Uncharacteristically, my father added in his own starkly factual
hunting diary, in brackets: 'Dorian going very well on Toll Gate.'

A few weeks later my father decided that it was time that the
horizons of my hunting experiences were widened and took me for
my first hunt with the Whaddon Chase, with which, later on, I was
to be so closely associated. It was a tremendously exciting occasion
for me. The horses went by train the evening before, being
accommodated at Redfield, the home of the 'Dolly' Lambtons. We
drove over next morning in time to ride into Winslow, where
hounds were meeting. Compared with anything that I had ever seen
with the Grafton, the field was enormous and very smart: but Toll
Gate acquitted himself well and, again, according to my diary 'went
brilliantly'. Lord Dalmeny, later Lord Rosebery, was the autocratic
Master, and very fearsome he was, particularly in the field, especially
if anyone dared to jump a fence in front of him, as on one occasion
did my father. Despite the fact that he was a recently retired
neighbouring Master, Lord Dalmeny sent him home. An hour or so
later, when my father was boxing up, the Hunt rode past. Dalmeny,
having obviously been told that he really should not behave in such a
way to a neighbouring Master, called out: 'You must come and have
another day with us sometime,' to which my father regrettably
replied: 'Thanks, I'd like to very much when they've got a gentleman
as Master.' Fortunately Lord Rosebery showed no resentment when
I became Master of the Whaddon Chase myself over twenty years
later.

My only regret hunting Toll Gate that season was that my father
would not allow me to wear proper hunting kit, in which I felt I
could have cut quite a dash. His real reason was probably the cost
and the fact that I was still growing, but I was disappointed, never
being too happy in jodphurs, covert coat and bowler hat, which was
exactly the same as my younger brother, Maurice, wore on his pony.

A particular highlight that year was the Derby, when a large party
of us enjoyed a delightful day out on the downs, tickets for the stands

being out of the question. It was made all the more exciting by the victory of Tom Wall's April the Fifth. My father always loved the Aldwych farces with Tom Walls, Ralph Lynn, Robertson Hare, Winifred Shooter and Mary Brough, and had somehow become quite friendly with Tom Walls. His son, of course, had been at Harrow with me, so we felt that we had a proprietary interest in the horse and backed it – at 25-1! Another highlight that holiday was the magnificent lunch which preceded the famous Bertram Mills Circus to which my father took me. I sat next to the artist, Gilbert Holiday, whose exceptional talent is deservedly earning late recognition. He seemed very pleased when I told him that his picture of The Fifth Dragoon Guards charging, in full dress, hung above my head at Greens Norton. Underneath were Kingsley's lines:

> Then hey for boot and horse, lad,
> Around the world away:
> Young blood shall have its course, lad,
> And every dog its day.

For this young blood the last term at Harrow was approaching all too fast. ('Thank God it *is* the last term,' my father said. 'The fees are going up again. They're going to be £70 a term now.') Though so happy at Harrow, we nevertheless dreaded the end of the holidays, which is hardly surprising considering the wonderful life that we were lucky enough to enjoy, despite my father's financial problems. But the end of those holidays in 1932 was particularly sad. My mother's health – the result of her breaking her spine in a hunting accident – and the economic crisis had finally forced my father to sell our home at Greens Norton, where we had been so happy for nearly fifteen years. All too soon the day of the final departure arrived, on the eve of my father's forty-seventh birthday. 'Goodbye to Greens Norton for the last time. Left at 8.30,' is my diary's laconic comment.

In one year I had had to say goodbye to Green Norton and to Harrow, both of which I had so loved, at both of which I had known such great happiness. Lines from a famous Harrow song seemed strangely appropriate:

> Life in front of me, home behind:
> I felt like a waif before the wind,
> Tossed on an ocean of shock and change.

Chapter 3

The Ocean of Shock and Change

That first year after I had left school was somewhat indeterminate. As Greens Norton had been sold, I was homeless. Having led such a sheltered life, suddenly to find myself without roots was quite a traumatic experience. My parents were 'following the sun', which meant that I would join them for short periods when the opportunity arose. I spent a fortnight in Jersey which I did not enjoy, other than the few days when I was allowed to use Jersey College sports ground to practise my hurdles in preparation for the Public School Sports. Estoril, a then newly discovered resort just outside Lisbon, was much more fun, especially when my sister, Barbara, and I introduced surf bathing there, having surf boards specially made for us. The Atlantic rollers were ideal, but it was very cold. Lenzerheide, the unfashionable 'annexe' to St Mortiz, where we went for the ski-ing was not cold enough, and there being no snow I and a boyfriend of Barbara's, Ander Henderson, who had just won his blue at golf and was to become a great friend of the family, were threatened with expulsion from our hotel for appearing at a fancy dress party dressed in beach wear carrying a placard 'Lenzerheide winter sports'! I did not really enjoy ski-ing, but that may have been because I dislike snow.

It was at Lenzerheide, however, that I first fell passionately in love. The object of my attention was a very attractive seventeen-year-old German girl with short blonde hair and a *retroussé* nose, called Heidi. She spoke hardly any English, which did not greatly matter as we only met on the dance floor at the hotel at which she was staying, which was not the same as ours. My aim each evening was to ensure that I had the last dance with her, when the lights were lowered and the band played 'Goodnight Sweetheart'. But I had a rival: not only was he a fellow Old Harrovian, but his name was Blennerhasett – no less – and being a little older he was rather more sophisticated than I was – and considerably better off. He won.

To occupy six weeks in the autumn, Barbara, who had also not long left school, and I were despatched to a course on Citizenship at Ashridge College – then run by the Conservative Party – at Berkhamsted, only a few miles from my old family home, Pendley. In fact, the course which provided us with the opportunity of hearing many extremely interesting speakers had no little influence on my later turning Pendley into a Centre of Adult Education. Being even then an enthusiastic student of history, I enormously enjoyed meeting and listening to such as Professor Namier, a greatly respected historian, and Sir Arthur Bryant, the famous author. Even the Prime Minister, Sir Stanley Baldwin, attended one weekend in honour of some anniversary. I was invited to take part in a review to be presented before him having, amongst other items, to sing 'Loch Lomond' – 'Ye'll take the high road' – with the senior tutor, Laurence Sutton, which went down very well, he being well covered while I was tall and skinny. Afterwards, the Principal, a bluff, rather pompous retired General, Sir Reginald Hoskins, introduced me to the Prime Minister. He was very friendly and approachable, showing genuine interest when I told him that I had connections with Hawtreys, of which he was an Old Boy. Many years later, when I had to write to him about an appeal or some business connected with Hawtreys, he replied in his own hand: 'Any communication from Hawtreys must have my attention. I remember so vividly my days there. I loved the school and was very fond of Edward Hawtrey, and I rejoice to hear of its prosperity. Yours sincerely, Baldwin of Bewdley.' I am the proud possessor of personal letters – the signatures at any rate were personal – from four Prime Ministers, Sir Winston Churchill, Lord Douglas Home and Margaret Thatcher being the others. I also once had an unexpected meeting and a very congenial chat with Jim Callaghan at, of all places, Hickstead.

Inevitably the emphasis was very much on the social side at Ashridge. We were all young, bursting with healthy energy, determined to live life to the full. Once again I was fortunate to make friends, though with the exception of Mary and Jo Garton, whose brother John captained the Oxford Crew and whom I met again many years later as High Sheriff of Buckinghamshire, they more or less passed out of our lives once the course was over. Two attractive brunettes on the course who particularly appealed to me were Betty Robson and Sanchia Whitworth, the latter's father being Robin, Director of the British Drama League who, by coincidence, was the very first speaker we had at Pendley in 1945. A pretty young blonde, Susan Armour, however, seemed rather more interested in me. One Saturday afternoon, both Betty and Sanchia being otherwise engaged, I took Susan to the cinema. On our return we went to the library, which was usually quiet at weekends. Susan began to make slightly amorous advances, which were not altogether unwelcome, finishing by sitting on my lap in a very deep leather armchair. Suddenly the door opened and the Principal walked in. He looked appalled at finding two of his students in such a compromising position, but struggle as we might we could not get out of the chair. Next morning I was sent for, the General telling me that never in his experience – which must have been very limited for a soldier – had he seen such a disgraceful carry on. 'I will keep a careful eye on you in the future,' he said. It seemed politic to dismiss poor, pretty Susan from the cast of the play that I had been asked to produce at the end of the course, lest he might see more than his moral rectitude could stand, but I was over-ruled by the rest of the cast and we all survived. I could not help feeling that it would have been a little fairer had I been caught with someone who mattered more to me.

I also spent a short time at a Crammers at Westgate-on-Sea, ostensibly to assist me in obtaining School Certificate credits in French and Maths which it was thought might assist me in finding a job: but probably it was just as much to keep me occupied. In those days it was essential to get one's School Certificate passes in English, Latin and Maths. In two attempts I gained credits in every subject that I took except in Maths, in which I failed completely. Rightly, my parents felt that although I was not intending to go to University, a School Certificate would be useful. Hence, ostensibly, the Crammers. I was already keen on tennis: at Westgate I became obsessed with it, even being selected to play for Thanet, which was no very great achievement, though better than just playing for one's local tennis club. But I fear that I lacked the application really to succeed: which as I have hinted already, has not infrequently been my story.

A year after I had left Harrow I still had no job, nor had I really decided what I wanted to do. Perhaps the fact that by then I had my own bank account made me feel a false sense of security, allowed me to believe that there was no great urgency to earn money. My father had taken me to the Westminster Bank in Threadneedle Street, introducing me to the Manager, explaining that I was the fourth, possibly the fifth, member of my family to bank with the

Westminster. It was then arranged that my father would pay into my account £100 each year. In addition, in the first year, he gave me an extra £200, to set me up in a bed-sit in London where it was hoped that I would extend my education (having by now acquired my School Certificate) by learning typing and shorthand, attending the Berlitz School of Languages and enrolling as a part-time student at the Guildhall School of Music. Unfortunately the following year, owing to his critical financial situation, my father was only able to give me half of the £100 that he had promised me if I could tell him truthfully on my twenty-first birthday that I had never smoked a cigarette in my life. I had not; nor have I to this day. Cigars are a different matter. When that winter my father took my mother to the sun in Jamaica he bought no less than two thousand four-inch Jamaican cigars, in little boxes of four, at a penny each. Almost as soon as he had a home of his own again, some two years later, he gave up smoking altogether, handing over the cigars to me!

Before my father left for Jamaica he told me that I really must make every attempt to find myself a job. I assured him that I would do my very best: but where? How? I had always enjoyed writing, had even had two or three articles printed in the parish magazine and one in a local paper. Perhaps I should go in for journalism. Through my contact with the Berry family, who owned the *Daily Telegraph* – Sir Gomer had leased the home farm at Pendley and his sons were at Harrow – I obtained an interview at their Fleet Street office, I remember little about it, however, and obviously it was not fruitful. Through my cousin Beryl Cautley, who was very friendly with the Robinson family (John, the son, being at Hawtreys and later representing Harrow as a spin bowler four years in succession), I was offered a position, starting at the very bottom, with Foster Robinsons, which, at that time, made paper bags at Bristol. I could not bring myself to accept it, much to Beryl's and to my mother's disappointment, but whether it was because living at Bristol did not appeal to me, or because starting at the very bottom was not at all what I was looking for, or because I was afraid of the embarrassment of telling my friends that I made paper bags, I do not know. It could well be that in turning down such a good opportunity I made a big mistake.

When, because advertising was a career that had certain attractions for me – perhaps because of my gift for telling a story! – I went for an interview with Crawfords, the most important advertising firm in the country at that time, I certainly did not get offered a job. Having been kept waiting about half an hour, I was ushered in to the presence of a quite terrifying German lady, who I understood later to be a senior executive. Having asked my name, age, address and so on she came straight to the point: 'Why on earth,' she said, 'should you think that with your background and your apparent lack of qualifications of any sort, you could be of any value whatever to us?'

To which I could only stammer: 'I really have no idea. I thought perhaps you'd tell me.'

Inevitably her sharp retort was: 'Well, if you haven't any idea I am quite sure that I haven't.' End of interview: not very helpful, and extremely deflating.

At Harrow I had taken singing lessons. I had also been taught by my great friend John Wyld's godfather, Roland Jackson, himself a professional singer. When first I lived in London, encouraged by Roland Jackson, I enrolled at the Guildhall School of Music to have lessons with an old friend of his, the great Victorian ballad-singer and teacher, Dr Plunkett Green, by this time elderly but still very distinguished. I could never, however, seriously see myself as a singer though my time at the Guildhall was very worthwhile. As it had often been suggested that my voice might be my fortune, I was quite keen to get into broadcasting. Over the months I had three different interviews. On one occasion, according to my diary, I was 'tentatively offered a job', but I cannot think what it was for I never accepted it. At the other two interviews I was firmly turned down, which genuinely disappointed me. There was some slight compensation in my occasionally being offered a few lines in a Radio Luxembourg advertisement, but I could never persuade any firm to offer me a permanent contract. After eighteen months or so I was beginning to worry, to think, even, that I might be unemployable, which was quite alarming at the age of twenty. I began to blame my lack of qualifications; I even resented the fact that my father had sent my brother to Oxford rather than me, though I knew well enough that Maurice had long before made up his mind that he was going to be a lawyer, needing a degree, while I had never had any clear idea of what I was going to do.

I had always been interested in the theatre, of course, and managed to get interviews with a number of eminent people. Sybil Thorndike and her husband Lewis Casson very kindly invited me to lunch with them at the Great Western Hotel, Paddington. They were charming, she never drawing breath, he nodding his head sagely at all that she said. A few weeks later, to my surprise, I was offered a part in a play going on tour with their daughter, Joan Casson: but, though I do not remember why, I could not bring myself to accept it. I was lucky enough, too, to see Sir Gerald du Maurier in his dressing room at the Princess Theatre. He was very friendly and easy, being particularly interested when I told him that I was related to Sir Charles Hawtrey, 'on whom,' he said, 'I have quite unashamedly modelled myself,' which pleased me. He asked his faithful secretary, Sybil Beaumont, to give me tickets for his play and arranged for me to see his casting director, but it did not lead to anything. I also had an interview with Basil Dean, who had seen me as Abraham Lincoln at Harrow, his own son being in the play. He had also seen me in a production of *The Brontës* at the Guildhall. He even offered me a part in *Cornelius*, which he was presenting with Ralph Richardson, but when I turned up at the first rehearsal I found that J.B. Priestley, the author of the play, had already given the part to somebody else, though I suspected that the attractive young actor who was lucky enough to get this small part was really a boyfriend of the obviously homosexual stage manager.

Would I have accepted the part if I had been seriously offered a contract? Frankly I doubt it. In the first place, being naive and still rather innocent, I was a little scared of the homosexual element that everybody warned me I would find in the theatre. Secondly, I realise, looking back, that I lacked the self-confidence. My life had been so secure. I was not sufficiently sure of myself to embark on such a hazardous career as the theatre. Nor was I convinced that I could succeed. My successes had been in character parts – Abraham Lincoln, the Reverend Patrick, the father in *The Brontës* – but in the professional theatre there were plenty of people of the right age to play such parts. I doubted whether I could ever make a success of young men parts. I was self-conscious concerning my badly shaped head and Williams nose, and while I could imitate or impersonate people quite cleverly, I was inclined to be embarrassed as myself. Disguise helped me.

I see in my diary that I also had a film test at about this time, but who arranged it or what happened I now have no idea. I was at about that time, however, considering – a little vaguely – two other very different careers. The first was the Indian Army, my interest having first been aroused by Willie Stevenson, a master at Harrow of whom I was very fond, and who had himself been in the Indian Army. I even went for a medical, but was turned down because of my chronic skin trouble; as, indeed, I was to be in 1939 and again in

1942. I thought, too, very seriously about joining the police. Shortly after leaving Harrow I had decided, on the recommendation of a cousin, George Rodwell, to join the Special Mounted Branch, just as others at that time joined the Territorials. Requiring no special qualifications, one just applied and hoped to be accepted. Arriving at Imber Court for my interview, I was both pleased and disappointed when the Commandant, Colonel de Chair, called me out in the middle of the riding test, saying that he had seen enough: pleased obviously because he appreciated that I was a good enough rider – after, I have to admit, he had discovered that I was my father's son; disappointed because I was denied the opportunity of showing him just how good I was! I enjoyed the Special Mounted Branch enormously, especially the State occasions, even though once I may have missed a great opportunity. Escorting an army unit up the Mall for the Armistice Parade at the Cenotaph, my horse suddenly stumbled, going down on its knees. I just stepped off over its head, remounted and carried on. Having arrived at Whitehall and taken up position opposite the Cenotaph, I noticed when I looked down that my horse's legs were covered with blood. Somehow I informed a superior, who told me to take my horse into reserve, at which moment I recognised the young officer in charge of a platoon of Guards in front of me: it was Raoul Charles Robin from Hawtreys days. Would he say 'Platoon wight turn?' My place was taken by a regular, fortunately, perhaps, for suddenly a shriek from a woman drew his attention to a man pushing his way through the crowd holding a revolver. He hurled himself from his horse, landing on top of the man, bearing him to the ground. That officer was awarded a medal. Might that medal have been mine? Or might the end have been even more dramatic? Sadly the Special Mounted Branch was not revived after the war.

I was tempted to become a regular, but when I found that one could not join the Mounted Police direct, but had to start 'on the beat' my ardour cooled. Later I was to have a long and happy association with the police, but in a very different capacity. Shortly after I had started my Adult Education Centre at Pendley, the Chief Constable of Hertfordshire, Arthur Young, arranged for officers from his force to attend courses there. As a result I was asked to advise on the setting up of the Senior Officers Police College at Bramshill. When it was opened I became a regular lecturer, either on the written and spoken word or on Adult Education. I never missed a course in twenty-five years. As a result I made many good friends in the police, often being fortunate enough to receive invitations to their social functions, at one of which, the E Division (CID) Dinner at The Savoy, Harry Secombe was a fellow guest. He not only drew a picture of me on his menu while I was speaking, adding an amusing caption, but was later to help me in a number of activities with which I was involved.

Another six months passed, taking me up to my twenty-first birthday, and still no job: and I have to admit that this was at least partly due to the fact that I was still enjoying a very hectic and varied social life. London, when I was living there, provided more than enough entertainment – cocktail parties, dances, tennis, visits to Lord's, Twickenham, Wimbledon, Hurlingham (for the polo), Brooklands (for the motor racing), and, of course, the theatre. With seats so cheap I reckoned to go to the theatre at least twice a week. Perhaps the most memorable production at that time was *Escape Me Never*, with the exquisite, gamin Elizabeth Bergner, to which I went at least half a dozen times. There were also plenty of visits to the country, frequently to our dear friends round Greens Norton, with tennis parties, swimming, at the end of the summer a morning's cubhunting; and visits, too, to Westgate-on-Sea where I spent much time at Hawtreys, joining in the school's activities or playing tennis with the masters. I also went to Henley, where my parents had taken a house for a few months. It was at Henley that my most important romantic liaison that year was to come to an end. I had been introduced to Leila by a distant cousin who used to act as a debs' chaperone. After a few weeks she assured me that Leila could never be persuaded to go to any dance unless I was in the party – her way, perhaps, of ensuring that I would accept her invitations, there being the usual shortage of young men, or debs' delights! Leila was exceptionally attractive in an unconventional way and very intelligent, which was not the case with all the debs I met! We became genuinely fond of each other, apparently only content in each other's company, the climax of our affair being the night that we rapturously danced until dawn in Cadogan Square, Carrol Gibbons's music floating out to us through the windows of the house where the dance was being held. 'Little white lies" was the tune that summer. Inevitably it became 'our tune'. Even today when I hear it – !

I invited Leila down to the Leander Ball at Henley. It was a glorious summer night and after the ball we drove around the town, she sitting on the hood of the little open Triumph I then had, her copper-coloured hair floating in the breeze and entangling with the white silk scarf that I wore raffishly round my neck, a champagne bottle in her hand. It was all gloriously 'thirties'; but unfortunately it resulted in her getting pleurisy. She was quite ill, having to stay in bed at our house for a week or more. Her mother came over several times, on the last occasion leaving her some money to give to Dorothy, the young maid who had devotedly looked after her day and night. Sadly, Leila departed having spent the money on herself, leaving Dorothy not so much as a shilling. That was it: I really resented her meanness, so it was the end of our affair, for ever! Rather priggish of me? It certainly seems so now. Later she was to marry a millionaire, so I doubt if my callous behaviour had any lasting effects.

The gap left in my affections was quickly filled by Deirdre. I had gone to a dance in London with Diane Wake, of whom I had been very fond ever since Greens Norton days, her family at Courteenhall being very friendly with mine. She was very pretty, exceptionally athletic, being good at all games, particularly tennis, and ran like the wind. Everyone loved Diane. It was a great shock to the neighbourhood and far beyond when shortly after the war, having returned to Courteenhall with her brother Toby – then unmarried, now Sir Hereward Wake – she was killed in a fall at a local point-to-point. In 1935 she was certainly one of the most lovely and popular girls around: an invitation to Courteenhall or to accompany her to a dance, therefore, was much appreciated. We dined at the Criterion and before going on to the dance went to the cinema, *The Bengal Lancers*: yes – all in full evening dress, white tie and tails! Not surprisingly, when we reached the dance everyone was keen to dance with her, while I, not being a regular debs' delight, knew few people. Before long I found myself on my own. I spent a couple of dances at the Champagne bar, then wandered back to the ballroom, leaning against the wall hoping that Diane might suddenly become free. While standing there I noticed a girl standing by the door. She was so pretty that I could not possibly believe that she was a wallflower.

There was a pause in the music before it started up again for the next dance. I noticed Diane whisked away. I also noticed this girl still standing by the door. I looked at her more intently. She was small, in a simple white dress, had short dark hair – and an unbelievably pretty little face. I just could not believe that she was left on her own. Surely she was waiting for somebody.

The next dance was an eightsome reel. No one collected her. I moved towards the door and as I passed her, as if by chance, stopped and made some obvious remark, such as, 'Hot, isn't it?' or 'Eightsomes are too energetic for me in this weather.' She responded in a natural and friendly way and started chatting. When the skirl of Scottish music was replaced by the more appropriate Cole Porter, quite naturally I asked her to dance. She was enchanting. I just could not believe my luck. It seemed incredible that anyone so outstandingly attractive could be without a partner.

Apparently she lived in London, did not go to many dances but loved music. Her name was Deirdre Wilson, so she had the same initials as mine – was this significant? My parents, I recalled – Vivian Williams and Violet Wood – had had the same initials; so, for that matter, had I and Diane Wake!

We danced happily for the rest of the evening; in the early hours I took her home. What had happened to the escort, whom she must initially have had, I do not know. Diane, I had no doubt, would be all right. Daringly I invited Deirdre to tea in my bed-sit in Warwick Road the following day. A week later I escorted her to a dance at Claridges.

For the rest of the summer we saw a good deal of each other, increasingly enjoying each other's company despite the difference in our backgrounds. She was a music student, was, indeed, an outstandingly talented pianist: her performance of Debussy's 'Catédral Englouti' at an entertainment that I organised in aid of the Church at Wicken near Greens Norton, where a friend had just been installed as rector, was highly praised by everyone, including some who had a real knowledge of music. We went occasionally to the cinema or theatre, but usually she used to come round to my Warwick Road bed-sit, where we played records.

In November her father invited me to join his party at the Savoy on Election night. There was a National Party landslide. Two days later I took her out in the country to meet my singing-teacher friend, Roland Jackson, and to play the piano. When I dropped her home she invited me in, for the first time; but it was the last time that I ever saw her. Suddenly, probably quite wrongly, I sensed that her parents saw me as a suitable match: which was not at all what I had in mind at that time, being barely twenty-one and with no job. In December I joined my parents for Christmas at the house that they had rented in the West Country. After Christmas I went up to Banbury to stay with Moyra Lubbock, who was to become my first wife, and discovered, perhaps, that I had far more in common with her than I

had with Deirdre: we hunted seven days in a fortnight and went to
two Hunt Balls. I did not return to London until mid-January and
then, due to unexpected circumstances, for only a very few days,
during which I made no contact with Deirdre. So ended a brief yet
somehow rather touching little interlude. Looking back fifty years
later it is not easy to condone such callous behaviour by a young man
of twenty-one; yet, however regrettable, it was not, I believe,
unique. Today it might be even less so.

Spending so much time at Hawtreys, I gradually became aware of
two factors which, inter-related as they eventually became, were to
have a great effect on my life. The first was that my old aunt, Mrs
Hawtrey, the proprietress of the school, was now well into her
eighties and increasingly concerned about the future of the school.
She probably knew, as I did not, that her daughter Beryl was dying
of cancer. She respected rather than felt any great affection for her
son-in-law, Frank Cautley; her only son, Michael, had died of
infantile paralysis while up at Cambridge and she had no grandchild-
ren. What then would happen to the school? Almost imperceptibly
I came to realise that I and my brother, her great-nephews, were her
nearest relatives. At the same time I was becoming aware of the
enjoyment that association with the school was bringing me. I loved
joining in all the activities with the staff and boys – and not only
because Miss Sparshot had been succeeded by a rather more
attractive young lady. The time I spent with the masters in the
common room or on the tennis court was always fun. Hawtreys
itself as a school meant a great deal to me, and I was genuinely
attached to the remarkable old lady who still so completely
dominated it.

As so often in my life, I made an impulsive decision. I was going
to be a schoolmaster. I realised that I had no qualifications, but I
believed that if I could get a job in a prep school, where qualifications
were still not absolutely essential, I might be able to prove myself
and eventually become capable and worthy of taking over Hawtreys.
Having learned of their existence from Frank Cautley – who, not
surprisingly, was somewhat sceptical – I made an appointment for an
interview at Messrs Gabbitas and Thring, Scholastic Agents, of
Sackville Street, London, W1. I do not know whether I saw Mr
Gabbitas, or Mr Thring, or, indeed, either of them, but I found the
gentleman who interviewed me sympathetic and helpful, and
impressed by my connection with Hawtreys. He would be pleased,

he informed me, to put me on their list, would forward information of
vacancies and would circularise my name to preparatory schools
looking for junior assistant masters. Much to my surprise, within a
fortnight I had had several notices of vacancies and four firm
invitations to interviews. One sufficed. The headmaster of Beachborough Park, near Folkestone, Mr F.E. Chappell, would, I was
informed, like me to meet him at the Garrick Club on 7 November. I
spent the afternoon at Oxford watching a memorable game of rugger
between the university and the All Blacks, with my brother Maurice,
Roger Pulbrook, a Harrow friend, and Michael Denison, but still
arrived at the Garrick Club in plenty of time – and immediately
decided that it was the loveliest club in London, an opinion that has
not changed. Fred Chappell duly appeared, tall, elegant, a neat
moustache, and sparkling eyes, the edges of which wrinkled
attractively when he smiled, which he did frequently. His voice was a
little precise and he obviously enjoyed language. I took to him
immediately.

He led me to a small room in which there were no other people and
sat me in a leather armchair while he himself perched on the fender
seat. He drew out a silver cigarette case – he was a heavy smoker – but
having selected a cigarette he did not close it. On one side, beneath the
thin wire holder, there was a card on which it was obvious that he had
written all the questions which he wanted to ask me, as he had,
presumably, other candidates. He put his questions to me in such an
informal and charming way that I soon felt completely at ease, until he
said: 'I see that you have a credit in geography. That is excellent, as I
would want you to take the bottom two forms in geography.'

What was I to say? Not only had I no credit in geography but I had
given it up my second term at Harrow as I so disliked it. I was silent. I
did not like to lie but was afraid of damaging my chances if I told the
truth. I was fairly confident that I could keep one jump ahead of the
bottom two forms by mugging it up in advance: Paris is on the Seine;
Amsterdam is the capital of Holland; Brazil is famous for nuts; a
peninsula is a – and so on. Fortunately, without waiting for an answer,
he spoke again: 'And, of course, you speak French. You would be
taking the third form in French; possibly the fifth.'

French! What was it that K.P. James had taught us at Hawtreys
when I was there as a boy? '*Me, te, se, nous, vous, le, la, les, lui, y, en*' –
the prepositions: the joke, of course, was *y en* at the end – 'he-haw',
like a donkey. No problems there, surely, but as for *speaking* French –
'Well, er, yes, sir.'

History, which I would also be expected to teach to the third form, worried me not at all. I had always enjoyed history; moreover, only the previous summer Maurice and I had toured the mediaeval castles of Yorkshire and Wales.

To my astonishment, less than fifteen minutes after the interview had commenced, he had offered me the job. Could it have helped that I happened to mention my connection with Hawtreys? No doubt. I was confident, nevertheless, that I could do the job adequately, and looked forward to it.

King George V died at 1155 on 20 June 1936. The following day I drove down to Beachborough to begin my first term as a schoolmaster and one of the happiest periods of my life, brief as it was. The school was totally different from Hawtreys, very free and easy, yet such was the natural authority of Fred Chappell that the freedom was never abused. At first I was a little intimidated by the senior master, one N.C. Wood, a crusty bachelor and firm disciplinarian, but after one big row – the result of my using his precious cricket pitch for sports practice! – we became great friends. In fact, I found him to be an extremely helpful as well as a human and amusing companion: he used particularly to enjoy the fact that he was an Etonian and I a Harrovian. The teasing, though perhaps rather puerile, was incessant. I encountered no problems, I am glad to report, with my geography; nor my French: while not a little to my satisfaction my talk to the third form on the mediaeval castles of Yorkshire and Wales was so successful that I was asked to repeat it to the whole school. This was a proud moment for me, though Woody rather resented it: 'At Eton, of course, we have always regarded classics as more important than castles.' At the end of my first term I received from Fred Chappell a most encouraging letter in which he was kind enough to say that he thought that I had the makings of the ideal schoolmaster, as I had the gift of treating young people as equals, never talking down to them, 'eschewing any suggestion of condescension' – he loved such language: I like to think that he was right. 'You have an exceptionally promising future,' he concluded. Enclosed with the letter was my first term's salary: £90! I was ecstatic. At last, it seemed, I was launched on my career.

Ironically at about the same time I received a letter from an agent offering me a comparatively lucrative contract to advertise regularly on Radio Luxembourg, which could well have led to successful careers in either broadcasting or advertising, or both; but I turned it down, without hesitation. I was too happy with my life as a schoolmaster. Teaching, I now had no doubt, was something at which I could succeed, something which could absorb the rest of my working life. The two happy years that followed did nothing to disillusion me. Rather, when I left Beachborough to go to Hawtreys, I had become more than ever convinced that teaching was my metier.

Chapter 4

TV Times

Whether or not at the age of twenty-three anyone can really be sure what their metier is I do not know. I am inclined to doubt it. Certainly in 1938 nobody could be certain what the future had in store for them. Already the Munich crisis loomed, but despite the hopeful if naive 'Peace in our time' reaction from Neville Chamberlain that followed it, most people felt that war was now inevitable. Like most of my contemporaries I did not concern myself too much with the distant future. It never occurred to me even to hesitate when I was asked to join Frank Cautley as joint headmaster of Hawtreys and had my old Aunt Nellie's share of the school – the major share – made over to me. Nor did I hesitate to bring forward my marriage to Moyra, with whom I had become increasingly involved after Deirdre and to whom I had become engaged the previous year. Young as she was, she seemed the ideal wife for a very inexperienced headmaster for whom, as I was frequently reminded, there were considerable advantages in being married. Older people could probably see clearly – as, I suspect, they did – the inadvisability of a young man of twenty-three embarking on both marriage and a new, responsible – and, in all likelihood, difficult – job when war was so obviously just round the corner. 'But,' slightly to adapt A.E. Housman, 'I was three and twenty: no use to talk to me.'

Certainly life was so full and exciting, if occasionally frustrating, that one never had the time or inclination to speculate on the future, let alone the 'post-war' future, even though it might have been wise to do so. Had I been told in 1938 that in less than ten years' time I would have abandoned being a schoolmaster and embarked on three totally different careers, virtually all at the same time, I would never have believed it: my commitment as headmaster of Hawtreys was, I thought then, for life. How could I have foreseen that after five wonderfully happy years at Hawtreys, apart from the occasional ructions with Frank Cautley, I would have found myself becoming more interested in the education of adults rather than children, eventually pioneering a Centre of Adult Education at Tring? How could I have known that within a year of taking up hunting again, as a respite from a very taxing job, I would have become a Master of Foxhounds? Or that these jobs between them – education and horses – would have resulted in my becoming a BBC commentator? In 1938 it would have seemed absurd, yet, in fact, it proved quite logical, even inevitable.

Having moved Hawtreys at the beginning of the war to the delightful North Wales estate of Sir Watkin Williams-Wynn, Llangedwyn Hall, I became, within a very short time, as busy in the holidays as I was in the term. This was because, although it had never in any way been planned, in 1940, after the real war had succeeded the phoney war, all sorts of people – parents, old boys, friends of parents or old boys – started to use Llangedwyn as a retreat. Having come once, they began to come regularly, attracted by the peace and beauty of the old Elizabethan manor with its terraced gardens, its woods and the delightful valley through which ran the little river Tanat. To keep them happily occupied in a world without television and insufficient petrol to make a visit to the local cinema ten miles away anything but a rarity, I started organising simple activities of a broadly cultural or educational nature. Before long I found this 'adult education' excitingly, unexpectedly rewarding, more rewarding even than teaching children. To see the response in people who had thought themselves to be beyond an enjoyment in music, or art, or drama, or history, or what you will, was inspiring. To provide for them was a challenge and, one ultimately felt, a responsibility. But even in a place as delightful as Llangedwyn one cannot work seven days a week, fifty-two weeks of the year.

In 1943, exhausted, I had something of a breakdown, initially brought on by a bad attack of jaundice. While recuperating at my parents' home in Somerset it was discovered that I had an internal growth which might or might not be malignant – it was less easy to be specific in those days. Treatment was obviously necessary, but as it was then thought that the Westminster Hospital was the most suitable place, I had to leave Hawtreys in charge of the senior master and arrange to live in London. Fortunately, it being wartime, my parents-in-law seldom used their flat so this was made available, Moyra dividing her time between the school at Llangedwyn and me in London. To pass the time, particularly the evenings, I accepted invitations to give talks, first at the Nuffield Services Centre in Leicester Square, then at the Gordon Services Club in Vauxhall Bridge Road. This so increased my interest in informal adult education that immediately the war was over I arranged for Hawtreys to move to Savernake Forest, appointed a headmaster – later forming it into a company, of which I am still Chairman – and proceeded to develop my ideas on residential adult education at Pendley Manor, my family home at Tring.

Here again after a few years, working at extreme pressure, I had another breakdown: nothing very serious, but enough to make me ease up, accepting the fact that I, like anybody else, needed proper relaxation. So I decided to take up hunting. This led, within a year, to my becoming, much to my surprise, a Master of Foxhounds and very much involved in the horse world. This, later, was to result in my long association with the British Horse Society, the BHS being the result of the merger, engineered by my father, of the Institute of the Horse and the National Horse Association of Great Britain. One of its first activities was to organise a horse show at the White City. The job that I did there for my father, Chairman and Director of the Show, was to lead directly to my becoming employed by the BBC.

Thus it was that within a few years of the end of the war I found myself developing three entirely separate, yet parallel, careers: careers which ultimately, I have always liked to think, became complementary, there being an educational content behind each of them. But they were all very far removed from the prep-school career on which I was embarking in 1938.

As far as the general public is concerned, of course, it is principally television and show jumping with which I am associated. How often have I felt, when introduced to speak at some function, that the audience expect to see half a horse! They are surprised to learn, if they ever do, that I am so closely involved in education. How, they wonder, could this horsey type, this voice identified with horse jumping, become associated with education? Perhaps the real question should be: 'How did an educationalist become a sports commentator?' It has often been quoted how Mike Ansell – Colonel Sir Michael Ansell, the remarkable blind man so long responsible for Britain's show jumping successes – told me that I could 'bloody well do it' myself when I criticised the public address at the Victory Championships which he organised in 1945. That is true: although I was really criticising the show communications, not the announcer. But there is rather more to it than that. My becoming a commentator was due more to my father than Mike Ansell, though I doubt if either of them set about it intentionally. It was natural that my father should be invited to organise the first big show, known as the National Horse Show, to be held after the war in 1946. He was the only survivor of the Committee that had run the old pre-war International Horse Show at Olympia, in addition to which he had already earned a considerable reputation as an organiser, organisation always being an art which had greatly interested him. In notes made by my mother, only discovered after her death, she had written:

> His Colonel [George Ansell, father of Mike Ansell] recognised not only his horsemanship but his organising ability when in March 1914 he appointed him Riding Master. He put all his heart and energy into it, and the wonderful Musical Ride which he produced that year, and which was I believe the first ever, was really the first thing which gave him the opportunity of displaying his extraordinary gift of organisation, which, I think, no one had suspected before, but which has proved one of his greatest powers since.

The week before the show my father was telling a friend of all the arrangements that had been made for the show, how to ensure its efficient running even more detail had been considered than at Olympia itself, when he was asked who was doing the public address.

'The what?' For a moment my father was stumped.

'The announcer, for the show classes.'

It was the one department that had been forgotten. Mrs Yeomans, who had announced the jumping at the Victory Championships the year before, would do the same for the one jumping class of each performance at the National Show, but an announcer was required for the show classes, a fact that had eluded my father. He was not the sort of person, however, to admit defeat, let alone confess to inefficiency. 'That is in hand,' he assured his friend confidently, hurrying off to a telephone to contact me.

'I've got a job for you,' he said. 'You're to be the announcer at the National Show next week.' When I said nothing, being completely taken aback, really knowing very little about the show, he went on: 'Well, you're supposed to be educated and know how to speak: and you've been brought up with horses. You'll love it.' Although he made it sound as though he were doing me an honour, knowing him so well I guessed his problem and, of course, agreed, inconvenient as it obviously was. It would only last three days, I thought, furthermore, a break after such a hectic twelve months at Pendley would possibly be good for me. So I agreed to do the job, thus becoming part of the team which the following year, 1947, mounted the first International Horse Show at the White City. Charged with interpreting this little-known sport to a largely lay public, I now undertook to be responsible for the show jumping commentaries as well as the show classes. At this show my father invited Mike Ansell who, with Phil Blackmore, had been a BSJA representative at the 1946 show, to become joint Show Director with himself and Frank Gentle, Chairman of the Greyhound Racing Association, which owned the White City. Thus commenced a partnership which Mike Ansell and I were to enjoy until his retirement some thirty years later.

At the beginning, the BBC's interest in show jumping was luke-warm, to say the least, but when in 1952 at the Helsinki Olympic Games Britain in the very last event won a gold medal, their attitude changed – as did that of many others in the media; just as, many years later, they were to seize upon snooker as a new popular sport. In 1952 they quickly – and successfully – set about establishing show jumping. As none of the BBC's regular sports commentators knew much, if anything, about horses, let alone show jumping, it was not altogether surprising that, having established myself on the public address at major shows, I should be invited, in 1952, to become the BBC's first official equestrian commentator. I saw no reason why I should not accept, imagining that it would only involve me in two or three major shows each year. Before long, however, it had built up to about seventy days a year, not including all the homework and travel involved: more than I had bargained for, perhaps, but how much pleasure and enjoyment it was to bring to me; how much drama, how many exciting trips all over the world – and, ultimately, how much frustration.

My long association with the BBC comprised four distinctive periods. There was the first ten years before ITV came into being. There was the period between the beginning of ITV and the BBC taking over the televising of Hickstead in 1969. Next came the period between 1969 and 1976, the year of the Montreal Olympic Games when, having worked for the BBC for twenty-five years, I made a firm decision to retire after the Moscow Olympics. Finally, there were the last four years up to my retirement. The difference between the first period and the last was so great that one might have been

3a.
With brother
Maurice and
grandfather,
Canon Wood,
on the front
at Westgate-on-Sea.

3b. Aged 13 with
Toll Gate, the
first horse of my
own, at Greens
Norton.

4a. Nostalgic view from my room at Harrow
(ten miles from Marble Arch as the crow flies!).

4b. Llangedwyn Hall, in the magical Tanat Valley,
where Hawtreys found peace in the war.

5a. With the family in Somerset at the beginning of the war.

5b. Brother Maurice, killed at the end of the war.

6a. Presentations from Michael Clayton, Editor of *Horse and Hound*,
to Jennifer and myself to mark my twenty-five years
as Master of the Whaddon Chase.

6b. The card accompanying the presentation
when I retired as the BBC's equestrian commentator.

30 YEARS AND 'CLEAR'!

BBC tv

operating in different centuries. When first I broadcast for the BBC in the early fifties, television had only recently been revived after the war. It was, therefore, very informal, very unsophisticated, still in its uncertain infancy; from a broadcaster's point of view great fun. One could certainly get away with far more than one could today. I doubt, for instance, whether I would be able to insist, as I did in 1952, that I did both the public address commentary *and* the television commentary: though, in fact, it worked quite well as one could make the two commentaries complementary. Today, if one is on the PA one is sh! sh!-ed if one starts speaking at the same time as the television commentator. On the TV one's most apt comment is drowned as the PA booms in. Why I insisted on doing both was because since starting at the White City in 1946 I had made something of a reputation for myself as a public address announcer; this was due firstly to my having the necessary knowledge about a sport which was to most people unfamiliar and secondly because I was fortunate enough to have a voice well suited to a microphone – it is all a matter of timbre, apparently – and easily recognisable. As a result, people attending the major shows expected me to be on the PA and felt cheated if it was anyone else. Naturally, therefore, I did not want to risk losing this reputation. After all, television was, at that time, new and not very widespread. Nor could anyone be sure that the BBC would continue to televise show jumping. Moreover, Mike Ansell left nobody in any doubt that he expected me to continue to provide the public address commentary at the two major shows for which he was responsible: the two shows, of course, that the BBC wanted to televise, the Royal International and the Horse of the Year Show. What is more, he expected me to operate from the control point in the centre of the arena at the White City, at the ringside at the Horse of the Year Show, then at Harringay, where, because he regarded me as his No. 2 – his liaison with other departments – he very much relied on me.

Our first producer, Bill Duncalf, presumably with the then head of sport, Peter Dimmock's agreement, was quite happy about this. Having little knowledge of horses or show jumping, Bill Duncalf also depended on me. We used to plan together, arrange the camera positions, even decide which events were most worth televising. He also expected me to act as his link between Mike Ansell and himself. I remember one evening when we were running late, the producer – on that occasion Bill Wright – told me through my earphones that television would have to leave before the end of the competition, information that I passed on to Mike Ansell, who, predictably, was furious, even instructing me to inform the BBC that if they pulled the plug on us now there would be no television the next day; he would so change the programme that during transmission time there would be no jumping. I passed this on to Bill, who not surprisingly sounded most indignant. Two minutes later he came back to me to say that 'presentation' had agreed to an extra fifteen minutes, which was the time that we required to finish the event. When, with relief, I told Mike, he insisted, to my astonishment, that I inform Bill that he would only agree if the BBC paid an additional £100 for the extra fifteen minutes: this I could not bring myself to do. A moment later, as I feared, he came up behind me, demanding that I connect him with Bill Wright on the telephone. Bill, poor man, was stunned and embarrassed. It just was not within his powers, he said, to offer another £100; it was not his department – only 'contracts' could agree payments; but Mike was determined and slammed down the receiver, returning to his seat at the other end of control. This was too much for me. Putting down my microphone I climbed out of my seat, walked across to him and told him that I wanted it on record that I did not agree with him as I thought he was being unrealistic and unreasonable. A minute or two later he came up behind me again: 'Tell them that they can carry on tonight: we'll discuss it in the morning,' muttering as he turned away, 'I run this show, not the bloody BBC, nor anyone else.' I got the message. All this was during a transmission. If only the great British viewing public could have known! Can one imagine such a thing happening today?

The BBC representatives, and most other stewards, came to the twelve o'clock conference the next morning trembling and expectant: Dorian and Mike, who were like Tweedledum and Tweedledee, had had a row. Mike had defied the BBC, then had had to climb down; Dorian had argued with him: what on earth would happen? But they need not have worried. Mike and I had very quickly patched it up over a drink after the performance the evening before; now he was charm itself, apologising to the BBC, admitting that it was our fault for running late, gently rebuking the course builder for getting too many clear rounds, thus causing the over-run. Everyone relaxed. Like most strong men, Mike did not resent it if one stood up to him, as long as one was on firm ground.

In 1956 the equestrian Olympic Games were televised from Stockholm – the most enjoyable Olympics that I remember. Only the equestrian Olympics were held at Stockholm, horses being banned from Australia because of the quarantine regulations. The Queen, who owned Countryman, one of our Three-Day Event team, was present, based on the Royal Yacht: the Swedish were charming hosts. My producer was Ronnie Noble, with whom I was very friendly, and who again used to plan everything with me as though we were partners which, of course, we were. There being no television amenities for the coverage of the cross-country phase of the Three-Day Event, the BBC simply mounted a camera on a Landrover, dashing round the course, taking shots wherever they encountered a competitor, eventually producing about forty minutes of film, to which later I added my commentary. Thanks to the skill of Ronnie Noble it eventually made a delightful transmission, viewers at home being far more satisfied with the coverage of the cross-country, even though it was a day late, than so often they are today when all they see may be a few haphazard minutes slotted into 'Grandstand' or 'Sportsnight', lost amongst a dozen other sports. Ironically Moscow in 1980 was, I understand, to have provided the same sort of excellent every-fence coverage that one expects from Badminton or Burghley, but because of the Afghanistan invasion there was no British team there to be televised. It should, perhaps, be appreciated that when the BBC, or ITV, is televising a programme from overseas, on Eurovision, they can only use the pictures provided by the television service of the country in which the event is being held.

Rome, in 1960, proved a somewhat hilarious experience, its informality and lack of pressures making it almost as much fun for me personally as Stockholm in 1956. On this occasion, attempting to cover the Three-Day Event, I was to record my commentary, on an ordinary tape-recorder, as the camera on the Landrover took its pictures. The edited film was to be transmitted that evening at ten o'clock. Unfortunately, when the crew returned to the studio they discovered that my tape was blank. I must have pressed the wrong button – I usually do! I was urgently summoned to the studio, arriving only just before transmission, to be told that I was to put on a commentary as the film was transmitted, making it sound, as Ronnie Noble insisted, as if I were actually there. There was no time to see it through first. Hardly had the film started than I heard a curious thumping sound. I could not look round to see where it came from, not daring to take my eyes off the screen in front of me, or the 'shot-list' which the producer had given me so that I would have some idea of what was likely to appear on the screen. A few minutes later I was startled by a weird, even bloodcurling, scream from somewhere behind me: again I dared not look round. Came the moment when a competitor jumped into a hard-bottomed lake – and I was drenched! I then had to look round, only to see positioned behind me a little Italian effects man whom I assume had been instructed to add local colour to my blank tape. The thumping was a horse galloping, the scream was a horse neighing, and when the horse jumped into the lake the little Italian, unbelievably, hurled himself fully clothed into a tank of water! How I managed to complete that broadcast I do not know, so convulsed with laughter was I. Yet I have seen that film several times since 1960 – and noticed nothing wrong!

Not that in those days it would have mattered at all that much had one failed to control one's laughter. One evening in 1956 at the Horse of the Year Show at Harringay there was a competition called the Gamblers Stakes which developed into a match between a great character called Nugget, a short-tailed Welsh Cob – docking was then still legal – ridden by John Walmsley, and the Irish rider, Seamus Hayes, on Waving Corn. I do not think that I can do better than to quote from an account of the event that I wrote at the time:

> Of the twelve fences in the ring only seven had to be jumped, and each competitor had to choose for himself which he would jump. The more difficult fences carried higher scoring cards – and the greater risk: the easier fences were only sevens and eights. The most difficult of all was a big treble of single poles down the centre, and to negotiate this successfully won a rider thirteen points – the ace. Competitors could jump any fence more than once, but must jump only seven fences in all.
>
> John Walmsley came in on the stocky, short-tailed Nugget – a personality horse if ever there was one. He is a horse that it is useless to try to put right, but left to himself he will adjust his stride and jump prodigious obstacles. John Walmsley rode old Nugget straight into the big treble on a loose rein. Down the line he went, faultlessly; turned in a couple of strides and started again; and then again – and again. Sometimes he bucketed so close to one of the parts of the combination that he must have taken six strides in between instead of the expected two. But on he went. And if, by mischance, he hit the third part, he just swung out, jumped the gate – the king, twelve points – and back to the treble. It was more comical than anything I have ever seen in the show ring, and I was helpless with laughter, so much so that I had to apologise to viewers for my complete loss of self-control. But worse was to come: Seamus Hayes arrived with Waving Corn. Fully cognisant of the rules, he knew that if a

competitor knocked part of a combination he had to go back and jump the whole thing again and that in this competition it was only a fence cleared that amassed points: there were no faults for refusal or fall. He therefore employed the same tactics as Nugget, but whenever he hit a part of the combination he made his horse stop at the next part, dashed back to the start and held up his hand, to show the judges that he was ready to begin again as soon as the fence was rebuilt and they had rung the bell. His seven fences seemed endless! On and on he went: clear; clear; fence down; back to the start; hand up. Off again: clear; fence down; back to the start; hand up. Off again – by which time I, together with the whole audience, was convulsed and had had to abandon my microphone completely.

At last he finished. Cascades of laughter and applause. But then – to crown it all – to heighten the ridicule of something already unbearably ridiculous – he was disqualified! He had jumped the fence just once too often, having lost count of the number of times he had held up his hand.

And he wasn't the only one who had to leave the room! I finally collapsed in hopeless giggles.

Far from being reprimanded I had a letter from Ronnie Noble next day in which he said: 'I think that I can say without any exaggeration whatever that last week we had some of the best television that I have ever seen and your 'playing card' programme just had us completely hysterical at home.'

He went on, incidentally, to thank me for my help with the Three-Day Event at Harewood. Here again, the producers, knowing little about Three-Day Events – the first ever held in England was in 1949, only six years earlier – very much relied on me for guidance and advice which, liking to be involved, I enjoyed. I cannot deny bias, but I often think that, although it was only in black and white and very unsophisticated, those early days saw some of the best transmission of equestrian events that we have ever had. Certainly the sport quickly became very popular with an ever-increasing viewing public: I personally enjoyed every minute of it.

In 1959 the BBC found itself faced with a rival, Independent Television. This produced immediate changes. Understandably, the BBC realised, as did ITV, that there was now an emphasis on technology. The channel that produced the cleverest pictures, exploited the most advanced equipment, developed the most sophisticated techniques, would get the acclaim, at least from the 'trade' and the critics, if not necessarily from the general public which is, perhaps, less demanding than the industry appreciates. The

general public, I believe, just wants to be entertained, not impressed
with technology. In his book *Chatterboxes*, Brian Johnston makes the
same point. Regrettably and, in my opinion, unnecessarily, there
was an immediate battle for viewers with, almost inevitably, a
deterioration in standards, a levelling down rather than up. I soon
became conscious of a subtle change in the BBC's attitude, even in
my own sport. It was becoming apparent that the BBC now
required what they would describe as a more 'professional' performance from their commentators, but what I would describe as a more
'journalistic' approach, 'punchy', brash, attacking, the emphasis on
the sensational. When 'Grandstand' was first introduced into the
Saturday afternoon schedules I received a telegram from Paul Fox,
then Head of Sport, which read: 'DELIGHTED HAVE YOU
FIRST GRANDSTAND PROGRAMME STOP APPRECIATE
THERE ARE CHANGES FROM NORMAL ROUTINE BUT
SINCERELY HOPE YOUR EFFORTS WILL MAKE THE FIRST
PROGRAMME A SUCCESS STOP THANKS IN ADVANCE
YOUR COOPERATION STOP REGARDS = PAUL FOX'.

I could read between the lines. The message was clear: my
whisper-over-the-shoulder technique was no longer what was
wanted. Perhaps it was not so much the BBC as a whole that was
demanding a different approach: rather it was the new Sports
department. When I first started television my producer, Bill
Duncalf, was also producing the excellent medical programme from
Bristol, 'Your Life in Their Hands'. Now there were producers who
concentrated only on sport for the Sports Department. Many of
them, being ex-journalists, were looking for something more
'hard-sell', more aggressive. I did my best to accept the change, but
was never again quite so relaxed or contented.

In fact, I was approached by ITV when they were founded, but I
was already under 'exclusive' contract to the BBC. Fortunately, I
was able to advise Raymond Brooks-Ward to apply for the position.
I had first met Raymond at Jennifer's twenty-first birthday party, the
year before we became engaged. During the evening a young man
approached me, suggesting that I might be able to help him. His
father had recently died, leaving him a little money. He could not
quite make up his mind whether he should go into the hotel business,
for which he had been trained, or become a commentator. He
thought that I might know a hotel near Towcester that was for sale;
or possibly might help him become a commentator. How fortunate
for Raymond that I was able to warn him that by purchasing

Cornhill, near Pattishall – the house where Dick Hobson had locked me in the cage! – he would be throwing good money after bad, as it had already failed twice as a hotel, and was to fail again. On the other hand, I had to tell him that there was really no such job as a commentator, it being very much a part-time job unless one was on the staff of the BBC. Raymond, not one to give up easily, then told me that he had recently bought a Sunbeam Rapier in which he was prepared to drive me to every show at which I was officiating, acting as my assistant. I declined the first part of his offer, but was happy to have his assistance, which I did for many years. At some time I introduced him to Peter Dimmock with a view to his becoming a racing commentator. A little unkindly, however, for his 'trial' Peter gave him a Maiden Two-Year-Old five furlongs at Newmarket with twenty-seven runners. Raymond tells how he just managed to recognise the colours of the favourite as it passed the post. When ITV came into being I was pleased to recommend Raymond and in no way hold him responsible for my brush with the BBC which almost immediately followed. A letter which I wrote to Harry Middleton, who had been at Hawtreys and was a senior executive at the BBC, sums up the situation. Having deplored the fact that the BBC had lost the magnificent show at Windsor, I went on: 'ITV now cover Richmond, the Royal, Hickstead, Great Yorkshire, Wilmslow and Devon County, all of which the BBC used to cover. At all of these Raymond Brooks-Ward, quite properly, is their commentator. In addition during the last two years the BBC has failed to take up Eurovision options for Rome, Aachen, Geneva, Rotterdam, Amsterdam, Paris and Brussels, leaving many of these now to be covered by ITV.' I pointed out further that when the BBC was covering a show, Raymond was usually doing the public address, and was even being billed as a commentator in the *Radio Times*; in addition the BBC used him on radio.

I had nothing whatever against Raymond Brooks-Ward personally – we remained close friends – but I was well aware that my reputation was inevitably being eroded. I had for many years been on my own. Now not only was Raymond doing more than I was, though not, admittedly, at peak viewing times, but the BBC was falling into the habit of using anyone who might be on the scene to do the commentary when there was transmission from overseas: Michael O'Hehir in Dublin, for instance. When I heard that Raymond, who had already arranged to be in Tokyo for sound radio at the 1964 Olympics, had been asked to do the television commentary as well while I stayed at home, it was the last straw. I immediately pointed out that since 1955 the BBC had agreed to a clause in my contract whereby 'the BBC undertakes not to engage any other commentator for equestrian events broadcast on its Television Service whether such events take place within or outside the UK without first offering the engagement to Dorian Williams'. Obviously they had no option but to accept this, and arranged for me to join the rest of the BBC team at Tokyo forthwith. Ironically, just hours before I left there was technical trouble in Tokyo which resulted in their losing the sound, so I had to stay behind after all, commentating off the screen in London. One morning after such a transmission I was out cubhunting and was asked by an old farmer's wife who, as she thought, had been listening to me in Tokyo the previous evening, whether I had come over by satellite! Generously the BBC apologised, even, of their own accord, paid me compensation; but it was an unhappy incident, unlike anything that I had experienced in my relations with them over the previous ten years. From that time onwards, by coincidence ITV televised progressively less show jumping, eventually in 1969 abandoning Hickstead, which they had covered since 1960. The BBC immediately picked it up, landing themselves with another thirty hours' television each summer. As a transmission usually lasts about an hour, this meant another thirty days. As some of the Hickstead shows run close to shows such as the Royal International, already being televised by the BBC, this could entail as many as ten consecutive days of show jumping on television. I now found myself seriously worried about over-exposure: not so much, to be frank, of the sport itself, but of myself. It seemed obvious to me that another commentator was needed. The obvious person was Raymond Brooks-Ward, as the BBC itself had appreciated, so long as I was happy about the arrangements, which I was. Raymond was too, so he became a BBC commentator, leaving ITV to Tom Hudson. It was assumed that Raymond would in particular be responsible for Hickstead. Indeed I insisted from the start that Raymond was the commentator for the Hickstead Derby, which he had very much made his own.

During the early seventies I began to feel that, intentionally or unintentionally, I was being pushed to one side. At one point I felt it so strongly that I demanded an assurance from the BBC that this was not the case, and obtained it. It was not just that I felt that I was being persuaded, subtly, to agree to Raymond increasingly taking over major events: it was also becoming evident that the BBC now had a policy of reducing the importance of the commentator, a point which Brian Johnston also makes in his book. Whereas it used to be a case of 'and over now to the Horse of the Year Show where Dorian Williams is waiting at the ringside', and then my taking over, setting the scene, describing the event, working up to the climax, now the programme was 'introduced' first by the outstanding broadcaster and personality, David Coleman, later by the very professional David Vine. Nor did it end there. Producers seemed obsessed with the need for a plethora of commentators. At one time or another we had, in addition to Raymond and myself, Richard Meade, Michael Clayton, Hugh Thomas, Michael Tucker and Ann Moore – all very competent, but one felt that one could hardly get a word in edgeways, though mercifully never more than three, just occasionally four of us, were all operating during one transmission. Fred Viner, my producer – and friend – for many years was, I am sure, right when he said that a good commentator had to have a sense of theatre. But with so many involved, with so much recording and editing, it was not easy to achieve this.

It all came to a head in 1975 when my agent analysed the transmission times at both the Royal International Horse Show and the Horse of the Year Show. The figures speak for themselves. Out of a total transmission time of 7 hours 28 minutes at the Royal International, I was commentating for 3 hours 13 minutes, Raymond for 3 hours 11 minutes, the remaining time of just over 1 hour being taken up by introductions and interviews. At the Horse of the Year Show, out of a total transmission time of 8 hours 20 minutes, I was commentating for 3 hours 23 minutes, Raymond for 3 hours 37 minutes, the remaining 1 hour 20 minutes being taken up by introductions and interviews. Out of a total 15 hours 48 minutes, my 6 hours 35 seconds was considerably less than 50 per cent of the transmission, which hardly suggested that I was the BBC's No. 1 equestrian commentator. Worse, I found that this new style of presentation made it impossible for me ever to build up an event, make it exciting, dramatic.

I wrote again to the BBC, my letter couched in straightforward, factual rather than aggressive terms. I discussed the matter with Alan Hart, the sympathetic Head of BBC 1: but there was no improvement. I decided it was best that I retired after the Montreal Olympic Games the following year. To my surprise, every pressure was brought upon me to reconsider. Cliff Morgan, Head of Sport, wrote me a charming and persuasive letter urging me to stay until

after the Moscow Olympics in 1980. Alan Hart himself insisted in a
letter that I was and always would be their No. 1 commentator, as
long as I wanted to be. Somewhat reluctantly, I agreed, hoping, a
little naively, that it would be back to the good old days. But it
never was, which left me feeling that there must, behind the scenes,
be some unknown factor, something that was virtually invisible
and therefore, from my point of view, insoluble. Two other
broadcasters who have had similar experiences to myself – both
household names – used a similar phrase to explain it: 'no one is
bigger than the BBC'.

So there it was: after nearly thirty years I had come to the end of
my commentating days. I finished without any rancour: indeed it is
my proud boast that in my long association with the BBC I never
had a real row with anyone at any level. If I did not like the way
that things were going, I accepted unreservedly that the BBC was
boss, the producers made the decisions. Either one accepted what
they decreed or one departed. I chose the latter because I did not
think that I could fit in comfortably, or successfully, into the BBC
Sports Department's new approach. My reputation could only
diminish, as, indeed, was already the case. I was no longer Mr
Showjumping, as I had been dubbed in the sixties; my photograph
no longer appeared, almost automatically, in the *Radio Times* in the
Royal International or Horse of the Year Show issues; not
infrequently my name appeared below other commentators, often
in smaller print than David Vine's. Significantly, show jumping
was being featured less and less in the *Radio Times*, which reflected
another aspect of the whole matter that was beginning to worry
me.

Gradually show jumping was becoming a circus just as surely as
golf or tennis had. It was the same few who were seen in every
televised jump-off; and because it was the BBC's policy to televise
part of two or three events, to satisfy the sponsors, one did not see
very much more than the jump-off. It was, of course, the
commercialising of the sport that had brought this about. Because
of their indirect advertising value, top-class show jumpers – the
horses – had become enormously valuable, a jumper, proven or
with potential, being worth anything over £100,000. Naturally
enough, if a generous patron or sponsor lays out that sort of sum he
expects a return on his money. Obviously, therefore, he wants only
one of the top riders to ride for him. Only the top riders get the
best horses, and to jump today's big courses they certainly have to

be exceptionally good horses, of which there are a limited number. From the public's point of view this can become monotonous; from the riders' point of view it inevitably increases the pressures.

Perhaps I saw the writing on the wall. I began to suspect that show jumping might lose its popularity. I became convinced that the way that it was being presented on television was not helping the sport. I may be biased, but I believe that the viewing figures bear me out. In a charming letter that I received from Brian Cowgill, then Head of B B C Sport, congratulating me on my first broadcast after the serious illness that I had in 1973, he wrote: 'The Royal International was seen by an astonishing total of 63 million people on B B C 1 over the six days – over 13 million on the Friday night – and all of them, like me, will echo the general delight that you were once again able to be our commentator.' The official viewing figures of the Royal International in 1982 were only 377 million; one evening at the Horse of the Year Show in 1983 attracted a mere 3 million viewers. It should be stated, however, that viewing figures for most sports have been falling. My retirement, surely, came at the right moment. Sadly, it was marred by ill health.

The week after the Horse of the Year Show in 1981 I collapsed with what is known as a 'frozen shoulder', both the cause and the cure of which seem to defy the medical profession. I can only say that the pain in my right shoulder was excruciating, necessitating endless pain-killing drugs which in themselves have a deleterious effect. A sojourn first at Stoke Mandeville and then at Guys Hospital brought little relief: gradually my right arm became paralysed, I lost a great deal of weight and was uncharacteristically listless. I was still in a poor way when in December it was time for my final broadcasts. I survived a special item on 'Grandstand' with Frank Bough, though the recording being delayed an hour created a problem. The programme from my home, produced by Johnny Watherston, was something of an ordeal, too, being filmed in a straight run, lasting some seventy-five minutes, the film later being edited down to forty-five minutes. Under Raymond Brooks-Ward's Chairmanship, Jennifer and I chatted round the fire with our guests, Pat Koechlin Smythe, Peter O'Sullevan, Ted Edgar and Frank Weldon, the Director of Badminton Horse Trials. After an hour the pain was so bad that I was about to ask the producer to stop recording when, fortunately, we reached the end of the reel. Not surprisingly, I did not look my best, nor, when I saw the programme, could I remember much of what we had talked about. I had an encouraging letter, however, from Alan Hart: 'I am writing to say how much I enjoyed the programme from Foscote, and also to put on record my sincere and heartfelt appreciation for all you have done for BBC Television. Words cannot really convey what we all feel, and how much we shall miss your commentaries.'

I was more myself for the Olympia International, the show at which I was to make my last commentary, surviving a fairly demanding programme without incident. At the very end of the final event – which, surprise! surprise! was running late – a camera was turned on me, showing me, as rarely happened, in vision. I just said: 'Well, now it's time for me to say goodbye. Thank you for putting up with me for so long,' which, to my genuine astonishment, produced a quite surprising number of letters from viewers saying that they had been in tears! Frankly I myself was too exhausted to be emotionally affected, though I enjoyed the end-of-show party afterwards, attended by some two hundred people, generously on this occasion being turned into a farewell party for me. It was just coming to an end when Harvey Smith walked in. What was going on? he demanded. Someone told him.

'Who's speaking for the BSJA?' he asked.

'Well, nobody really,' at which Harvey seized a chair, leapt up on to it and made a hilarious speech lasting twenty minutes. He reminded a delighted audience of the numerous mistakes that I had made, quoting particularly – and erroneously – the time that I referred to somebody knocking over the water jump! 'He may make mistakes,' he concluded, 'but everything he's ever done has been only for the good of show jumping: and whatever you may think of him, I just want to know who the hell is going to take his place?' Not surprisingly, I was then much moved.

Such regret as I experienced in ending my long relationship with the BBC was compensated for by the many friendly letters that I received both from those who were unknown to me and those with whom I had been corresponding for many years, but who in most cases I had never met. One very old correspondent from Leicester wrote: 'I will not, of course, be watching show jumping any more: it would seem disloyal.' I hope that I persuaded her to reconsider her decision. Equally affecting was a request from a twelve-year-old from Merseyside that I should become her pen-pal! I did. But most gratifying of all was a letter from Margaret Thatcher in which she said: 'I am so sorry to hear that you are retiring this year. You have had a marvellous career and are a credit to British show jumping.'

A few weeks after Olympia, Alan Hart, and Cliff Morgan, who took the chair, invited Jennifer and myself to a wonderful lunch at Television Centre. All my friends and colleagues, some of whom I had not seen for many years, were present, most of them making speeches, as is the custom at such functions in Wales. I was presented with two beautifully framed engravings from the Duke of Newcastle's *General System of Horsemanship* which had been used in a television programme featuring Princess Anne and Mark Phillips in their home. The warmth of that gathering and the generosity of both the speakers and the present certainly helped me to forget my frozen shoulder.

By an extraordinary coincidence it was a damaged shoulder that marred the grand finale to my career as a Master of Foxhounds – which had also lasted almost thirty years: but this time it was the left shoulder. In over fifty years of hunting I had been fortunate enough only to have broken one bone, a collar bone, in 1968. Now my final day was ruined by another broken shoulder, but one which, in a most galling manner, was not connected with hunting at all.

Chapter 5

Master Pieces

To analyse one's enjoyment of hunting is not an easy exercise. People like hunting for so many different reasons: the air and exercise; the social; the challenge of crossing a difficult country; an escape from pressures in business; just the pleasure of riding a horse; a minority for the joy of watching a pack of hounds working. As far as my own enjoyment is concerned it is very much an amalgam of all of these, in addition to one or two very different ones that I experienced during my years as Master.

My love for the sport started at a very early age, due naturally to the influence of my father who was Hunt Secretary of the Grafton, later Master. Such was my obsession with hunting that not only did I devour each Christmas holidays the W.G. Ogilvie books, *Scattered Scarlet, Galloping Shoes* and so on, all illustrated by Lionel Edwards, learning many of the verses by heart, but every evening after hunting I used to fill sketch books with hunting pictures. The interesting point was that the pictures were all correct, by which I mean that even at that early age – I was still at my prep school – I liked everything in the hunting field to be right: the huntsman up with his hounds, one whipper-in 'on', the Master at the head of the field, but a decent distance behind the hounds; only people towards the back would be making for the gates, and the second horsemen would be on the road. I was certainly no artist: my efforts, one assumes, were a kind of manifestation of my absorption with hunting, as others might be absorbed with football or cricket or collecting cigarette cards. From my very first day each hunt was scrupulously written up in my diary: but even at the age of ten my style was still somewhat immature, it seems:

December 18th, 1925. We drew Kingthorne: they drew upwards and a fox went off towards Abthorpe, then turned left-handed. I with Whiteman [my father's second horseman] went down alongside of a wood, then turned to the right, then to the right again, through a gate, then round to the left, rushing straight away through two gates and on to the brook where we attempted a deep black ford but could not get through so turned back across the railway. Then after a few fields we came out on the road, turned left, trotted down it a bit, then turned in a gateway to the write [sic], jumped a couple of quite small fences and up to Bucknells. There I left Whiteman and joined Daddy. We then ran to Stowe Ridings, past Stowe School and all the way to Tytes Copse [sic] so I came home.

According to my father's account it was a hunt of eleven miles with a furthest point of six miles, which was quite an achievement for my 14 h.h. pony, Freckles, and his ten-year-old rider, who, according to my diary, had hunted the same pony the day before, riding on to the meet at Syresham which was eight miles from home. Horse boxes at that time were unknown: horses and ponies had to be very fit – and were.

I do not think that I appreciated how enormously more enjoyable hunting would be when, promoted from a pony, one was riding something on which one could not only keep up with adults but could jump any fences that they did. Inevitably as a teenager one was still a little diffident, hesitating to go in front of people wearing red coats and top hats, but at least one was not at the back. It was, I think, at a special meet for members of the Pony Club that I first experienced the thrill of really riding to hounds. On 15 January 1931 my father, who was Master, thought it would be appropriate if I took on the role of field master, despite the fact that when I had been entrusted with a similar responsibility the previous year I managed to have the whole field left – but that was in big woodlands where such an experience can happen even to the most knowledgeable field master. This time it was a meet in the 'fashionable' part of the country, Astwell Mill. There was a field of fifty children, with about ten adults. My own diary had become somewhat terse by this time: 'Children's day, super fun. Field master, but only six finished.' My father, in his diary, described the day more fully: 'Pope [the famous Grafton huntsman whom my father had appointed in 1928] took hounds to a holloa on the Syresham road. Settling down they ran very fast to Astwell Park, rather slower but prettily to Priesthaze and Wappenham Lodge, then back to Astwell after an excellent hunt of one hour, ten minutes: only six up, apart from Pope and myself.' He does not say who they were or even that I was one of them. The others included Teddy Lambton, son of the famous trainer, George

Lambton, later to train successfully himself, and sadly to die at a comparatively early age in 1983, David Wallace, Janet and Gay Margesson. The latter was an extremely attractive young sixteen-year-old whose father, David Margesson, was the Government Chief Whip, later War Minister, and who is now married to Lord Charteris, for many years the Queen's Secretary, later Provost of Eton. After leaving Greens Norton, Gay and I were not to meet until Princess Anne's wedding, more than forty years later. In 1980 she came with her husband to Hawtreys to present the prizes on Speech Day.

That particular hunt, free from the interference of grown-ups, only a handful of us up, was my most exhilarating experience in the hunting field so far. It had been almost like a race, the challenge to keep with hounds, the determination not to be beaten by these two sisters, on their brilliant cock-tail ponies, however attractive they might be; proudly giving a lead to the younger Teddy on his smart grey pony, and to get to the end. Alone with hounds! At least with only five or six others. I re-read Siegfried Sassoon's *Memoirs of a Foxhunting Man* from cover to cover almost at a sitting.

Toll Gate being bred for racing, I naturally wanted to point-to-point him. In fact, he was entered for the Whaddon Chase meeting at Weedon that year, but for some reason he never ran. It may have been because he was lame or possibly he was not fit enough, as I had only returned from school the week before. Disappointed as I was not to be riding, I nevertheless remember the meeting well enough. Except for the Open Race, all the riders wore hunting kit, either red coats or black, with no crash helmets, some even in top hats. The invincible Sir Richard Cruise, the King's occulist, won both the Heavyweight and Lightweight Races with War Gratuity and Eaglebrook, second in the Lightweight Race being Major Steddall who as the result of losing a leg in the war rode side-saddle. Some of the names of riders in other races are still well-known in the Whaddon Chase country today: Glen Boyd Thomson, for so long Hunt Secretary during Lord Rosebery's Mastership and, indeed, Secretary my own first season; Cliff Beechener, the well-known trainer; Harry Bonner, for many years doyen of the show ring; Bill Conolly, the famous dealer whose clients included the Prince of Wales, who was himself riding at that meeting. Another was Leslie Jones, who used to act as field master for Lord Rosebery, and about whom a delightful story used to be told. A long, wide avenue runs up to Mentmore from the village of Cheddington, each verge being some twenty-five yards wide, all, in those days, immaculately kept. One day as the whole of the Whaddon Chase field was riding up the avenue a careless rider allowed his horse to stray on to the grass.

'For heavens' sake!' cried field master Leslie Jones. 'Come off that grass at once. Don't you know that his lordship mows it all himself?' conjuring up a wonderful picture of the portly Earl sweating up and down the avenue pushing his mower.

Some of the owners of runners at that point-to-point in 1931 included such familiar Buckinghamshire names as Merrick and Terry, whose descendants still live and hunt in the district: indeed, Edward Roads, whose mother was a Terry, is married to Diana, Albert Buckle's daughter. It was on land owned by the Terrys that the famous F. C. Turner Vale of Aylesbury pictures, prints of which are so well-known, depicted.

From the day I left Harrow until the outbreak of war I still hunted whenever I could, although we had left for ever our home at Greens Norton. I was particularly fortunate in hunting a good horse belonging to old Lady Penrhyn who lived at Wicken and whose husband had once been Master of the Grafton; also some wonderful horses owned by Lord Wardington, stepfather of Moyra, my first wife. In those days I was prepared to hunt anything on four legs; some of those loaned to me by farmers were certainly not in quite the same class as Lady Penrhyn's Horatio or Lord Wardington's Diane or his appropriately named Moneymarket (he was Chairman of Lloyds Bank). After my parents had bought a house at Castle Cary I also had great fun with the Blackmore Vale. Whenever I was at home my father generously used to let me have a day on one of his horses: Romeo, Ile Rousse or Echo, the latter being a brilliant, bright chestnut which my father had successfully shown as a hack. Tragically it was killed under me in a very good hunt from a little covert by our home at Hornblotton. It was my first experience of a horse that I was riding being killed in the hunting field. Mercifully the experience was only once to be repeated.

From 21 January 1939, when I rode a good horse of Moyra's with the Bicester, I did not hunt again until 10 November 1950 with the Grafton – 'easily the wettest day I ever remember,' according to my diary, but sufficiently enjoyable for me to buy the horse that I was riding and to take up hunting again, as a relaxation from the very busy life that I was then leading at Pendley. At first it was just one day a week. By Christmas it had become two days a week. Before the end of the season, as much to my own surprise as everybody else's, I had agreed to become Joint Master with Colonel Neil Foster. It had been my intention, originally, to be a Master for just two seasons, to see out Will Pope, the huntsman who had been appointed by my father in 1928 and who now, having run the Hunt almost single-handed during the war, had become a little difficult to manage. Having for so long been his own boss, he did not now always find it easy to take orders – especially from people he did not know. Everybody wanted him to complete his twenty-five years as huntsman of the Grafton, as not only was he one of the outstanding huntsmen of his era, but he was immensely popular, especially with the farmers. Perhaps – it was, I understand, Will Pope's own suggestion – a 'chip off the old block' might ensure an amicable and happy end to his great career.

I knew, of course, that I barely had the time, but I knew too that in Neil Foster I had a Joint Master of great foxhunting experience. Since my earliest childhood, it must also be admitted, I had nurtured a secret ambition to be a Master of Foxhounds: my father's approach to the job some twenty years earlier, with the emphasis on organisation, had made a great impression on me. He held strongly the view, as I was to later on, that good sport, which must always be the priority in any successful hunt, depends on good organisation. Having worked extremely hard for five years, almost without a holiday, in establishing my Centre of Adult Education at Pendley, I felt entitled to follow in my father's footsteps, even if it was only for two years. I had worked it out that with Neil as my Joint Master I need not hunt more than two days a week. My conscience, therefore, was clear. As it happened, however, at exactly the same time I suddenly found myself a television commentator with very quickly increasing commitments, and equally suddenly Pendley became busier than ever before, thanks to an unexpected opportunity to run a large number of courses for British Railways and the welcome, if surprising, popularity of the annual Pendley Shakespeare Festival. Taking on a pack of hounds, therefore, was not quite as easy as I had anticipated: but I will never regret those two wonderful years. With Will Pope right back to his very best form, with the little bit of beginner's luck that is always so helpful, the Grafton enjoyed two great seasons. It was only a matter of time before I was out every one of the four days hounds were out, each one being so enjoyable that I could not bring myself to miss a single meet: yet I still managed somehow to run Pendley and commentate for the BBC, though most of our show jumping broadcasts were, of course, in the summer. From our first opening meet sport was outstandingly good, the conditions ideal, being mild and damp, so untypical of the usual November, which is not, as a rule, a good scenting month. Within weeks we seemed to have made a reputation for ourselves, similar to the reputation that my father and Will Pope had made back in 1928, their first season. People came from all over the country to have a day with us. They were seldom disappointed. I remember one great day towards the end of November, in 1951, when we met at Culworth crossroads, our visitors including Captain James Hanbury, who as a boy had been brought up in the Whaddon Chase country, now the very successful Master of the Belvoir, and Major Tony Murray-Smith, who had just taken on the Mastership of the Quorn: their wives came with them, Tony's then wife, Ulrica, later becoming one of the most popular and longest-serving Masters of the Quorn. It is, I think, worth quoting part of the account of that day from *Horse and Hound*:

> Finding in kale above Sulgrave they ran at top speed towards Alithorne which they missed by half a field, swinging as if for Stuchbury, which they also missed, then racing for Greatworth where for the first time they checked after thirty-five minutes. They were soon on again but the fox was twisting badly until they came up to Thenford, in the Bicester country, where the fox was seen less than a field ahead of hounds: unfortunately a fresh fox jumped up and they flew to Halse Copse, straight through, over the Radstone road, across to the railway as if for Whistley, but turning in a left-hand sweep round Helmdon they were eventually stopped at Stockings Farm before entering the Whistley stronghold: just over three hours: seventeen miles as hounds ran.

This account of a wonderful day's hunting is evidence, surely, of the priorities for most people in a day's hunting: 'tearing a fox to pieces' just does not enter into it. Killing the requisite number of foxes in a hunting country to ensure that the fox population is properly controlled is just one of the justifications for hunting. There are many others. When I became sole Master of the Whaddon Chase in 1954, having been persuaded to continue for one further season with the Grafton to see in Joe Miller, Will Pope's successor, I was to discover, too, that Mastership was a great deal more than putting on a velvet cap, riding at the head of the field and enjoying oneself, important though I have always felt it to be that the Master should be able to lead his field.

There is, admittedly, something anomalous, even anacronistic, about both a Hunt's standing in local society and its Master's. The indisputable fact is that even today the existence of a local Hunt is often of greater relevance in a neighbourhood than that of a local council, in many ways it being more influential in a larger area. Both Trollope and Surtees insisted that a local Master was of more importance – and, indeed, more enviable – than a local Member of Parliament or even a Lord Mayor. A hundred years ago that may have been logical: it should not be so today, yet frequently it is. The relationship between landowners and farmers and the local Hunt is often as important as their relationship with the local Council: the ordinary country people who follow the hounds in cars or on foot are usually more concerned with what sport the Hunt is having than with what happens at a parish council meeting. The chairman of the parish council holds sway over the environment of the village; the mayor of a town holds sway over the environment of the town; the Master of the Hunt holds sway over as much as a whole county, for a Hunt's playground is the countryside of Britain.

The responsibility of a Hunt Master, therefore, is considerable. He not only has to satisfy the Hunt subscribers who are paying for their sport – and when all is taken into account paying for it in thousands of pounds rather than hundreds; he not only has to maintain good relationships with the farmers in his country, thus ensuring that the Hunt is welcome on their land; but today, if he is to have a happy Hunt he has also to be accepted by all those who, because they live in the country, often following on foot or in cars, look upon the Hunt as their own property – in other words, the Hunt Supporters Club, which, happily, most Hunts now boast. Thus, the Master has to be accepted and respected by the whole local community, which not only involves his giving a great deal of his time to the Hunt, but necessitates his being consistently diplomatic, tactful, patient, sympathetic. Not surprisingly, this paragon of all the virtues is something of a rarity. A Master can but do his best.

When first I became Master of the Whaddon Chase I did not find it easy. The Grafton country had had a tradition of hunting going back two hundred years, to the 2nd Duke of Grafton. The major part of the Whaddon Chase country had, since the middle of the nineteenth century, only known the Rothschild family's private pack which hunted the carted stag, almost entirely on their own land, owning as they now did their great estates at Tring, Aston Clinton, Halton, Waddesdon, Mentmore and Wing. The north end of the Whaddon

Chase country had been hunted for some eighty years, equally privately, by the famous Selby Lowndes family of Winslow, later of Whaddon Hall. The row between the two packs when the Rothschilds started hunting foxes as well as the carted stag during and after the First World War is now history. It was all more or less satisfactorily patched up when in 1922, after a short interim Mastership of Lord Orkney, Lord Dalmeny (Rosebery) took over the whole country: but for a long time it left much bad feeling. The situation had probably been exacerbated by the fact that compared with most Hunts the Whaddon Chase hunted a comparatively small area. Very roughly most Hunts have a territory of some two hundred square miles. The Grafton, for instance, has exactly this amount of land over which to hunt, all in the southern half of Northamptonshire, whereas the Whaddon Chase, all in North Buckinghamshire, has only half this area: even less now, with the spread of the new city at Milton Keynes. When visiting farmers my first few seasons I would frequently be asked whether I was a Dalmeny man or a Selby Lowndes man. One had to move very cautiously. Gradually, largely due to the forming of our Supporters Club, appropriately called the Whaddon Chasers, in 1955, and the little committee of hunting farmers that I invited, in 1956, to organise an annual dinner, the country became united. The Whaddon Chase country has, I am proud to think, been singularly free of those factions that can so bedevil the well-being of some Hunt countries. I was fortunate enough, therefore, to have, with Albert Buckle, whom I appointed as huntsman in 1954, an extremely happy regime. Nevertheless one never ceased to be aware of the immense responsibilities of being Master: rather one became increasingly aware of them. If a Master is properly conscientious then it is scarcely an exaggeration to say that for twenty-four hours a day, fifty-two weeks a year, he is at the Hunt's disposal. An experience of my own on Christmas Eve 1964 effectively illustrates this fact. It was 6.30 p.m. I had not long returned from hunting, was still in my breeches and boots; the children, then very young, were eager and excited, hanging up their stockings, wrapping up presents; carol singers were expected. The telephone rang. It was Bill Manning, who, having lived in the country all his life, as his father had before him, was one of the most respected of Whaddon Chase farmers: he was also a senior member of the Hunt Committee.

'Sorry, Master,' he said. 'I'm afraid there's trouble. Morris, Rowsham, is hopping mad. Some idiot riding home has taken down

his electric fence, letting all his cattle into the kale. I'm afraid you'll
have to go and see him.'

'Tonight?' I asked, not very happy at the idea.

'Fraid so. That's an important farm so close to Aston Abbots [one
of our best coverts]. You can't afford to upset him, can you?'

'No, of course not.'

Half-past six on Christmas Eve: off I went.

Walking up the path to his front door – I feared that to go to the
more generally used back door might be considered familiar – I could
see the delightful domestic scene in the old-fashioned farmhouse's
living room: the decorations, the children round the fire, Mrs Morris
busying herself with parcels, Christmas music coming from a radio.
Nervously I knocked at the door. After several minutes and another
knock I heard the shifting of bolts, the unlocking of the door, then
slowly it opened. The moment Mr Morris saw who it was he
slammed the door in my face, but not before I had put my foot in,
still, fortunately, wearing my hunting boots.

'I don't want you here,' he shouted at me. 'Get off home. I've
nothing to say to you: nothing at all.' He was furious, red as a turkey
cock, his hair bristling. Still with my foot in the door, I explained
that I had simply come to apologise: I knew that there was nothing
that I could now do, but that if I could find out who had taken down
his electric fence then I could assure him that whoever it was would
not hunt again with the Whaddon Chase this season. My efforts were
punctuated by his incessantly shouting at me, telling me to go home,
but I stood my ground, continuing to apologise, asking if I might
come in and explain fully, rather than stand out in the cold.
Eventually he called back over his shoulder:

'Shall I let him in?'

To my great relief one of his teenage daughters called back: 'Better
let him in, Dad.' Reluctantly he pulled back the door, and in I went
to join this cosy, charming, Christmas-card scene.

Before very long he had offered me a drink. An hour later I left,
wishing them all a happy Christmas. At the door I held out my hand.
He took it, to my delight shaking it warmly.

'I appreciate your coming,' he said, 'on Christmas Eve:
goodnight.'

Mr Morris, Rowsham, always had to be treated with respect: but
from that Christmas Eve onwards respect, I believe, was mutual.

At the Olympia International in 1980 I was told that a member of
the choir taking part in the finale, which I was producing, would like

to meet me. It was one of the pretty teenage daughters who had persuaded her father to let me in, now, of course, married and a mother herself. That summer I had the pleasure of opening her village fête at Wingrave!

Another Christmas, ten years later, was also to provide me with a moving, yet strangely rewarding, experience. At about eight o'clock on Christmas Eve the telephone rang. When I answered it, a voice said: 'You need not know who I am, but I am speaking from Stoke Mandeville Hospital. Eric Hancock, as you know, is very ill. He is nearing the end now. It would mean everything to him if you could come and see him.'

'Do you mean now,' I asked, 'or will the morning be better?'

'He's sleeping now. I suggest the morning.'

I did not know to whom I had been talking, but I knew that I had to go.

Eric Hancock ran a small agricultural machinery business, owning a few acres near Winslow. He was a devoted supporter of the Hunt. I was aware that, although no great age, he was now dying of cancer. I was at the hospital by ten o'clock on Christmas morning. Had it not been for the fact that a mutual friend was by his bedside I would scarcely have known him. His face lit up when he saw me: he became quite animated. I stayed for an hour or so, only getting up to go when I could see that he was tiring.

'I'll come in and tell you how we manage on Boxing Day,' I told him.

'That's right,' he said, 'Have a good day.'

I knew, of course, that I would not be telling him about Boxing Day. He knew it, too: but he looked relaxed and at peace when I left him. He did not last many more hours. How pleased I was that I had been to see him: and how humble it made me feel.

Two further brief ancedotes illustrate the point that I am trying to make: the responsibility of being a Master. Although John Morris, no relation to my old friend at Rowsham, had only recently taken up hunting, he had not only become very keen, but put in most useful work opening up that part of the country in which he lived, making jumping places, taking down wire, seeing that foxes were not disturbed. His two teenage daughters also hunted, being made to feel very welcome by the whole Hunt. One morning John phoned me to say that his wife, from whom he had not long parted, had died the previous night: his daughters were very upset. 'I'm ringing to ask you to write to them, Master,' he said. 'A letter from you would mean more than anything in the world.' Again I felt very humble and, not unnaturally, very flattered; just as I did when a few years ago one of the Supporters Club's keenest members, Leslie Berry, telephoned me, just as I was getting up, to tell me that during the night his wife had died. 'I wanted you to be the first to know,' he said. No less moving was it to learn, when I was seriously ill myself in 1973, of the prayer circles that had been formed in a number of villages.   .

To relate such incidents may appear arrogant, but it seems the easiest way to emphasise the scope of a Master's responsibilities. It may not be logical that someone only chosen by an informal body that has no constitution or legal standing can enjoy such standing. It may not make sense; it is certainly an anachronism which those outside the world of hunting must find difficult to understand, yet it happens to be a fact just as much today as it was one hundred or two hundred years ago. The Master is still regarded, as it were, as the head of the tribe to whom members of the tribe feel entitled to turn, to whom they can bring their troubles.

Although at times a Master may feel that the burden is almost too onerous, there is still, fortunately, the great compensation of:

> That best of bounties, the gleam of a wintry sun,
> The far-flung English counties and a stout red fox to run.

Yet even here there can, for a Master, be plenty of worry and anxiety. From the public relations point of view the two outstanding occasions each season are the Opening Meet and Boxing Day. The Opening Meet always attracts a large crowd of both mounted and car followers, which makes a Master particularly keen that they should be fortunate enough to have a good day. If sport has been good, if everyone, both mounted and car followers, has enjoyed himself, then morale is high – which counts for much at the beginning of the season. The second great occasion is Boxing Day, when all over the country huge crowds assemble to see the local hounds. With so many cars following, a Hunt is lucky if it can provide anything but comparatively moderate sport (there is no such thing as a bad day's hunting: some are less good than others). Most Hunts accept this as long as they know that all those in cars and on foot have enjoyed themselves, seen some fun, appreciated the countryside, for if they have they will be more likely to identify themselves with hunting in general, their local pack in particular, and support it. Occasionally, however, one is fortunate enough, despite all the problems, to enjoy a good hunt, thanks to a fox taking a line which, probably as much by good luck as good management, avoids all the crowds. I well remember such a hunt, on Boxing Day 1973, perhaps because it was to mean a great deal to me.

At the beginning of that year it had been discovered that I had cancer. Thanks to successful treatment and a major operation I survived, even starting to ride again at the beginning of October. During the first few weeks of the season, when I was virtually riding with only one arm in use, I had to be careful, but I had decided that at Christmas I would, all being well, start hunting properly, hoping then to carry on as if nothing had happened. It depended, of course, on my being completely fit: this I had to prove. Leaving the vast throng in the square at Winslow, hounds were taken to Tuckey, the little covert that for a century has traditionally been the first draw on Boxing Day. I held the field back on the Claydon road, which meant that the cars were all behind us, except for those which had tried to anticipate the hunt by going round to Addington, where the Tuckey foxes usually run. A fox was quickly on foot, going away almost immediately, across the road in front of us, in the opposite direction to Addington; thus we had a wonderful start, ahead of the hundreds of cars queuing up behind us. There was a good scent; hounds soon settled, and after a few fields they were streaming away ahead of us, difficult indeed to keep in touch with. Leaving Granborough to their left, they flew past Hogshaw and Fulbrook in the Bicester country, heading for the Quainton Hills, which they skirted, making as if for Waddesdon. By this time the field was strung out all the way back to Winslow, but the horse that I was riding, a big grey seven-year-old, Monty, one of the best that I had ever owned, was giving me a tremendous ride. Never for a moment did hounds check: there was no respite for horse nor rider, but the best was to come in the last ten minutes. We were galloping up a road with hounds running on our left when, meaning to be helpful, someone opened a gate for us, but as he did so a visiting Bicester farmer shouted that there was no way to get out of that field. Unfortunately, or fortunately as it turned out, Albert Buckle, the huntsman, two or three others and myself were already through the gate. While everybody else thundered along the road we had six fences in a line, out of grass into grass, most of them with barbed wire in them or behind them, but, galloping on, our horses just ignored the wire. For a few minutes it was like a steeplechase, with the bonus of a pack of hounds to follow:

exhilarating, again, is the only word to describe those few minutes –
one might have been in the nineteenth century. The fox found a
convenient culvert under the main road below Waddesdon, and it
was all over; but for me personally it had been a memorable sixty
minutes, convincing me that I was 100 per cent fit – the perfect
Christmas present.

Though not consciously aware of the fact, there can be no doubt
that after my illness I slowed up a little, certainly tired earlier. Nor
was I conscious of any deterioration in my nerve. I noticed,
however, that I had developed a greater concern for my horses. I
began to worry more than hitherto about their hurting themselves:
as a result I found myself jumping difficult or unenticing fences with
less relish, even avoiding them altogether if possible. Gone,
understandably perhaps, was the first, fine careless rapture that I had
enjoyed for fifty years.

Nevertheless, I was to continue for another happy five years as
Master, with Peter Stoddart as Joint Master and Albert Buckle as
Huntsman. Then, both Albert and I being sixty-five, we decided that
it was time that our regime, which had extended over twenty-six
seasons – allegedly the longest partnership between Master and
Huntsman on record – should come to an end. Peter Stoddart agreed
to carry on with Lady Zinnia Pollock, now Judd, an extremely
successful exhibitor in the show ring and, farming locally, very
popular with the farmers. David Barker, who was European Show
Jumping Champion on Mister Softee in 1962, was invited to hunt
hounds. Our final meet was arranged for 18 March 1979 at the farm
of Mr and Mrs Will Stone and their son, Richard, who throughout
our regime had been dedicated helpers where anything with the
Hunt was concerned. With all the neighbouring Hunt Masters and
Huntsmen invited, together with many other friends, a meet worthy
of the occasion was anticipated.

The previous weekend I had gone down to stay with old friends at
Brighton, Ronnie and Marjorie Evers, who had been such a help to
me at Pendley, particularly with the Shakespeare Festival. Ironically,
I never accepted invitations on Saturdays during the hunting season,
but to please a close friend I agreed to speak at his Rotary Conference
at Eastbourne. The Evers live in one of those tall, narrow houses
with just one room on each of its four floors. The staircase,
therefore, is narrow and twisting, especially at the top, where on the
inside there is virtually no tread. Coming down them early on the
Saturday morning I missed my footing on the top stair and fell right

to the bottom, splitting my head open. I had to have nine or ten stitches, and gave my talk at Eastbourne looking as though I were wearing a turban. In some discomfort I then drove home to be greeted by Jennifer who, having overcome her disappointment that I was not some Arab sheik arriving to buy one of her ponies, decided that I did not look at all well and phoned the doctor. He arranged for me to go to Stoke Mandeville where it was discovered that my shoulder blade was broken in three places and I had cracked three ribs. Obviously, to my great distress hunting on the Tuesday was out of the question. However, I struggled into my clothes, was driven to the meet, where with difficulty I was heaved on to my horse. As I rode up to join the others a girl on a pony rode up to me and handed me an envelope. Assuming it to be a 'get-well' card I put it in my pocket. After we had all posed for photographs, hounds moved out into Dorcas Lane where it had been my intention briefly to address the field, thank them for all their support over the years and wish them luck, before leaving them to enjoy themselves. I had just started to speak when further down the lane there was a holloa. Away they all gallivanted, carrying me with them: for a moment I thought that my horse was going to follow, willy-nilly, but I somehow managed to stop and then had the humiliating experience of watching my beloved Whaddon Chase disappear into the distance. My feelings can be well imagined. Nor did the debacle end there: at the first fence Peter Stoddart had a crashing fall, breaking *his* shoulder! At the end of the day Igor Nares, who had come over specially from the Dordogne, in France, for my last day, having, until he retired, hunted all his life with the Whaddon Chase, drove me to the farm of an old friend, George Simms, at Quainton, where the survivors had assembled.

Peter Stoddart, his arm too now in a sling, arrived at the same time as I did. Not surprisingly as we entered the house we were greeted with, 'Here come the geriatrics,' but disappointment at such an unedifying end to nearly thirty years of Mastership was soon drowned in champagne. On arriving home I took out of my pocket the card that I had been given at the meet. In neat but childish writing it simply said: 'Thank you for being such a good Master: Love from Yvette.' I could have asked for no greater accolade.

Chapter 6

Companions of Honour

I have been fortunate enough to ride many good horses – first putting my leg across one when I was twenty-six days old! In the thirty odd years since I first became a Master I have ridden more than a hundred different horses, and, of course, owned many more, providing horses for the hunt staff to ride being one of the responsibilities of a Master. My policy of selling my hunt horses every two years was often criticised on the ground that it was unkind for a huntsman or whipper-in to lose a horse after two seasons just when mutual confidence had been established. As I saw it, if I kept a good horse indefinitely it would eventually either break down or, as it grew older, lose its speed. It would then be virtually unsaleable, which would mean that I would be unable to afford new horses of a high enough standard to carry the hunt staff in front across a big country. Although I have to admit that over the years I sold some very good horses, nevertheless I think that I can claim that during my Mastership my hunt staff were always extremely well mounted. As a rule, I bought six or seven-year-olds from various sources – punctiliously I never bought all my horses from the same dealer, believing that competition is healthy, since dealers always like to sell horses to a well-known Hunt – then sold them at the Warner and Shepherd April Sales, held at Leicester, invariably making money on them. Obviously over the years a few broke down and, patched up as well as possible, were sold very cheap. But in fourteen years, through seven sales, I almost broke even. Had it not been for the tragic death of perhaps the best hunt horse that I ever owned I might have finished up with a handsome profit.

One day, during a very good hunt in my second season as Master of the Whaddon Chase, Albert Buckle, my huntsman, and I had been greatly impressed by the way Bill Manning was going on a big, hog-maned bay horse. Albert told me that he thought I might be able to buy it; which I did. Called Lantic, and standing nearly seventeen hands, it was certainly one of the best horses that Albert ever rode – 'looked through a bridle,' as he used to say. People often suggested that I should keep it for myself, but much as I might have liked to I had the sense to realise that it was even more important for a huntsman to be well mounted than for the Master, for out on his own in front with his hounds, the huntsman has to lead the way. Nothing is unkinder than to mount hunt staff inadequately: nor more short-sighted, for sport largely depends on the huntsman being well mounted.

As Lantic was only six when I bought him, I did not sell him with my other hunt horses at the end of that season but kept him until my sale two years later, by which time Albert had had three wonderful seasons on him and he had made a tremendous reputation for himself. Any number of people wanted to buy him, often offering me very large sums, but I always refused, insisting that he must go to Leicester. If it is once thought that one is holding back or selling one's best horses privately it is quickly assumed that one is only selling one's less good horses, which obviously affects the sale. The presence of Lantic in the sale would assure good trade and probably the top price of the whole sale for Lantic himself, so many people – wealthy people at that – being anxious to buy him.

On 5 February – it was 1957, towards the end of my third season as Master, just eight weeks before my sale – Albert was cantering along the side of a covert at Wing, within a few hundred yards of the kennels, when suddenly Lantic lurched sideways and went down, pinning Albert beneath him. Albert, fortunately, was unhurt but Lantic was dead: he had suffered an aneurism. In an effort to salvage the sale I replaced him with a good horse of my own, Top Gallant, that I had bought the previous year from the legendary dealer and riding-school proprietor, Horace Smith, father of the equally legendary Sybil, who taught the Queen to ride. It fetched a fair price, but nothing near what I had anticipated getting for Lantic.

Occasionally for one reason or another I would ride one of the hunt horses, but believing that, like a car, a horse goes better for one person, I always tried to ensure that the hunt staff had their own horses and I had mine. What is interesting is that almost without exception every one of my own horses has been an individual, with its own personality, its own character, its own mental attitudes and reactions. Some have been instantly loveable, with some it has taken time to know and understand them. One or two have been elusive, making it difficult if not impossible to establish a good mutual relationship, probably as much my fault as theirs, not being sufficiently patient, perhaps, for patience must surely be the vital quality in a horseman – patience and firmness. A horse appreciates a positive approach, a decisive control: dithering only confuses it, just as it is frightened by a frightened rider.

Occasionally I have found myself wholly *en rapport* with a horse from the very moment that I saw it: Monty, for instance. At the end of the 1969–70 season a well-known dealer from whom I had bought one or two good horses phoned me to say that he had a useful five-year-old that he thought might suit me: would I like to have half a day's hunting on it? Although I knew that, having to lead the field across a stiff country, a five-year-old was not really what I required – I needed a horse with experience – having recently lamed all but one of my horses, I decided to accept his offer: at least it would be something to ride on the very last day of the season. As the horse was unboxed at the farm where I was collecting it my immediate impression was that I had been very foolish. This was not my horse at all: it was poor, a dirty grey, very immature – it turned out to be only a four-year-old – yet there was something about its outlook that at once appealed to me. It had such an honest eye, its ears were always pricked, it held high its attractive, alert head. Despite its condition, it had definite personality. Against all logic I took to it. Nor did its outlook belie its performance. We had a nice hunt in the morning during which it gave me a great feel, jumping everything we came to with enthusiasm, yet it was so kind, so generous. I decided there and then to buy it, convincing myself that I could always sell it on at a profit, which would not have been difficult as it was one of the cheapest horses I ever bought. I learnt that it had been sold to a lady in Leicestershire, but being too strong for her, she had returned it. The dealer did not want to be saddled with it all summer, so decided to sell it cheap. I was the fortunate purchaser.

Because he was so strong, the horse had obviously been kept short of food, hence his poor condition. He soon began to put on weight, and having a big frame was to grow into a very fine horse. As he was only four years old, I decided to let him have a season's show jumping in Foxhunter classes before turning him away for the whole winter, only hunting him properly a year later when he was coming six. Ridden by Kathy Kennet, a girl with some experience, he quite took to show jumping, qualifying for two regional finals. He was bold, clever, full of character and by now snow white. He really loved his hunting, being, I very soon decided, the second best horse that I had ever hunted: perhaps in fairness to others I should say that he was the equal second best horse that I had ever hunted. In six seasons he never fell, only twice refused. The first time was his first season. Coming up a hill at the top of which there was a fairly hairy fence with a dry scooped-out ditch in front of it, I chose what seemed to me to be the easiest place, by the side of a tree. To my surprise, Monty stopped, having presumably missed his stride – or perhaps it was the first time that he had encountered a big ditch in front. I turned him round quickly and he jumped it perfectly. Six years later I found myself galloping up the same field towards the same fence. I chose the same place by the tree: to my amazement Monty stopped again! Was there something that he did not like about it, something that frightened him, that he did not understand? Or was it I who, remembering how he had refused this same fence six years earlier, anticipated the possibility of his refusing it again, and communicated my doubts to him? At any rate he stopped, and then, as before, jumped it without hesitation.

One day, later that year, when I went to see him and his companions out at grass in the summer he was not, as was usually the case, the first to trot across the field to greet me. When I walked up to him he seemed listless, not himself at all. The next day he looked even less himself: obviously he was ill. We brought him back to the stables, arranging for our veterinary surgeon to see him immediately. Sadly, cancer was diagnosed and within a month he was dead. I owed him much, if only because he had carried me so brilliantly that first Boxing Day hunt after I had been ill. I was to miss him greatly.

If Monty was the second best or equal second best horse that I ever had, Blaze was without any doubt the best. He started life between shafts in Southern Ireland. Colonel Joe Dudgeon, an international show jumper of great renown between the wars and proprietor of a famous riding school in Dublin, bought him blind on the recommendation of a friend who had seen him out hunting one day. After a week or two Dudgeon sold him on to the wealthy father of a young girl who wanted to take up show jumping. He proved too strong for her so her father ordered her to sell him, which she was reluctant to do, having become very fond of him despite his unsuitability. She was, however, prepared to lend him to me. After one hunt I knew that I would never be satisfied until I owned him. Eventually I did and had ten wonderful seasons on him.

Standing still, especially before he had been clipped out for

hunting, he was no beauty with his big head and his hairy heels. But
once in the hunting field, with his high head-carriage, his magnificent outlook, his tremendous strength and action, it was a
different story. He was strong, but had no vice; no fence was beyond
his powers; his stamina was bottomless. The Master of a Leicestershire pack sent me a blank cheque, telling me to fill it in as I liked:
he was determined to buy him. 'I am not the sort of person,' he
wrote to me after a day that I had had with the Quorn at Upper
Broughton on 2 March 1952, 'to allow myself to be pounded as I was
in that hunt from Ellers on Monday.' But I would not sell. The
following year my father, who at that time was training the British
Three-Day Event riders, asked me to loan him to the team, as he had
learned of his reputation, both in the hunting field and in Hunter
Trials, in which I do not remember his ever being beaten, except
once in a Championship by Lantic, which I also rode on that
occasion. Selfishly, I could not bring myself to let him go for
someone else to ride. From the very beginning there was, I believe, a
genuine affection between us. He would make a strange murmuring
sound the moment he heard me enter the stable yard or, indeed,
according to the groom who worked for me at that time, when he
heard my car. More than once when out at grass in the summer, on
hearing me or seeing me approach he would, from a few strides, pop
over a post and rails or a wall to greet me. Did he associate me with
the galloping and jumping that he so loved? Whatever the reason I
have had no closer affinity with any other horse, with possibly just
one exception. He had a very special place in my heart, as he does in
my memory. He broke down after a day with the Pytchley in 1959. I
had one day with him the following season but he pulled up lame, so
after a few years' contented retirement was put to sleep when we
moved from Pendley to Foscote in 1964. I still have one of his hooves
to remind me of the best horse that I ever owned.

An eccentric friend, a parson with a passion for racing, informed
me one evening that he was sending to the meet next day a horse
which he intended to give me if I liked it. Belonging to a local dealer,
it was called Pancho, but he would tell me no more. My first reaction
was to assume that my old friend had had a little too much to drink,
though knowing well his impulsive generosity it did not surprise me
when, true to his word, the horse turned up at the meet next
morning, making an immediate impression on me. It was one of the
most beautiful horses that I had ever seen: obviously thoroughbred,
or very nearly so, the brightest of bays, with black points, a fine,

7a.
Bosses:
Joint Masters
Peter Stoddart
and myself,
riding Kingsway,
lead the field
with George Simms
in close attendance –

7b.
– and Workers,
the backbone of
foxhunting:
Richard Stone and
his father, Will,
earthstoppers and
terrier men, with
George Simms,
a genuine hunting
farmer.

8a. The beginning of the end. 1980: the last Whaddon Chase meet for Albert Buckle and myself after twenty-six seasons. Albert's successor, ex-European Show Jumping Champion David Barker, is on the extreme right.

8b. The end – of an era. Albert Buckle, flanked by the winged Masters, surrounded by friends.

generous eye – and long, sensitive ears. I could not wait to ride him, though the dealer told me, as I mounted, that I might find him 'just a bit on the strong side', adding reassuringly that he was sure that I would be all right in front. It so happened that from the first covert we had a fast, straight hunt, lasting thirty minutes, during which he virtually ran away with me the whole way. But how could I refuse such a magnificent gift horse? With the usual horseman's conceit, I was sure that I could steady him, find the right bit for him, generally settle him down: but although my initial affection for him grew, during the next six years he pulled harder than ever. I had one or two terrible falls on him, usually on the flat, but he jumped brilliantly, his sensational, almost abandoned style giving me both elation and confidence. Except while galloping, when it was as though he had completely lost control of himself, he was one of the kindest, most gentle horses one could ever ask for. Why, then, did he try to run away? Why was his behaviour on these occasions so irrational, so untypical of him? I could never find out very much about his past, other than that he was well-bred and came from Ireland. I doubt if the dealer himself knew much more, but realising that he had acquired a horse that was going to be very difficult to sell, decided to let him go very cheap to my old parson friend, who genuinely wanted to show his appreciation of the fun that he had had with me with the Grafton and sincerely believed that I would be able to manage Pancho all right in front – which I more or less did, though sometimes it was definitely less rather than more.

While he was still alive I wrote a little novel entitled *Pancho, The Story of a Horse*, which was published in the United States, Germany and Holland as well as in Britain, selling very well. It attempted, in a story which was pure fiction, to explain his strange behaviour, but in reality I never did discover what it was in the mind of this otherwise placid, gentle horse that made him try to run away, sometimes even at the trot out exercising. Once again the inner workings of a horse's mind had proved elusive: yet there must have been some logical explanation could one ever have discovered it.

The most valuable horse that I ever owned, though he did not cost me very much, was Orator. He was also a horse to which, because of his noble appearance and delightful temperament, I became very attached. Out hunting one day I noticed a visitor going extremely well on a big, attractive bay horse. Apparently it belonged to Lord Astor, whom I knew to be a sick man. Convinced that he would never be strong enough to manage such a horse, I rang him up and asked if he would be prepared to sell it. To my delight he said that he would, if I could find an easier horse to replace it. It so happened that I had a very honest horse which I had bought for my whipper-in. It was a quiet ride, a reliable jumper, but very slow. It was sound, good in the stable, but a dull horse. Having, not altogether surprisingly, failed to reach its reserve at the Leicester Sales, I was trying to sell it privately. Might it, despite its somewhat plebeian propensities, suit Lord Astor? He came to see it, decided that it was suitable and at once suggested that we should do a straight exchange. Reluctantly I pointed out, as I felt I had to, that his was a very much higher class horse than mine, but he insisted that a horse was as valuable as its suitability to its owner.

A few days later I drove over to Cliveden to see Orator. What a horse! I could scarcely believe my good fortune. It was even more impressive standing still than out hunting. Bill Astor then told me the horse had been Dublin Champion two years earlier. This I doubted, as I had been judging at Dublin that year. When I rode the horse, however, I could believe it: it rode like a champion. Indeed, I began to feel that there was something familiar about this horse. Sure enough, back at home I discovered that I had myself given Orator the four-year-old Championship at Dublin. More than that, reporting on the show in *The Horseman's Year*, I wrote that it was one of the best young horses that I had ever ridden and that it would be a long time before I forgot the style in which it had galloped round that great main ring, the Jumping Enclosure: for a four-year-old it had been most impressive. In the two years since I had seen it and ridden it at Ballsbridge it had, of course, grown and furnished, but even so I could not help feeling guilty that I had failed to recognise it. Sadly, Bill Astor died before he had even had the opportunity to try out his side of the bargain, but I was fortunate enough to have three seasons on this great horse, which can genuinely be described as the perfect gentleman. Despite his great size and proud presence he was one of the kindest horses that I have ever owned, yet one of the boldest and most courageous. His end was tragic. At the Opening Meet at Stewkley in 1968 we were enjoying a good hunt from High Havens when we ran up towards the back of Swanbourne. As I was approaching a quite straightforward fence on the outskirts of the village a rider on my right suddenly swerved across me. Orator never for a moment thought of stopping or running down the fence, but we were forced to swerve to the left, jumping the fence at an angle. Orator never touched a twig, but he landed on the end of a stake that was lying on the grass. The other end, the sharp end, shot up, piercing him through the heart. He staggered, then fell, dead. It was a cruel trick of fate: a million to one chance. To return to one's yard without one's horse is a horrible experience. For many weeks the sight of his empty box haunted me. I felt that I had truly lost a friend: one that I shall never forget.

Three chestnuts, each in a different way, have given me as much pleasure as any of the many good horses that I have been lucky enough to own. Fair Sue was a liver chestnut that a farmer friend kindly offered to loan to the Hunt stables, as he knew that we were short of horses. The moment I saw her I decided that this time she was for me, to replace Orator, rather than for Albert for whom I was fortunate enough recently to have bought as good a horse as he had ever had; but it was the best part of two years before I was able to buy her, by which time her reputation had made her very expensive. She was an old-fashioned looking mare, the sort that one would have expected to see carrying King Henry V at Agincourt. Riding her one always felt that one was on an unusually high-class horse: she had scope, quality, style, and was the envy of all who saw her. At the end of her hunting career I tried, unsuccessfully, for three years to get her into foal.

Kingsway, a bright chestnut, came from Yorkshire as a six-year-old. He is now over thirty, looking at least fifteen years younger. Until 1981 I still occasionally rode him cubhunting, which he loved, pulling as hard as ever, even taking the odd jump with all his old enthusiasm. Now his role is that of nanny. He loves looking after my wife's young ponies, disciplining them if they get too saucy, playing with them, protecting one if it is bullied by the others. Everybody in the Hunt knows Kingsway, members of the Hunt Supporters Club often driving up to see him in his field at Foscote. Surprisingly, when in Yorkshire in 1980, I only learned for the first time that he had broken his leg show jumping as a four-year-old. That he survived that as well as breaking down twice, finally, in 1978, shattering his sesamoid bone in his off fore testifies to his great courage.

When eventually Kingsway was retired I bought a horse called Punch, which looked so like Kingsway in colour, outlook and performance that most people out hunting thought that it was still Kingsway, though, in fact, he was a horse of greater substance. Punch had been show jumped by Mallory Spens, even doing a clear round at the Royal Windsor Show in the Ladies' National Championship, but had suddenly decided very firmly that he did not enjoy show jumping, declining even to enter the ring. He loved hunting, however, his jumping being nothing if not exuberant: hurling himself into the air, he seemed determined to clear every fence by at least two feet. Being, also, beautifully balanced he gave one a lovely ride. I have always thought that he had as much character and as great a sense of humour as any horse that I have ever owned. In the yard he loved being given an apple or a carrot, but as he saw one approaching his box he would pretend to go all coy, even bad tempered: back went his ears, his head swaying from side to side, his upper lip curling or quivering, then suddenly he would withdraw his head inside the box, just from time to time peeping over the top. If one played him at his own game, walking up to one of the other boxes first, he would stamp angrily or kick his door, then within a few moments put his head out again, all smiles. He also used to show his displeasure in no uncertain way if another horse was boxed up for hunting while he was left behind: but when it was his turn he just could not wait to get into the box, proudly tossing his head and swishing his tail. If the box did not start immediately he would kick out at the partition: 'For goodness sake let's get going,' he seemed to be saying – a very different attitude from his latter show-jumping days. Why, one wonders? His temperament was unusually generous and, like Orator, he was a very kind horse: but obviously he had a mind of his own.

After some eight seasons, during which he never gave me a fall, he put his foot in a rabbit hole out hunting one day, so badly damaging a tendon that two highly respected veterinary surgeons assured us that he would never go hunting again. But he did. After a long summer out at grass he came up sound and gave me two more seasons, going as well as, if not better, than ever. More accurately, he gave me one and a half more seasons, for on a beautiful January morning in 1984, shortly after the start of a hunt from Liscombe, at one time the official residence of the Master of the King's deerhounds, when thanks to a lucky turn I found myself leading the field, he suddenly dropped dead. In fact, he slumped into a ditch as I was going through a gate. At first I thought he was but winded, having just ridden round the side of a heavy wheat field: but he was gone. He had died suddenly, painlessly, doing what he loved most. Walking back to my box across three large fields of wheat, his saddle on my arm, seemed at the time the longest journey in the world. I missed him greatly – still do – as there had always been a rapport between us only equalled by that which I had had with Blaze. Punch was a great character, loved and admired by so many; but although his death was an experience which none who have known anything similar would ever want to repeat, it was a merciful end for a great horse who went leaving a lovely memory for which one can only be grateful.

There is a sad element, though fortunately with a happy ending, about another chestnut, not as big as Punch but very much more famous. This was my father's Sea Breeze which, ridden by Michael Bullen, had three times won the Tony Collings Cup for the leading Three-Day Eventer and represented Britain in the Tokyo Olympic Games in 1964. His story seems to emphasise how little is really understood about the mind of a horse.

When Michael Bullen retired from competitive riding, my father found for Sea Breeze a very promising young rider in the Army, which necessitated the horse being stabled away from home. Sea Breeze had had a reputation for being awkward in the stable and, therefore, needing careful handling, which at my father's home he always had. This regrettably was now lacking. Not only did he quickly lose condition, but worse, he quickly lost his form. There seemed to be problems, too, in keeping him sound. After several months my father understandably decided that it was a waste of money paying for the livery of a horse which was now a liability, giving nobody any pleasure. He therefore suggested sending him to me as, should he fail to return to his old form, we could always send him to the kennels to be put down.

His arrival at Foscote certainly distressed me. When we opened the box Sea Breeze just stood at the top of the ramp, shaking. He had no flesh on him, his eyes were hollow, his coat staring. It took us thirty minutes to get him down the ramp and into his stable, in which he immediately tried to savage Deirdre, the girl groom, who was to look after him, finally kicking her out of the box. He would not feed, could not rest, just stood there shaking, his eye wild, his ears laid back. It was obvious to us that the horse had suffered a complete nervous breakdown. After a few days, as we could do nothing with him, we decided to put him out in a field with my wife Jennifer's old retired show hack, Reynali Arabesque.

Gradually, the poor horse relaxed; slowly but surely Deirdre gained his confidence. At the end of the summer we brought him in and started riding him, step by step helping him to regain his self-confidence. Finally, a little apprehensively, I took him out hunting, riding him as second horse. That was all that he needed, the finishing touch to his cure: he enjoyed every minute of it, not surprisingly, with his eventing experience, proving himself a brilliant performer. He not only became one of the easiest horses in the yard, but also one of the most sentimental. He would happily hang his head on one's shoulder for as long as one allowed him. That he had been badly treated there can be no doubt – we even found that he had two holes in his chest, the result of being pierced with a pitchfork. Being a very sensitive horse, he had worked himself into such a state that eventually he went to pieces: once his confidence was restored, he recovered, relaxed. He even survived unscathed an extraordinary incident that I experienced with him in the hunting field. Leaping over a fence I saw, to my horror, that we were about to land on or in an ordinary domestic bath which a farmer was using as a water trough. Sea Breeze made a great effort to clear it, but could not quite do so, turning a somersault as the bath tipped over. He was quickly on his feet and galloped off, leaving me on the ground, a little shaken – as much by the experience as the fall – but unhurt. Someone kindly caught him, bringing him back for me to remount. Being in the middle of a good hunt, I quickly set off after those in front, soon catching them up. When, after thirty minutes or so hounds marked at a drain at the back of Thornborough village, I dismounted, discovering to my astonishment that in hitting his jaw against the side of the bath Sea Breeze had snapped in half both bars of his bit. I had been riding him with nothing in his mouth at all. As he was reputed to be a strong puller, I had always hunted him in a fairly severe double bridle. Thereafter I used only a snaffle, with the result that he never pulled again. So often a horse pulls against a bit, frightened of being hurt: pulling then becomes a habit. Having given me five great seasons, Sea Breeze was retired and lived to a contented old age.

Reynali Arabesque, who, as his constant companion, had so helped Sea Breeze in his rehabilitation also provides a rather sad and revealing story. Jennie Loriston-Clarke had sent one of her famous Bubbly mares to one of Jennifer's stallions. As for some reason Jennie wanted the mare to winter at Foscote first, Reynali, now twenty-four, was chosen to share her field and keep her company. Horses, being originally herd animals, hate being on their own. Reynali and this beautiful mare became devoted to each other; it was a real Darby and Joan relationship, neither ever leaving the other's side. In due course the mare foaled, her newly born foal naturally then becoming the focal point in her life. Suddenly Reynali was no longer her friend, rather, thanks to her maternal instinct, she saw him as a danger. Summarily she rejected him. Within days old Reynali had deteriorated beyond recall. Before the week was out it was only merciful to put him out of his misery. That a horse can be unhappy is certain, though happiness or unhappiness in a horse may well be a subtly different emotion from that in a human: what one must never forget is that a horse does possess feelings, possibly intense feelings, which are neither easy wholly to understand nor detect, knowing, as we do, so little of the workings of a horse's mind. It is in our own interest as much as in that of our horses to take the trouble to acquire an understanding of them to the very best of our ability.

In his interesting autobiography, *On The Level*, Henry Cecil reveals his conviction that horses suffer mental breakdowns – just from being tested too hard. Like humans, every horse has a different personality which needs knowing.

A dog, of course, is able to express its feelings more easily: it is more demonstrative, more spontaneous. A closer, more personal relationship, therefore, is possible between a dog and a human being. For many, therefore, to live without a dog in the household is unthinkable. Only when I was away at school and when I was ill in London at the end of the war have I ever had to live without a dog. Of the many that I have had I am writing of only two because it was from these two that I experienced first-hand evidence of the interdependence of a dog and its master.

The first dog that I owned personally was a little Australian terrier puppy I bought in 1938 shortly after I had taken over Hawtreys. Naturally, when I brought this tiny creature back to the school the boys showed great interest – there had probably been no dog at the school since the day that I had arrived with the puppy in its wicker basket sixteen years earlier.

'What's its name?' I was asked.

'What do you suggest?'

'Mike the Tyke,' said a rather facetious small boy, later to become a distinguished Member of Parliament. He was standing next to Michael Savernake, who today, as the Marquis of Ailsbury, is our landlord at Hawtreys at Savernake Forest. So Mike the Tyke it was: it seemed appropriate, too, in that Hawtreys had originally been called St Michaels. If one has a dog in an institution, it has to be very much a one-man dog, otherwise it belongs to everybody, with no real identity of its own. Mike was certainly a one-man dog. He never left my side, lay silently at my feet in the classroom when I was teaching, slept on my bed, waited patiently for hours in the car, even sat obediently on the touch-line when I was taking a game of football. He was, indeed, my shadow.

In 1942, my mother being seriously ill, I decided to spend the major part of the summer holidays at my parents' home in Somerset. In wartime there was not, of course, sufficient petrol for me to drive from North Wales to Somerset, and trains in wartime were understandably unreliable, especially on a cross-country journey. I decided, therefore, to cycle down to Somerset, taking with me little Mike, who used to sit happily enough in his basket strapped to the handlebars. As my 150-mile cycle trip aroused considerable amusement amongst both staff and boys, for a joke I had little cards printed: 'Mike, my Bike and Me. Spent last night at . . . . Now proceeding to . . . .', which I intended to send to various friends from various stops. All went well the first few days: the weather was good, there was a following wind; all my visits were enjoyable, both Mike and I receiving warm welcomes wherever we spent the night. I stayed the fourth night of my trip with the Elliot Smiths at Cheltenham, where Elliot, previously a master at Harrow, was headmaster at the College. My next stop, on 11 August, was Badminton, where I was to stay with the Westmorlands, both sons being old Hawtreys boys: David today is Master of the Horse, Julian (Fane) a very successful author. The weather had by this time broken; it was wet and gusty, with a strong cross-wind. I was nevertheless making good progress, finding myself at about three o'clock in the afternoon cycling steadily along the road between Birdlip and Cirencester. On one of the few straight stretches of road, slightly down hill, I was overtaken by a bus, which seemed to me to be travelling very fast. A lorry coming the other way forced the bus to swerve, leaving me very little room. Such was the wind displacement as the bus passed that my cycle heeled over so severely that I all but fell off. For a moment as the bus sped away I did not realise what had happened – then I saw Mike lying in the road. He had fallen out of his basket right under the back wheels of the bus. He was dead, killed outright, mercifully – but what a shock! It was all so sudden. One minute – and then – ! I was desolate. Rightly or wrongly that little dog meant more to me at that time than any human being. The Westmorlands were kindness itself. My parents' home, which I reached by train the next day, was as welcoming as ever, but I was inconsolable. A sentence in my diary sums it up: 'Mike dead: too desperate for words: why, oh why!' There was nothing else that one could say. Doubtless many people find it difficult to comprehend the affection a human being can feel for an animal: it can, in fact, dominate one's life.

Before the end of the holidays my mother gave me a delightful little terrier, Tiger, who was succeeded seven years later by Leo, a Norwich Terrier, who did not at all approve of my getting engaged: he was so hostile, in fact, that it became a case of him or her. She won. In 1956 Jennifer herself gave me a little terrier bred at the kennels by Albert Buckle. It was so small that we called it Goliath. 'Golly' was a most faithful companion for ten years until, much to our dismay, he contracted cancer of the throat, after a few months having to be put down. It was only with the arrival of Coco in 1969, however, that the painful memory of Mike was wholly erased. Coco, bred in the village, was exceptional: not only had he a particularly attractive personality, but he was a wonderful companion, completely loyal. When I was ill in 1973, for many months he spent all his time, except when I was in hospital, on my bed or sharing my chair. He was also great fun, always enjoying life to the full. He could catch a ball effortlessly from even the most difficult angle; indeed, he loved to play ball for as long as he could get anyone to play with him. Such was my affection for him that I wrote a short novel, called *Lost*, using him as I had used Pancho, as the fictional centrepiece of a story. The book, nicely produced, with delightful line drawings by Michael Lyne, went very well, being serialised in the *Sun*. It was reissued by Methuen in 1983.

Coco had a chestnut patch over his left eye, but otherwise he was completely white. Strangely, during my childhood, my parents had a little terrier, all white but for a chestnut patch over its left eye. They called it Grock after the clown, which was why I called my little terrier Coco. Recently I came across a photograph of my grandfather with my father and one of his brothers, all mounted. In the picture is his little terrier – also completely white, but for a patch over its left eye. I do not know what its name was.

At the age of thirteen, while still very sprightly – as indeed he had to be with three of his own offspring in the house – Coco began to lose his hearing, which had always been exceptionally acute, as is that of his progeny. A veterinary surgeon told me that deafness is one of the worst afflictions a dog can suffer, depending, as it does, so much on its hearing, which is apparently eight and a half times as effective as a human being's. Whereas Coco had always known exactly where I was, being able to hear me if he could not see me, now with his hearing impaired it seemed that all the time he had to have me in his sight. Whenever it was practical I took him with me wherever I was going, but obviously he often had to be left behind, which although he might be disappointed did not worry him all that much with the other dogs and other members of the household at home – until he went deaf. In July 1981 I had to go to London for the Royal International Horse Show at Wembley. On the Thursday evening Jennifer phoned me to say that she was very worried about Coco, who was pining to such an extent that he would neither eat nor drink. She went so far as to say that she was afraid that he might not be alive if I could not get home before the Sunday. I drove straight home that night, arriving at about 1.00 a.m. My presence seemed to revive him: mentally if not physically he was for a day or two his old self. But it was too late: either being very weak he had contracted some virus or the lining of his stomach was sufficiently damaged to make it impossible for him to retain food, or even water. Within a few days he had become so emaciated that we were convinced that in the very near future he would just not wake up, which is what one would have wished. Such was his courage, however, that he would not give in. Finally, despite his still bright, luminous eyes, which followed me everywhere, the sight of his pathetic little frame was so distressing that we decided it kinder to have him put to sleep.

I have never had a dog of my own since Coco: but he left his progeny, all of which have inherited his exceptionally loyal, affectionate character. He already had a son, our daughter Carola's Lucky, out of a Jack Russell bitch, and while we were away in Australia in 1979 he managed, astonishingly, to put Jennifer's lurcher – Piaf, named after the singer – into whelp! She produced eight puppies – on our daughter Carola's bed! She, like her parents, being devoted to animals, had transferred to a sleeping bag on the floor when she realised what was happening. We kept two, both brindle, calling them Miss Piggy and Miss Muppet: the others were fawn, rough gold and black; all of them being the shape and size of a fox. Quick, obedient, affectionate, they are delightful dogs, happy reminders of Coco. Though so different in shape and colour, they yet possess many of his qualities and characteristics while very much retaining their own individuality.

It is, of course, this individuality, in any animal, that is so fascinating. Unless we attempt to understand animals as individuals we are missing so much. Anyone fortunate enough to achieve this mutual understanding can enjoy a uniquely satisfying relationship, which can, like Macbeth's sleep, be the balm of hurt minds – and much, much more.

Chapter 7

Mens Sana

It was, perhaps, fortunate that the horse I was riding at my last meet as a Master of Hounds was kind and well-mannered, though very keen and free going. Had he not stopped when I asked him to as the whole field galloped past at the start of the hunt, I might have suffered a serious injury, for I was in no fit state to ride and must inevitably have fallen off before long, which would not have been very good for my stitched-up head and broken bones. Fortunately, although that tiresome tumble ruined my final meet, it did not keep me out of the saddle for long. The damage done then was in no way comparable to the three or four serious illnesses with which I have been afflicted during my life, at least two of which could have proved fatal. Despite which I can honestly claim to have been blessed with an unusually strong constitution. It is not so much the illnesses themselves that are of any particular interest: rather it is what has caused them, even more what has cured them, that has led me gradually to certain beliefs which, because they are becoming increasingly accepted, may be relevant.

Healthwise I did not, apparently, make a very promising start. On 20 August 1914, when I was just seven weeks old, my mother wrote in the family diary: 'Dorian very seedy, being considerably troubled with his digestion: instead of gaining weight he is beginning to lose it rapidly.' My digestion has always troubled me, but I have not noticed that it has ever caused me to lose weight! Two months later there was, it is evident, little improvement. My father, seriously wounded at Messines Ridge, had just been allowed out of hospital and though still unable to walk came down to visit us at Westgate-on-Sea, where we had apparently taken rooms in a house near the front. He was not impressed by the appearance of his son: 'Dorian is now nothing but skin and bones though still cheerful. This upset his father who decided that there had been some mistake in his diet, and he is slowly but surely being starved.'

'Stuff him with porridge' was, allegedly, the down-to-earth advice offered by my father. Immediately I began to put on weight. Was this, in fact, the full explanation? It had been noticed that from the very day that I was born I had adored my father, had eyes for nobody else but him. Was it, moreover, coincidence that I had begun losing weight at precisely the time that my father had been so seriously wounded? Certainly it was no coincidence that I began to pick up as soon as he came home: from then on I made steady progress, developing quite normally until about two years later when my father returned to the front and there is mention in the diary, for the first time, of skin trouble. It was to continue intermittently until I was well into my thirties, as a rule, in the summer, generally confined to my legs, though there were periods when my hands were afflicted as well, once at Harrow so badly that I had to have both arms in slings at the same time, which was embarrassing enough, though not as embarrassing as when, only once or twice mercifully, my face was affected. It is generally believed that such conditions are caused, like asthma, by nerves, but I cannot imagine what could have affected my nerves at that period of my life, my childhood being so happy and straightforward. It is, nevertheless, a fact that, once grown up, as soon as I had successfully found myself a job which I enjoyed, at Beachborough Park, the skin troubles for a time disappeared. They were not to return until the end of 1938, about three years later, by which time I had for a year been in an awkward partnership as joint headmaster of Hawtreys with Frank Cautley and had realised that I had made a mistake in marrying Moyra when I was still so young and, as I now appreciate, so immature. Though the collapse of our marriage was inevitable, there was never any bitterness or quarrelling. We both admitted without openly discussing it that it had been a mistake. Ostensibly, therefore, we were able to carry on quite harmoniously, though I, at any rate, was distressed at its failure. It was the other problem, therefore, which at the time I found more disturbing. The relationship between two people who had only previously known each other as master and pupil, now attempting to share authority, was bound to be fraught: there was an almost permanent frustration which naturally led to considerable tension. Being by nature a go-ahead person, I was finding the rigid atmosphere at Hawtreys depressingly different from the relaxed atmosphere at Beachborough which, being young, I had so appreciated, and which I was so keen to introduce at Hawtreys. My efforts, however, were doomed to failure, the boys apparently being much happier knowing exactly where they stood, rather than offered a freedom which seemed to confuse them. In any case children do not like being pulled in two opposing directions and not surprisingly at Hawtreys the majority felt it safer, perhaps more logical, to accept the old system that they were used to rather than the new, introduced by a stranger not much older than themselves. In due course I learned that change cannot be introduced too quickly, that a compromise is often preferable to a clash: but at twenty-three I was impetuous and, like so many on the threshold of life, full of self-confidence and eager for change. As many years later I was to say in a talk at Bramshill, the Senior Officers Police College: 'At twenty-five one thinks one knows everything; at thirty-five one has begun to wonder if one does know everything; at forty-five one realises that one knows very little.'

The climax to my awkward relationship with Frank Cautley came just six months after I had joined him at Hawtreys. It was caused by the Munich crisis in 1938. Did we move the school from Westgate-on-Sea to somewhere safer, or did we stay put? Cautley was totally opposed to the idea of evacuating. 'We don't run away ol' man. Never have done.' I became increasingly convinced that, apart from the safety consideration, it was right that we should move: as a result of our staying at Westgate our numbers were dwindling. When eventually the school did move, to Llangedwyn in North Wales in September 1939, we were down to fewer than forty boys. The strain of all this resulted in a return of the skin trouble, in a very virulent form. For want of a better word we referred to it as a form of eczema or dermatitis, to which I was particularly prone due to my, allegedly, having one skin fewer than is normal: at any rate, all through my youth no cure for it had every been discovered. Apart from the inconvenience it was also very painful. That Christmas, 1938, we went to stay with Moyra's parents at Wardington, near Banbury. Her mother, who only died in 1983, being a very down-to-earth, no-nonsense type of person, insisted that I could perfectly well go out hunting if I wore a wellington instead of a top boot. Initially it seemed an impossible idea, but I did as I was told, four days each week for a month. The air and exercise, the enjoyment of my favourite sport, most of all the relief from all the stresses and pressures at Hawtreys, had a remarkable effect on my leg. Long before the end of the holidays my trouble was cured, which was all the more remarkable in view of the fact that my doctor at Westgate was seriously advocating amputation, the leg having gone septic!

There was no further trouble until the end of 1942. The school was happily and successfully established at Llangedwyn, a beautiful house in North Wales belonging to the Williams-Wynns, where it had been possible, without much dissension, to introduce a far more relaxed atmosphere, largely due to the environment. Apparently there had also been a much less formal routine when the school had moved to Surrenden Park near Ashford in the First World War. Llangedwyn, a charming Elizabethan manor house, was set in a gentle valley, peaceful, isolated, but friendly: one could not fail to feel relaxed in such an environment. It helped, too, that Frank Cautley, having decided to retire, was taking a much less active part in the running of the school. Nothing if not conservative, in strange surroundings he did not feel at home. Llangedwyn, therefore, was a very happy experience for me, many friendships started there having lasted to the present time. It was, however, very hard work, harder than one realised at the time, for in addition to the usual busy term-time commitments there were all the holiday activities that I had introduced: and, having failed to be accepted for the services because of my skin trouble, there were also the many local war efforts in which I was involved. It was literally all go: enjoyable, rewarding, but exhausting. I do not remember any proper holiday between 1939 and 1942, except for the one which had ended in tragedy with little Mike's death in the summer of 1942, and which may well have contributed to the breakdown of my health a few months later. It began with the skin trouble which first blew up again at the end of the summer: then, much more serious, in December I contracted jaundice. Unable, after a few days, to eat anything, I deteriorated so quickly that my mother was sent for. My belief, however, is that my eventual recovery was entirely due to the arrival of an old friend from Beachborough days, Sylvia Ellis. She was shocked at my appearance, but at first felt quite helpless: then when I told her that I knew that I would be all right 'if only I can keep something down', she decided that there was only one answer – brandy. The only brandy available was at a farm five miles away. Though well over sixty, she walked there and back on a freezing night, returning triumphant, but almost on her knees, with the brandy. Whether or not she realised that any form of alcohol is usually forbidden a jaundice patient I do not know. At any rate I took it, kept it down and was soon on the road to recovery, though feeling very low for some time – the usual after-effect of jaundice. My diary is blank for the whole month of December 1942, but there is a brief entry for New Year's Eve: 'Still weak: feel very old.' I was twenty-eight!

While recuperating at my parents' home in Somerset, there was further trouble. Suffering constant stomach pains, a barium meal disclosed that I had an internal growth, which could be malignant, or become so: this necessitated treatment at the Westminster Hospital in London where I went to live at the end of February, my in-laws kindly lending me their flat in St James's. Managing to get employment as a part-time lecturer at the Nuffield Centre, where I also did a disc jockey session, introducing simple classics to service personnel, I kept myself well occupied, though from time to time the flying bombs drove me down to the family home at Pendley where I had a little flat of my own, the house now being occupied by the Women's Land Army.

Those brief sojourns at Pendley were to have an important influence on my plans, now maturing rapidly, for turning Pendley into a Centre of Adult Education, as, in a different way, did the sessions at the Nuffield and Gordon centres. The latter convinced me that ordinary people were anxious to widen their horizons, to learn more: the former, Pendley, convinced me of the importance of environment. I quote from my diary for 23 April (St George's Day) 1944: 'Perfect April day, the park serene, blossom and daffodils everywhere, the soothing call of the woodpigeons, so much, for me, associated with Pendley: right across in No Man's Friend a cuckoo. Pendley is not only a retreat: it *heals*.' I had become aware that the health of mind and body were complementary: to provide education without relaxation was, in the long run, a waste of time. There must be thousands who needed Pendley, for whom Pendley could make a vital contribution in their restricted lives. Yet at this time I felt both frustrated and depressed. My brother, Maurice, with whom I had always been exceptionally close, had been killed in Normandy. The anticipated end to the war, like a receding mountain top, seemed always to be further away. My treatment was debilitating; my skin was troublesome again. Most of all, I was longing, now that the plan was so surely developing, to get my Pendley scheme off the ground.

Suddenly, I heard that, at very short notice, Pendley was to be derequisitioned on 1 July 1945, my thirty-first birthday. Typically impulsive, I persuaded my colleagues, Roger Pulbrook, who had been at Harrow with me, and Kenneth Bowden, both of whom were involved in education, that we could launch Pendley at the end of October. We had neither furniture, equipment, a programme, nor money, all of which somehow had to be produced in less than four months. To say that we worked round the clock seven days a week is no exaggeration. There was certainly no time for treatment, cysts, skin troubles, or anything else. Nor was there any need for treatment: my ailments had all disappeared. I also found time to appoint a headmaster to run Hawtreys, and turn it into a company. When Pendley opened on 31 October 1945, I felt fitter than for a very long time. Finding Pendley so stimulating, exciting and challenging, I retained excellent health for more than five years, despite the fact that during that time I had only one short holiday, with my great Harrow friend, John Wyld, who had, sadly, lost his first wife, Helen; and even then I was recalled from the south of France before the end of our fortnight to cope with a crisis at Pendley.

It was, probably, exhaustion as much as anything else that caused the unfortunate return of my skin trouble in 1951, this time affecting my face as well as my right leg. A fortnight's stay at a special clinic at Amersham helped, certainly as far as my face was concerned, but the final cure of my leg, which had resisted the treatment, came in a curious and, at that time, unexpected way. Brenda, my stepmother, had recently become convinced of the effectiveness of 'the box', radionic treatment by remote control. Not surprisingly, many people are sceptical about this 'alternative medicine', the principle of which is for the 'patient' to supply a 'contact', a drop of blood or a hair from the head, which is analysed and then treated by 'remote control': but then many people would have been sceptical a hundred years ago if told that before long they would be able to sit at home and watch a 'live' picture of something happening a thousand miles away. Certainly an increasing number of people, including Jennifer, are satisfied that 'the box' can both diagnose and cure: and not only humans but animals, which would seem to discount the cynics' view that any cure claimed is due entirely to the mind being persuaded of the cure. At present it is obviously a very inexact science, but it has many adherents. In 1951 it was something quite new.

My stepmother had no doubts whatever that both she and her horses had been helped by 'the box'. She insisted, therefore – and she could be very insistent – that I go on the box. Her own confidence being infectious, I was soon wholly persuaded, perhaps in desperation, that 'the box' could cure me. At Whitsun in 1951 I was staying with friends in Kent, having been invited to judge at Edenbridge Show on Whit Monday. My right leg being particularly bad, I was worried as to how I was going to ride some thirty different horses, so, recalling what had happened in 1938, I even took a wellington boot with me lest I could not get into a proper riding boot. After lunch on Saturday I suddenly felt so tired that I asked my hosts if I could lie down for an hour. No sooner was I on my bed then I virtually passed out, feeling totally drained. I slept for nearly four hours. When I awoke I was a different person, free from pain, full of energy, myself. Within twenty-four hours my leg was almost healed. I judged four classes on the Monday, riding nearly forty different horses. Since that Whitsun I have never, remarkably, had skin troubles of any sort. I later ascertained that I had in fact been put on 'the box' on that Saturday afternoon. One can but draw one's own conclusions. Coincidence? Mental influence? A genuine cure? There are more things in heaven and earth . . .

My most serious illness, of course, was the cancer with which I was afflicted in 1972 – though it was not diagnosed until January 1973. Again it may or may not be relevant but for some years I had been at full stretch. Apart from being Director of Pendley, I had had a big job in establishing, on behalf of the British Horse Society and the British Show Jumping Association, the National Equestrian Centre at Stoneleigh, which had encountered, to my surprise and disappointment, considerable opposition. I had only recently completed fifteen years as sole Master of the Whaddon Chase which, as I have suggested earlier, can be very time-consuming if one is conscientious. It would almost be true to say that I was attempting to do three full-time jobs. In fact I was lucky enough to have a first-class staff at Pendley, and being only 'Honorary' Director at Stoneleigh I was assisted by an experienced professional staff. As far as the Hunt was concerned, I had since 1961 had a quite exceptional Hunt Secretary in 'Puggy' Wyatt who, in 1970, I was to persuade to come in as Joint Master with Peter Stoddart. The latter had hunted with the Whaddon Chase since he was a child and was the son of Laurie Stoddart, who as Chairman of the Hunt had appointed me as Master in 1954. They made my job very much easier. Sadly 'Puggy' Wyatt was to die in 1976. But without him and Peter and, of course, Albert Buckle, my huntsman, I could never have carried on as Master.

I am of the opinion, however, that hard work, even over-work, can be less destructive than mental distress. By 1972 I had become very agitated at an unexpected development. After five years as Vice Chairman of the British Horse Society, I was unexpectedly opposed in an election for the Chairmanship, and defeated. This hurt, chiefly because it was so unexpected. It had been taken for granted on all sides that I was to succeed Mike Ansell, who had been Chairman for twenty years. Earlier in the year I had attempted to prepare myself for the position by giving up various other commitments, even resigning as Director of the British Equestrian Centre at Stoneleigh and as Chairman of the British Horse Society's Riding Establishments Act Committee, set up to cope with the implementation of the Act. I have to confess that at the time I did not find it easy to accept this rebuff, though with hindsight I can well appreciate that I allowed myself to be more upset than I should have been: more, perhaps, than if I had not been more tired than I realised. The fact of the matter is that, for a variety of reasons, in 1972 my resistance was low. When a lump appeared on my right breast early in 1972 I ignored it, even joked about it. When at the beginning of 1973 I realised the truth, it was nearly too late. When one is first aware that one has cancer one is, not surprisingly, in a state of shock. One finds it almost impossible to accept: it is something that happens to other people, never to oneself; it is something that happens to older people. One forgets, of course, that sixty is, for many people, old.

Naturally it is death with which one is most concerned. Despite the number – the ever-increasing number – of known cures, many people automatically regard cancer as terminal. One need not necessarily accept this situation for oneself, but one cannot help knowing that this is most people's reaction as one becomes increasingly aware of the fact that everyone, even one's friends, seem embarrassed to meet one. They do not quite know what to say, are uncertain how to behave. They appear to feel that they are looking into the eyes of death, so are uncertain how to react. They prefer, therefore, not to meet one at all. In my experience this tends to increase one's determination to overcome the disease. One is all the more anxious to prove that cancer need not be fatal: which I believe to be important, for determination must be a vital ingredient in recovery. Once one has recovered from the initial shock, accepted the situation, one learns to see the death aspect in its right perspective: more accurately nature produces its remarkable defence mechanism which somehow gradually obliterates death from one's conscious thinking. One is aware, of course, that at some time in the future it may prove fatal, but not tomorrow, or next week – only some time in the future, and that might be a long way off. One is much more concerned with the immediate future, the current problems: should one stay in London for the treatment? How long will one be able to stand the treatment? Should one carry on with one's social life – for how long? Should one arrange for a proper holiday after the treatment or wait until after the operation? Should one try to organise the operation nearer home, making it more convenient for one's family? Before one knows where one is, one is making plans for the future: with help from one's family and closest friends one is looking *forward*. I claim no particular courage in firmly providing myself with those targets which, I believe, were largely responsible for my recovery. After a time it never occurred to me that I might not be alive when the European Championships were held at Hickstead in July: therefore the BBC were informed that I would be available – and then I just had to make sure that I was, *assume* that I was. Having survived the treatment, probably the worst part of the cure, although aware of the operations to come in the summer it never occurred to me that I would not be out hunting at the Opening Meet in November. I knew that I had a strong constitution, was resilient: obviously, therefore, I would be fit enough, providing a suitable horse could be found, which by September it was. Then having bought a horse I had to be fit enough to ride it: so I more or less was, having swum in a heated pool almost daily all through September and October and started riding immediately after the Horse of the Year Show in October. Ironically, having been passed over for the British Horse Society Chairmanship at the end of 1971, a year later, October 1972, before it was confirmed that I had cancer, Mike Ansell had told me that, thanks to the ill health of Bill Barton, who had defeated me in the election, mine was the Chairmanship in 1974 if I wanted it. Having discussed the matter at length with Jennifer, I accepted, then almost immediately became ill. But after all that had happened I never lost my determination to take over the Chairmanship in 1974. At the British Horse Society's December Council meeting at the end of 1973, I was duly elected. On the same day I learned at Guy's Hospital that my surgeon and doctors believed my operation to have been completely successful.

Although there were many bad moments during my illness, the worst being the removal of the bandages from my thighs, from which the skin had been taken for my grafts, and the pneumonia bout a fortnight after the first operation, which was more nearly to prove fatal than the cancer, I never suffered such pain, even during the treatment, as when I had my frozen shoulder in 1980.

The week after the Horse of the Year Show I had driven down

from the north of England in ceaseless rain. Arriving home I told Jennifer that I felt so groggy that I thought I might be getting 'flu. She advised me to sit down in front of the fire with a stiff whisky, which I did. Having dozed off, I woke up an hour later with the most excruciating pain in my right shoulder. Great friends, Dick and Anne Hawkins, who were having supper with us that evening, insisted that we call a doctor, who tentatively suggested a frozen shoulder, a complaint of which at that time I had never heard. Worse rather than better next morning, I was taken to Stoke Mandeville Hospital where I remained for eight days during which there was little, if any, improvement, the medical profession it seems being as much in the dark where frozen shoulders are concerned as anyone else. So great is the pain that endless drugs and painkillers are essential, though one cannot help feeling that these drugs have a damaging effect on one. After a week or two my mind seemed scarcely to be functioning. I would fall asleep in the middle of a conversation, or over a meal. I could remember nothing that I had said or done a few hours earlier, which was frightening. Yet without drugs I could not possibly tolerate the pain. There was, during my time at Stoke Mandeville, at least one amusing incident – amusing even at the time. On a certain Sunday morning I woke up at 2.00 a.m. in agonising pain, it being four hours since I had last had one of my block-busting painkillers, which seemed to be effective for just four hours, but not a minute longer. I rang for the night nurse – who was new – to ask her for my next pill. To my astonishment she told me that I would have to wait another hour.

'But why?' I demanded. 'I had my last at ten o'clock.'

'Maybe,' she replied, 'but it's not yet two o'clock, the clocks were put back tonight, so it's only one o'clock and according to the book you're not due for your next pill until two o'clock.'

With difficulty I managed to persuade her that my internal clock had not been put back and that there was no way that I could survive for another hour. Somewhat reluctantly she agreed to fiddle the book.

With no improvement by the end of a month, it was arranged that I should return to Guys Hospital in case the trouble was in any way connected with my cancer. In fact, the authorities there were of the opinion that in the second operation that I had had to have, three years after the first, to remove another lump, (which happily proved not to be malignant), a gland probably responsible for lubricating my shoulder had been removed. But this, of course, was no solution.

Despite again setting myself 'targets' – in particular my final television commentary at the Olympia International Show at Christmas – I continued to deteriorate, having lost more than two stone since the end of October. Eventually, in desperation, Jennifer agreed to allow Ronnie Longford, famous for dealing with the backs of racehorses, to see me. She had heard that he had a theory that frozen shoulders were due to a nerve being trapped in the spine. Sure enough, he discovered that I had eight misplaced vertebrae, which he proceeded, there and then, to correct. To my enormous relief I woke next morning with practically no pain. At once there was a welcome improvement, though I still suffered a certain amount of discomfort, not being able properly to use my arm. Whether the improvement was entirely due to Ronnie Longford's treatment or whether the frozen shoulder had run its course, obviously I cannot be certain, but by the end of January I was well enough to go to Malta for a week to recuperate. On my return I was greeted with the news that a crisis had arisen at Pendley which was so serious that the Centre might have to go into immediate liquidation. This, after thirty-five tough but always rewarding years, was unthinkable. Suddenly the future of Pendley was far more important than my frozen shoulder. Just as at the very start of Pendley in 1945, so again in 1981 ill health had to be relegated to second place. It was, I believe, a case of priorities within the mind.

Naturally it was a shock when, in May 1983, I learned that I was to have a second mastectomy, though principally of a precautionary nature due, apparently, to an imbalance of hormones which had developed in my remaining breast. I was quite confident that I could cope, however, partly because I was at that time involved in important negotiations regarding the future of Pendley, the outcome of which was, again, far more important than any operation, partly because one's attitude to such setbacks is rather different in one's seventieth year than it is even in one's sixtieth. Or is it?

I do not dispute the fact that the cure of my eczema could have been due to the various ointments and treatments I had; nor do I dispute the fact that my cancer was obviously cured in part by deep-ray treatment and brilliant surgery; nor the fact that physiotherapy and manipulation partly solved the problem of my shoulder. I do not even dispute that as a small baby it really might have been porridge that turned an ailing baby into a healthy child. Nevertheless, I am sure that certain extraneous forces and conditions also contributed to these cures. It must be an over-simplification to attribute everything to mind over matter: what strength of mind had I at two months? Yet it is, I believe, a mental attitude, conscious or unconscious, that is frequently the essential ingredient in curing what appears to be incurable. It may be a determination within the mind to overcome: more often, perhaps, it is a diversion within the mind, the mind subconsciously distracted by some problem that seems more immediate, of greater importance than one's physical condition. That the health of the mind is inextricably associated with the health of the body cannot, surely, be denied.

Two further but quite differing experiences in support of this theory may be worth relating. One evening when I was in charge of Hawtreys at Llangedwyn, the matron, Mary Probert, a dear friend who was later to help me for a short time at Pendley, suddenly startled me by asking: 'Has it ever occurred to you that you might be a faith healer? Do you realise that in two whole terms we have not had a single boy in the sick room – something that I have never known in the whole of my experience? I put it down to your own enthusiasm.'

'That is hardly the same as faith healing,' I pointed out, adding that only the week before a certain boy had gone to bed with a bad cold: which she admitted was true, at the same time reminding me that when told that he had for the first time been picked to play for the First XI next day, his cold had miraculously disappeared. Miraculous is a word to be used with extreme caution: nevertheless, various experiences have led me to believe that it is possible for one person, so long as he has total confidence in himself, to stimulate another or others into improving their condition, whether it be mental or physical. Once that self-confidence is undermined, then little can be achieved. Obviously such a quality can be abused, as in the case of a charismatic dictator, but properly controlled it can be usefully infectious, even stimulate an improvement in a person's health – as can enthusiasm, as can humour, for surely it cannot be doubted that a good laugh makes anyone feel better, however poorly he or she might be.

While involved in the war effort at Llangedwyn, in particular with the Home Guard, I became very friendly with a certain Will Hughes who lived in the village. Almost every Sunday evening I called in at his cottage for a cup of tea and a good laugh. One evening, several years after the war, I received a phone call from Will's wife informing me that he was desperately ill, had only a short time to live, but would love to see me before he died. Next morning I drove up to Llansantfraid, where the Hughes now lived, found their little house, knocked on the door and went in, to be greeted by Mrs Hughes with great warmth and gratitude. I was just in time, she told me, as she feared that it was now only a matter of hours.

I went up the narrow staircase to Will's low-ceilinged, darkened room. At first I could scarcely see him, but he moved when I went in, slightly lifting his head: certainly he looked a very sick man. I took his hand and for a moment held it. Not at my best in the sick room with someone seriously, perhaps incurably ill, I was hesitant, not sure how to begin. I decided to try a little banter.

'You're going to be late on parade again, Will,' I said. 'Mr Taylor won't be too pleased.' Mr Taylor was the old keeper of whom we were all rather afraid. Will chuckled.

'You'll put in a word for me, won't you,' he murmured, just audibly, but loud enough for me to catch the attractive Welsh lilt in his voice.

'Why should I,' I replied, mock serious, 'after all the trouble you got me into shooting that old pig of Davies Bryn Mawr's, pretending you thought it was a German paratrooper – by the derelict barn, remember? And what about the time you hid Sergeant Miller's cap before the Armistice Parade?' He was chuckling now, spontaneously, though from time to time wheezing painfully. 'Nor have I forgotten,' I went on, 'the night that you were responsible for the Vicar falling into the bog, telling him that you thought his old mare, Juliana, which he used to put in a shed at Penybont, had escaped.'

'The old Vicar, Plas Ucha – ' he began, but I continued, reminding him of the time that we were to be visited by the Lord Lieutenant, Lord Davies, who turned up not, as we expected, in a Rolls Royce, but in an Austin Seven. It had been arranged that as his car turned out of the Mansion's gates, Will would signal to the Guard of Honour, our Home Guard Platoon, outside the village hall. They would then be ready to present arms as the car drew up. Unfortunately Will could not believe his eyes when he saw an old Austin Seven instead of a Rolls, so failed to give his signal, which meant that the Lord Lieutenant was greeted by a real Dad's Army, a slouching, smoking, giggling rabble. Worse was to follow when, on the Lord Lieutenant's departure, the Austin Seven failed to start and had to be pushed down the road to Llanrhaiadr-y-Mochnant by a somewhat irreverent Home Guard.

By this time Will was almost sitting up in bed with tears – of laughter – streaming down his cheeks. At the end of an hour, feeling that he had had enough, I made to depart.

'Nos da, Will,' I said, turning at the door.

'Bye-bye then, leg-puller-in-chief,' he retaliated, 'Cymry ambyth!' And laughed again.

The expression on Mrs Hughes's face when I came downstairs was a combination of anxiety and relief. Incapable of speech, she just clutched my hand.

'He's fine,' I told her. 'We've had a good laugh, talking about the old Home Guard. It's quite cheered me up.' Him too, I believed.

As I left, I said that I would phone her in the morning to hear how he was: which I did. He was a different man, she assured me delightedly, quite his old self. Will lived for another five years.

Recalling the humour and vitality of those past years enabled him, I am convinced, to adopt a more positive mental attitude to his present situation.

Though great advances have been made in the field of research into mental disease it is nevertheless true, I am afraid, that we still understand only very imperfectly the workings of the mind, let alone the importance of the mind in relation to health. Though from a scientific point of view there is insufficient proof that one's health can be influenced by one's mental condition, it is becoming increasingly accepted, especially with cases of cancer, that when for some reason or other a person is worried, his resistance is lowered: he is then more susceptible to disease. This is made very clear in the late Iain McLeod's book on Neville Chamberlain. Chamberlain had never had a day's illness in his life, but within weeks of Germany's invasion of Holland and Belgium on 10 May 1940, and his resignation as Prime Minister that same afternoon, he was afflicted with cancer. In six months he was dead. Can anyone doubt that his physical collapse was affected by his mental condition? His humiliation was total. Another example comes to mind. Albert Spanswick, leader of the 200,000 strong COHSE, was at the very centre of the bitter battle between his union and the National Health Service. According to Len Murray, General Secretary of the TUC, the eight-month struggle put an increasingly intolerable strain on him. Within a few months of the end of it, although only sixty-three, he had contracted and died of cancer. There are many, many incidents where it is obvious that strain and worry have led to illness, in particular cancer.

Chapter 8

From Pony Club to President

In *My Early Life*, Winston Churchill wrote:

> Don't give your son money. As far as you can afford it, give him horses. No one ever came to grief – except honourable grief – through riding horses. No hour of life is lost that is spent in the saddle. Young men have often been ruined through owning horses or through backing them, but never through riding them, unless, of course, they break their necks, which taken at a gallop is a very good death to die.

Sir Winston would no doubt have been pleased to hear my surgeon, Sir Hedley Atkins, say, after my recovery from cancer, that he thought he ought to recommend all his patients to take up riding as he had no doubt that I owed my recovery, in part, to my fitness from riding. He would also be pleased to know that something like two million people ride in Britain today: though whether none of them ever came to grief, 'except honourable grief', I am inclined to doubt. Certainly they can sometimes cause grief. Those involved with horses have the reputation of being unusually independent: some would say arrogant. It is true that the majority of horsemen seem reluctant to be properly taught, preferring to learn from experience. This, perhaps, is the reason why it is only a minority, and a small minority at that, of the two million riders in Britain who belong to any organisation or Society. My career in the British Horse Society started in the Pony Club in 1928. As the first to enlist in the Grafton Hunt Pony Club, which was one of the first three branches to be formed, it is conceivable that I can claim to be the very first Pony Club member. I was elected to the Council in 1952 becoming Chairman in 1974. Throughout my thirty years in administration I was increasingly aware of the fact that the horse world can only be led: it can never be driven. Indeed, thanks to this independence of those associated with horses – and ponies – it proved difficult enough even adequately to lead, which suggests, perhaps, that it is as well that the main membership, about 35,000, is no larger. Nevertheless, that the wider membership, including all the Pony Clubs and Riding Clubs, amounts to only 100,000 or one-twentieth, at most, of all riders must be regarded as disappointing, especially when one knows that the other four-fifths benefit from the Society's work in so many ways.

When Colonel Mike Ansell retired from the Chairmanship of the British Horse Society in 1970, it was the end of an era. His reign could be described as a period of consolidation. After the war, my father had been instrumental in bringing together the two existing societies, the Institute of the Horse and the National Horse Association of Great Britain. There were, in 1947, between the two societies some 4,000 members. Between 1950 and 1970, not only did the membership increase – doubling from 10,000 to 20,000 with the founding, in 1967, of the British Equestrian Centre at Stoneleigh which became the Society's headquarters (outside London, to most members' relief) – but its work also expanded greatly. Whereas in 1947 only dressage and combined training had come under its aegis, gradually responsibility for many other activities was undertaken together, of course, with the Pony Club, which had its own constitution: riding clubs, driving, welfare, riding establishments and so on. For the last ten years of Mike Ansell's reign, I had been very much his lieutenant, eventually being appointed Vice Chairman, though there was, in fact, no provision for such a position in the Society's constitution. When Mike Ansell announced his decision to retire, there was a natural if unspoken desire by the members of the Council for a change of emphasis. With hindsight one can see this as inevitable: Mike, with his international reputation, his great authority, his control of the whole horse world – he was also Chairman of the British Show Jumping Association and, of course, was Director of the two most important shows, the Royal International and the Horse of the Year Show – had been a giant. As so often happens when a giant leaves the scene there is, while acknowledging the greatness of the giant, a craving for something a little less dominant. I was well aware of this myself: indeed, had told Mike that when I succeeded him I would be a very different kind of Chairman. It would neither be possible nor wise for me to attempt to emulate his highly effective and successful style of leadership. Without my realising it, however, members of the Council had very much identified me with Mike and his style of leadership. They now wanted something quite different. They felt, too, that in the interests of the Society it was essential that there should be evidence that the election of Chairman was properly democratic, although in fact there had never previously been an election for the Chairmanship. Hence the very popular and successful businessman, Bill Barton, whose principal interest in the horse world was hackneys, was nominated to stand against me. He was greatly and rightly respected in the Society: he had been an excellent Treasurer and even, in 1964, had been President. In contrast, though I believed that I had done some useful work on the Council, in particular in setting up the National Centre at Stoneleigh and guiding, as its first Chairman, the Riding Establishments Act Committee through its early difficult years, I was merely regarded as Mike Ansell's shadow, a role incidentally which I had enjoyed, which had taught me much and of which I was in no way ashamed.

Looking back, it is hard to explain why I should have been so surprised at the result: disappointed perhaps, even hurt, but not surprised. In fact it made sense, for in 1972 Mike was to become President/Chairman of the newly-formed British Equestrian Federation, which had been set up to represent the British Horse Society and the British Show Jumping Association in dealing with the international aspects of the two Societies' work. In other words, Mike with all his knowledge and experience, his international standing, would still be around. The British Equestrian Federation, of course, was the ideal vehicle for Mike who, everyone believed, still had a great contribution to make. To have at the same time his lieutenant of ten years as Chairman of the Society smacked of an *embarras de richesses*. My defeat for the Chairmanship was, however, to have two valuable repercussions. The first was that the British Horse Society Council, well aware that it would be almost impossible for anyone to succeed Mike Ansell, who had made it virtually a full-time job, decided to appoint a professional Director – a wise step, in view of the failing health of Bill Barton. It was also to make my own job very much easier when I became Chairman – without an election – in 1974. Accordingly an able and popular soldier, Major-General Jack Reynolds, was appointed. After a short time he was to become Director General of the British Equestrian Federation, his place with the British Horse Society being taken by Colonel Nigel Grove-White, with whom I was to have such an excellent relationship for the next eight years.

The other advantage of my being in the wilderness for two years –

there being no official Vice Chairman, I was not even, after my defeat, a member of the all-powerful Finance and General Purposes Committee, though I retained my seat on the Council – was that when I became Chairman I was able to bring to it a much more detached approach than would otherwise have been possible. I was able to see the work of the Society in perspective: not only from the point of view of one department vis-à-vis another, but also from the wider aspect of the Society's position in the whole horse world – its limitations and its potential. After two years away from the Society, I was in a far better frame of mind to run the Society. I had overcome a serious illness, had eased the burden of Mastership by bringing in two excellent Joint Masters, had a long-established dependable staff at Pendley and generally felt regenerated. Best of all I felt wanted, even needed, by the Society. It was not quite a case of 'come back, all is forgiven', because there had been nothing to forgive, but I was conscious of the fact that the Society, or at least the Society's Council, genuinely believed that I had a useful job to do, a job which, being now more detached than anyone else, I could, perhaps, do as well as, if not better than, anyone else. I became Chairman within a month of my sixtieth birthday.

When taking the chair at my first Council meeting I made it clear that I had three ambitions which I hoped very much to achieve during my chairmanship: the first was to increase the membership; the second was to revise the Society's constitution; the third was to improve the welfare and educational side of the Society's work, giving greater consideration to the ordinary rider as opposed to the competitor or specialist. There was a fourth which I did not mention, knowing it to be impractical, though even today I still hope that it might one day be achieved. This is for the Society to have a home of its own, a dream that I had had ever since my father and I had offered Pendley to the Society in 1962, an offer which, unfortunately, had not been accepted. There are many advantages in being situated on the Royal Agricultural Society's showground, with all its amenities, its accessibility, its convenience from the staff point of view, but most people would prefer it if the Society's home could be entirely independent, preferably based on a country estate. A fifth ambition, which again I never stated publicly, knowing that it could never happen during my Chairmanship, was an amalgamation of the British Horse Society and the British Show Jumping Association.

My first ambition, to increase the membership, was satisfactorily achieved, the numbers rising from 22,500 my first year, 1974, to

35,000 when I retired in 1982. There has also been a considerable shift of emphasis towards welfare, made possible by the profit-making sections of the Society agreeing to a levy whereby money is made available for welfare, inspection of riding establishments, bridleways and so on. I doubt, however, whether either of these ambitions could have been attained without the new constitution.

The original constitution had come into being when the Society boasted only 4,000 members with just four committees, the General Purposes, or Executive, Committee consisting of the chairman of each of the four committees and four members elected by the Society as a whole. In other words, there were as many elected members as statutory. As the Society expanded, however, so the number of committees multiplied, until by 1975 there were, including sub-committees, no less than eighteen, each committee chairman being entitled to a seat on the General Purposes Committee: but there were still only four elected members. This meant that the General Purposes Committee was not only unbalanced, but was far from representative. It also meant that the chairman of each committee tended to express interest only in those proposals or discussions that affected his, or her, own committee and its members, rather than the Society as a whole. As the committee chairmen also dominated the Council, the result was that the Council became little more than a rubber stamp, any sense of real democracy in the Society being almost completely stifled.

While the Council agreed in principal that the constitution was now out of date and should be revised, there was, nevertheless, considerable opposition, reflecting, as I saw it, a reluctance by members of the Council to accept any reform that might erode their power or influence. The two planks on which the new constitution was based were, firstly, a drastic reduction in the size of the General Purposes Committee, all its members in future being elected, nobody becoming a member just because he or she was chairman of an important committee; secondly, the reduction in the actual number of committees.

General Jack Reynolds, by now Director General of the British Equestrian Federation and, therefore, suitably detached and independent, agreed to draft the new constitution. Throughout the three years before it was finally agreed, he showed remarkable patience and resilience. It was a dogged battle. Twice the Council sent it back to the Finance and General Purposes Committee, the stumbling block usually being either the proposed merging of certain committees or the reduction in the size of the General Purposes Committee. On more than one occasion there was a threat from one group or another to withdraw altogether from the Society, until Lord March, as President in 1976, summed up the situation at the Annual General Meeting when he told the Society that it must make up its mind whether it wanted to be a Federation or an Association – a Federation, of course, being a group of organisations each with its own autonomy, a solution to the Society's problems which at first sight might appear logical. After all, what had dressage to do with long-distance riding; or horse trials to do with the Riding Establishments Act? I, however, and others whose opinions I greatly respected, were strongly opposed to this, firstly because we believed that the horse world could only speak with a strong voice if it was united. Taking into account all the Riding Clubs and Pony Club members, the Society could now claim to represent more than 100,000 horsemen which, in dealings with Government Departments, carries weight: as has been proved on a number of occasions. No Government Department would listen to groups of a few thousand: to sacrifice the Society's unity could only, as I saw it, dissipate its influence and bargaining power. Secondly, to become a Federation seemed to be a retrograde step. Already the horse world is too fragmented, with those who hunt uninterested in dressage, show jumpers totally unconcerned with long-distance riding, racing a world of its own, polo something apart. To split it further seemed exactly the reverse of what was now required in the interests of the horse world as a whole. Equestrianism is, unfortunately, always going to court a certain amount of criticism, due, in part, perhaps, to envy or resentment. If it is going to withstand this criticism, then it must be united rather than divided. Made up of such independently minded people, however, this unity is not easy to achieve. I certainly had no wish, while I was Chairman of the Society, to preside over its disintegration: rather, I was prepared to work hard to prevent it. Eventually, after many hours of discussion and argument, the new constitution was agreed and is, I believe, now accepted as much more effective than the old one, its strength lying in the total independence of its General Purposes or Executive Committee. Whereas previously there was the continuing problem of vested interests, now the Committee is working for the good of the Society as a whole.

As an example, it is worth quoting the case of Hugh Thomas, the Olympic Three-Day Event rider, who as a member of the Horse Trials Committee was frequently critical of the Society – often with justification – especially as a member of a small Working Party set up to investigate the possible advantages of Horse Trials becoming an independent body, a plan which, after the Working Party had reported back, was not, in fact, proceeded with. Hugh was proposed for the new General Purposes and Finance Committee, duly being elected as one of its eight members. As Chairman of that Committee for three years before I retired, I know from personal experience what a loyal, industrious member Hugh was: but most of all, thanks to his integrity, he would invariably put the interests of the Society first. Indeed, on more than one occasion he supported a resolution which was not necessarily to the advantage of Horse Trials. He is now Treasurer of the Society and could well be Chairman one day. It would not have been easy under the old constitution for Hugh's talents to have been utilised so greatly to the benefit of the Society as a whole: nor expected. He would, to all intents and purposes, have been on the General Purposes Committee just to look after the interest of Horse Trials, and nothing else. Without doubt the new constitution achieved the adoption of a much more detached attitude being taken by members of the General Purposes Committee in dealing with the affairs of the Society. No longer was the Society hampered by the exploiting of vested interests. Which does not mean to say that with the ratification of the new constitution there were no further problems. Far from it. It takes time in any Society for change to be wholly accepted: even more so in a Society as complex and made up of so many disparate groups of independent interests as the British Horse Society. I have sometimes suggested that in each year of my Chairmanship I had to attempt to cope with a problem created by one or other section of the Society.

I have already mentioned Horse Trials' threatened independence: subsequently both Riding Clubs and the Pony Club were to express similar aspirations. The defection of either would have distressed me greatly. I had been much involved from the very beginning in the emergence of the Riding Clubs as a vital part of the horse world. Much of the pioneer work was done by David Satow, who was almost part of my own family. My father was his godfather. His mother, who died giving birth to David and his twin sister, was my mother's greatest friend. His father was my father's accountant. We had been at Hawtreys together. When the British Horse Society moved to Stoneleigh from London, David, who was the Society's Development Officer, lived in a cottage of ours at Foscote, where we had moved from Pendley in 1964. Against the trend at that time, he

9a. With admiring looks from Jennifer and 2-year-old Piers, Pancho returns from exercising in the snow.

9b. Monty leads the parade of a thousand British Horse Society members at Badminton in honour of the 10th Duke of Beaufort's forty years as Master of the Horse.

10a.
Faithful old friend Kingsway, over 30 years old, in contented retirement.

10b.
Pleased as – Punch!
As enthusiastic as ever in his last season.

worked very hard for the interests of the ordinary rider, something that very much appealed to me. I had always had tremendous admiration for the Riding Clubs, watching with delight their growth and experience.

As far as the Pony Club was concerned, it was part of my life, having been founded by my parents with Major Harry Faudel Phillips, Colonel Guy Cubitt and Mrs Hurst. Apart from my years as a member – I believe that I was one of the first to pass the A Test: I am sure that I could not now! – when I became Master of the Grafton in 1951 I became President of the local branch, as I did of the Whaddon Chase in 1954, my wife for ten years being District Commissioner. Fortunately the consultants employed to advise the groups on the feasibility of becoming independent recommended that it would not be to their advantage to break away from the Society, although there was, sadly, a breakaway bridleways movement.

There was an anxious moment, too, with Dressage. As long as I can remember, the Dressage Committee has always been 'sensitive', due, I believe, to what one might call a collective inferiority complex. They resent, understandably, the allegation that there is something a little precious about dressage. If there is, then it is not the fault of dressage enthusiasts, rather it is the ignorance of those riders who dislike any form of serious equitation. They possibly feel, too, that compared with the show jumpers and eventers, their representatives have been less successful internationally. This may be true, but dressage on the continent is a way of life, as it has been for centuries: overseas riders, both collectively and individually, are bound to be superior to British – for the time being. Whatever the reasons, the Dressage Committee were not happy about paying the 7 per cent levy which was required to subsidise the Society's welfare responsibilities and such activities as the Riding Establishments Act Committee's inspections and the Rights of Way Panel which particularly benefited the ordinary rider. But here again the new constitution proved its worth. The Council voted in favour of the levy: the Dressage Committee, finding themselves out on a limb, sensibly and graciously accepted it. But at one time, as with Riding Clubs and Pony Clubs, there had been a threat of withdrawal from the Society, bringing us ever nearer to the situation when the Society would be no more than a Federation.

In 1976 we had to cope with a major eruption in the Combined Driving Trials Committee. Alan Bristow, the extremely able Chairman of Bristow Helicopters, an outstanding pilot himself, had recently taken up driving, meeting with immediate success and quickly reaching international standard. Unfortunately, he fell out with the Committee of which Frank Haydon, Cynthia's husband, was the much-respected Chairman, determined to force his resignation. Possibly he had some right on his side – he certainly had one or two staunch allies – but his behaviour was unfortunate, only succeeding in antagonising people. Though I tried as far as possible to be impartial, I found his habit of ringing me at my home at eight o'clock almost every morning for two weeks somewhat irritating: almost a form of intimidation! Finally the matter came before a special meeting of the full Council which gave him permission to address it, despite the fact that he was not a member. His speech was a little unfortunate and succeeded only in alienating his own supporters. Whereas his intention was to criticise the inefficiency of the Committee, he somehow gave the impression that he was criticising Prince Philip, which, of course, was unwarrantable and unacceptable. That, inevitably, was the end of the matter, but it had dragged on for over seven months.

There was a sad episode, too, the following year with the Riding Establishments Act Committee, which relied for its existence on a very generous annual grant from the Home of Rest for Horses. It was unanimously agreed by the Council that the streamlining under the new constitution necessitated the work of this Committee being taken over by the Welfare Committee and carried out on a regional basis. This, not altogether surprisingly, was resented: in addition there was one of those personality clashes which no amount of diplomacy on the part of the Chairman or anyone else could overcome. Inevitably the strained relations resulted in the loss of our grant. Another Chairman might have been a little more accommodating, but having worked so hard for the new constitution I felt that it must not be allowed to be eroded. It is hoped that an improvement in relations will be achieved by the inclusion on the Council of a representative from the Home of Rest for Horses.

In the clash with the Training and Examinations Committee in 1980 I had no option but to climb down, but the circumstances stemmed from a very different, indeed unexpected, sequence of events. When John Blackmore retired at the time of the introduction of the new constitution after twenty-five years as the Society's Secretary, it was decided to replace him with a Company Secretary and a Finance Officer. With inadequate reserves, the Treasurer had rightly insisted that there must be very much more careful budgeting and no overspending. A small Finance Committee was set up with instructions to inspect the accounts monthly. In 1980 these were produced by the Finance Officer, whose figures up to the end of the third quarter gave no cause whatever for alarm. The fact that the figures, both for income and expenditure, were always exactly on target, caused little surprise, rather satisfaction. In fact we should have been alerted. Unfortunately, the Finance Officer had a breakdown in health and had to leave the Society. It was then discovered that the figures that had been produced monthly were unreliable. Pressures of work had prevented proper analysis of the different accounts. An urgent appeal to the auditors presented an entirely unpredicted and very alarming state of affairs.

The Council had been assured at their September meeting that we were on target: now, at the December meeting, it had to be informed that there was a likelihood of a loss of over £70,000 – not a very pleasant statement for a Chairman to have to make. It was made more difficult by the fact that we could not, for obvious reasons, explain fully the facts: we just had to appear incompetent and accept responsibility. As was to be expected, the Council demanded, first, that we produce very quickly a revised budget, second that we evolve a plan which would further streamline the Society, drastically cutting back future spending, our limited reserves being quite unable to survive another big loss. I was not to know, fortunately, that I would, within a few months, be trying to cope with an almost identical experience, but in a totally different context.

Colonel Nigel Grove-White, the Director, worked round the clock to draft a 'white paper' for discussion. It was agreed in principal by the Finance and General Purposes Committee, but was considered to be too radical – at least in parts – by the Council, which sent it back to be redrafted. This time, despite major changes recommended, it was accepted. One of these major changes was the transference of Training from the Training and Examinations Committee to the individual disciplines which were, in fact, already responsible for much of the training, while Examinations were to be organised and administered by the British Equestrian Centre's Management Committee at Stoneleigh. Training and Examinations had always been a very active and influential committee, contributing much of value to the Society. I had, therefore, had reservations about axeing it, although on paper it seemed logical. When the examiners had their annual conference at Stoneleigh, I was invited to address them to explain the thinking behind the new proposals, the urgent need for stringent economies. When I arrived at Stoneleigh anticipating opposition, but nothing that I would not be able to handle, I was surprised to find that although, so far as I knew, there were only a hundred or so examiners, no less than four hundred people were packed into the indoor school. I had to speak to them from the centre of the arena: a Daniel amongst the lions, indeed! First, however, the Chairman introduced me in a lengthy speech, which can fairly be described as hostile and hard-hitting. Almost from the moment I began to speak I was barracked. It seemed better to let the session take a question and answer form, though the questions, most of which appeared to have been planted, were without exception aggressive. I did my best: at least, having all the facts at my finger-tips, I was not like a wretched Minister in the House of Commons improperly briefed. But I knew that concessions would have to be made because I could not deny that these proposals had been introduced too hurriedly, without proper consultation. It was largely my own fault. I had been anxious to get the new proposals implemented before I finished my term of office as Chairman the following year. I was keen, too, that before I retired the Society should be back in a profitable situation: which, in fact, it was, thanks to the Herculean efforts of our Treasurer, Peter Fenwick, and the senior staff at Stoneleigh. To my great delight, and not a little to my relief, in the space of two years a loss of £70,000 was turned into a surplus of £140,000 – no mean achievement, surely.

Despite the fact that, according to the minutes, the whole Council had originally approved the white paper – the Chairman of Training and Examinations later insisted sincerely that he had dissented – we had no option but to re-draft it: Training and Examinations was reprieved, cuts in our expenditure being found elsewhere. I have often likened the British Horse Society to the Government: everyone is in favour of cuts and economies as long as it is not in their own department. In the Training and Examinations saga I could have asked for no better example. Different Government Departments, no doubt, can be as limited in their outlook as different departments of the horse world, which is, perhaps, no bad thing. Although ultimately consideration for the whole must be paramount, nevertheless people wholly dedicated to their own department or sectional interest have an indisputable contribution to make, even if it sometimes appears to be at another department's expense. Their outlook may be limited but, in my experience, they are usually worth listening to. It is, of course, the responsibility of the chairman or head of an organisation to weld the apparently disparate parts into a whole. The parts in the British Horse Society were very disparate indeed, with the profit-making departments, such as Horse Trials and Riding Clubs, on the one hand and those representing a cost to the Society, such as the National Centre, Road Safety and Welfare, on the other. Yet, despite the problems, the occasional setbacks, I always enjoyed my time as Chairman. I made many friends; I was repeatedly rewarded by cooperation and encouragement; I was frequently impressed by colleagues' loyalty and integrity, putting the success of the Society before any self interest. After I had been re-elected for my fourth two-year term of office, I decided that I would retire altogether when I had completed eight years. I was pressed to stay a further term, but I decided that apart from the fact that the whole role seemed to be becoming increasingly demanding, especially as I grew older, I had reached the conclusion that there was little more that I could achieve for the Society. I had done as much, I felt, as was within my capability: the Society was now in a healthy state financially – and as harmonious as it was ever likely to be; it was still steadily expanding with an increasingly important role to play in the horse world; it was efficiently and imaginatively administered. I accepted that for the Society to have a home of its own was still a pipe-dream, likely to remain that way for the foreseeable future. Nor was a merger between the British Horse Society and the British Show Jumping Association any nearer, despite the fact that no two Chairmen – John Blakeway of the BSJA and myself of the BHS – could have worked in closer cooperation. It was, I felt sure, the right time for me to retire, just thirty years after I had been elected to the Council.

For my service to the horse world I had the great honour to be awarded the Order of the British Empire in the New Year's Honours of 1978. I had, in fact, received a letter from No. 10 Downing Street the previous 22 November informing me that the Prime Minister intended to recommend my name to the Queen: would I confirm on the enclosed form my willingness to accept? Which, of course, I did. I heard nothing more until the morning of 31 December – New Year's Day was on a Sunday – when turning on the radio in the kitchen shortly after seven o'clock the very first item I heard on the News was: 'OBE's go to the Two Ronnies and Dorian Williams': good company! I assume that the reason that one receives no firm confirmation in writing is to ensure that one does not make public the honour until it is officially announced. In fact, one hears nothing further from No. 10 or the Palace until one receives a summons to an Investiture, any time between March and June. Finally, towards the end of the year, several months after the Investiture, there arrives a splendid document signed by both the Queen and the Duke of Edinburgh.

The Investiture itself is, it goes without saying, an unforgettable experience. On arrival at Buckingham Palace at about 10.15 a.m., one is directed up the magnificent staircase at the top of which one is politely separated from one's family. We were fortunate in that being recognised by Sir Eric Penn, Comptroller of the Household, Jennifer and our son and daughter, Piers and Carola, were taken to the special raised seats which run down the side of the ballroom where the Investiture is held. Being at the throne end, they were within a few feet of the Queen. The whole of the floor of the ballroom is taken up with some three hundred gilt and crimson seats. Those receiving awards are taken into a large gallery which is divided by plush red ropes into what I can only describe as 'pens': one for those to receive knighthoods and other senior honours, one for CBEs and OBEs and one for MBEs. One has anything up to one hour to wait, which can be quite an ordeal: not only is there very limited seating accommod-ation so that one has to stand for most if not all of the time, but, unlike almost any other occasion, the probability is that one knows nobody in one's own pen. It is like going to a cocktail party in a district where one is a complete stranger – but with no cocktails. We experienced a not dissimilar situation when we were fortunate enough to be invited to a reception at No. 10 Downing Street in 1983: it so happened that it was the very day that the June election was announced, which naturally greatly enhanced the atmosphere. We doubted if we would know anyone at all: nor did we, other than Peter and Virginia May, whose daughter, Suzanne, is a top-class eventer. Wandering through the magnificent state rooms on the first floor, however, we found that many of the eighty present were known to us by sight: Max Bygraves, Jimmy Tarbuck, Adam Faith, Bob Willis, Jayne Torvill and Christopher Dean, the skaters, Steve Davis, the snooker champion, Paul Eddington and Nigel Hawthorne from 'Yes Minister', Andrew Alexander, the political columnist, Winston Churchill and many others, all of whom were friendly and easy to talk to. By contrast, at the Palace everyone was very reticent, the importance of the occasion causing nervousness or shyness: nor, of course, was there any alcohol to drive away inhibitions. Other than a few words when good manners demanded them, or the occasional stilted greeting when somebody recognised one, most people kept themselves to themselves.

Not surprisingly, many people want to spend a penny before the end of the wait: having made known their problem to one of the ushers they are escorted down a corridor to a rather splendid loo. Eventually one is called – it is, as I remember, in alphabetical order – and led up a passage at the side of the ballroom to the entrance at the top end where the dais for the Queen is sited. An official prompts one on the procedure, having put a pin in one's lapel on which the Queen will hang the medal: one then waits one's turn. Now: six paces forward, turn left, facing the Queen, who it appears has a word for everyone, then proceed straight across the top of the ballroom to the passage on the other side. Here one is relieved of one's medal, which is placed in a box and immediately handed back to one, the pin being carried off to be pinned on somebody else's breast. One is then shown into the back of the ballroom, seating oneself on any free chair for the rest of the investiture. Soft music is playing throughout, often appropriate, the famous Mozart's *Musical Joke*, show jumping on television's signature tune, being played at the moment of my own investiture. In fact, the likelihood is that one is so nervous one is scarcely aware of the music nor, regrettably, does one fully appreciate what the Queen is saying. I do recall that she mentioned the *many* aspects of the horse world in which I was involved.

It was raining when we left the Palace a little after midday. Most of the photographers had left or were packing up their equipment, but Jennifer was determined that we should have a record of this great occasion. She therefore seized a photographer about to depart, insisting that he take a photograph of Dorian Williams.

'Who?' he asked blankly.

'Dorian Williams,' she repeated, 'the show jumping commentator. *Horse and Hound* will definitely want a picture,' which fortunately they did. Getting into our car, which we had been allowed to park in the courtyard of the Palace we drove out through that splendid arch and those famous gates. It was all over.

It is not easy to describe one's reaction on hearing that one has been nominated for an honour. I personally was so overwhelmed that I did not even allow myself to feel deflated when at the meet that Saturday morning a well-meaning friend greeted me with: 'OBE? But isn't that what they give to municipal gardeners?'

'Only very good municipal gardeners,' I managed to reply,

resisting the temptation to tell him that such as he would be lucky even to get a Scout's badge for dropping bricks.

I had only two regrets in receiving this honour. The first was that my father had never been similarly honoured. He had done so much more for the horse world than I had ever done. Founder of the BSJA with Colonel 'Taffy' Walwyn, co-founder of the Pony Club, responsible for reviving the International Horse Show in 1947, one of the architects of the BHS after the Second World War, he had also introduced dressage into Britain in the thirties when he formed the British Riding Club. He had even pioneered right back in 1914 the Regimental Trick Ride and Musical Ride. He had not only been Chairman of the Institute of the Horse when it became the British Horse Society in 1947, but in 1953 he had been President. My second regret was that my honour was not at least partly in connection with Pendley, for although I appreciated that as far as the general public was concerned it was my association with horses that had brought me recognition, I always believed that my work at Pendley was of far more lasting value. In commentating on show jumping from the beginning, I had helped to popularise the sport; in being responsible for the founding of the National Centre I had made a contribution to equestrianism, an important leisure time activity; but in founding Pendley I had, I liked to think, pioneered an aspect of education that could positively and lastingly affect peoples' lives.

Various other awards and presentations which I have received during my life have all given me great pleasure: none more than the exquisite silver goblet given to me by the British Equestrian Writers Association when I retired from commentating at the end of 1981. It was inscribed: 'The Most Famous Horse Voice of Them All'. Nothing can give a professional greater pleasure than the approval of his peers. Oddly enough I nearly missed the presentation. Suffering still from my frozen shoulder, a friend had driven me to the lunch at the Café Royal. As, thanks to the traffic, we were nearly late, my friend dropped me at the restaurant before parking the car – which took him an hour. When, as we reached the end of the meal, he had still not arrived, I went to look for him, only returning as Alan Smith, equestrian correspondent of the *Daily Telegraph*, Chairman of the British Equestrian Writers Association, was calling my name. It was a complete surprise.

I greatly valued, too, the picture presented to me when I retired from the Whaddon Chase and the little shield given to me by the

British Team after they had won the Three-Day Event Gold Medal in the Olympic Games in Mexico in 1968.

Towards the end of my last year as Chairman of the BHS, our President, Lavinia, Duchess of Norfolk, whose husband Bernard had been President twenty years earlier, phoned me one evening to ask me if it was the President's responsibility to nominate the next President. I explained that officially it was for the General Purposes Committee to propose a name for consideration by the Council. Had she anyone in mind, I enquired.

To my astonishment she said: 'Yes: you.'

That, I assured her, was quite out of the question. In the first place there was no precedent for a retiring Chairman being promoted to President. Secondly, and far more important, it had for the last twenty years or more been the policy to invite a national figure with equestrian connections, from royalty downwards, to be President of the Society. We had had Prince Philip and the Princess Royal; we had had people of great eminence such as the Duke of Beaufort, the Marquis of Exeter, the Marquis of Abergavenny, the Earl of March; soldiers of renown such as Sir Gerald Templer and Sir John Mogg. Mr Williams was hardly the appropriate successor to such people as these.

To my surprise she made it clear that it was no spontaneous suggestion on her part. She had discussed it with General 'Monkey' Blacker, President of the British Equestrian Federation, who, she insisted, had thought it an admirable idea. I told her that I would think about it, but I very much doubted whether it was viable. A few days later I received a long letter from 'Monkey' Blacker in which he urged me to accept Lavinia's suggestion. He and Lavinia had canvassed most of the members of the Council, all of whom thought it might solve a number of problems. If I would agree to be a 'Working' President I could be of great assistance to the new Chairman, Peter Fenwick, who, as a businessman responsible, with his brothers, for running Fenwicks of Bond Street and elsewhere, might well find it difficult to devote sufficient time to the many public relations demands on the Chairman, visiting regions all over the British Isles, attending social functions and so on.

It was true that the duties of Chairman had become extremely onerous. There was the danger that people of the right calibre might be deterred from accepting the position because of the amount of work now involved. With some diffidence, after very careful thought, I agreed, the outgoing President putting forward her proposal at the next full meeting of the Council: it appeared to be carried with acclaim. Not altogether surprisingly, however, the proposal did not find universal favour. At the following Council meeting a representative of the ever-vigilant Training and Examinations Committee queried the legality of the election – rightly, as it happened, the constitution making it clear that the President elect has first to be nominated by the General Purposes Committee, then to be elected, properly proposed and seconded, by the Council. Fortunately the Society's Director, Nigel Grove-White, had appreciated this and at a special General Purposes meeting, called to discuss another matter, immediately before the Council, had arranged for me to be properly nominated. At the Council that followed I was, to my relief, elected unanimously.

Even today I harbour doubts about the wisdom of that decision, anxious lest the Society might have felt a little cheated having an ordinary commoner, one of themselves, thrust upon them. I had always been aware that a few members felt strongly that the Society had already been downgraded having the British Equestrian Federation superimposed upon them. The Federation, being made up of an equal number of members of both the BHS and the BSJA, automatically took priority over the two component Societies, whereas when the BHS, prior to the formation of the Federation in 1972, had itself acted as the Federation, dealing with all FEI (Fédération Equestrien Internationel) matters on behalf of both Societies, it had been regarded as senior. Now it had been relegated.

If such apparent pettiness is difficult to understand, it has to be remembered that in any organisation members tend to be sensitive about their own status or that of their organisation: they are jealous of their rights, which they will protect with vigour. Considerable opposition had had to be overcome before the Federation came into being.

Even more of a problem, perhaps, was the fact that I had for so long been Chairman, and a member of the Council for twenty years previously. It was easy for people to regard me just as an upgraded Chairman, which, again, might be thought to diminish the position of President. Conscious of this, I certainly did what I could to be an effective 'Working' President, hoping that the help that I was able to give my successor as Chairman compensated for my not being a figurehead of great stature. At least being President enabled me to retain my contacts with an organisation with which I had been so long involved, and to which I had become very attached. In addition it naturally made me very proud to have attained one of the highest positions in the horse world, an achievement that would have so delighted my father, who had himself been President just thirty years earlier, the year of my election to the Council.

This does not mean that I had any inflated ideas about the importance of my being President of the BHS, or the importance of the position itself. As far as the personal side was concerned, any ideas of grandeur that I might have entertained were quickly eliminated when shortly after I had been elected President I received a letter from a member of the Society addressed to Dorian Williams, President of the British Horse Society, British Equestrian Centre, Stoneleigh, starting Dear Sir or Madam! As far as the position of the Society's President was concerned, I could have wished that it were more prestigious, for it would then have reflected a wider representation. I have already pointed out that even when one includes all the members of the Riding Clubs and Pony Club, the BHS is only supported by about 20 per cent of all the people who ride in this country. Obviously there are many who might be described as weekend riders, even suburban weekend riders, who are never likely to belong to any Society or organisation: but sadly, thanks to the fiercely independent nature of the equestrian community, it seems unlikely that the many breed and pony societies or specialist groups, such as the Hack and Cob and Riding Horse Association, the Ponies of Britain or the British Show Pony Society, will ever come under the British Horse Society's umbrella, any more than will the National Light Horse Breeding Society (until 1983 the Hunters' Improvement Society) or the BSJA, or indeed polo, Driving, Riding for the Disabled, however desirable it might be. Nor, it seems to me, would it be altogether illogical for hunting and point-to-pointing, under the aegis of the Master of Foxhounds Association, to come under the same all-embracing umbrella. They are 'associated' with the Society, of course: but if the work of the Society is to be really effective, if the whole horse world is going to be properly administered, then I doubt if that is really enough.

The value of a strong, prosperous Society reflecting every equestrian interest with the exception of racing, which is a world of its own, indeed a self-contained industry, is threefold. Firstly, it can speak with an authoritative voice as far as legislation and parliamentary matters are concerned. When in 1981-1982 I was involved, as Chairman of the Society, with Customs and Excise and the relevant Ministers in attempting to achieve a more realistic administration of the VAT system, it was not helpful to discover that other branches of the horse world, speaking for only a few hundred interested parties, were also making approaches to the Ministry. Not surprisingly, Civil Servants are unimpressed with these splinter approaches, suggesting the inability of a community to speak with one voice.

Secondly, only with complete unity will there be the strength of purpose to eliminate the prevalent ignorance in the horse world which often amounts to cruelty. A united public opinion in the horse world itself is essential if ignorance is to be overcome. Thirdly, with the sensational increase in the popularity of riding over the last two decades, it is vital that the relationship between the horse world and the public and local authorities should be properly handled. Particularly vital is it that publicity and public relations should be professionally managed. This can only be done if sufficient funds are available, which they never can be in a fragmented community. A single example will suffice to demonstrate how ineffectual an approach to local authorities can be if there is insufficient authority in the approach. Each year a large number of young people seek proper instruction and tuition so that they can take up a career with horses which, with the increasing popularity of riding, seems to them and to their parents an entirely feasible proposition. Unfortunately it is virtually impossible to get any assistance in the way of grants or even advice from local authorities for riding students, although they will help almost any other student. Frequently, in an attempt to help, the BHS will make an approach to a local authority, but it seldom achieves much, as the Society just does not carry enough weight. It has failed adequately to convince the public that riding is no longer an exclusive pastime, only available to the upper classes: it has failed because it has not been in a position to speak with one loud, authoritative voice, its very strength forcing people to listen. If it represented a million riders, instead of 100,000, and had available funds which such a large Society would be in position to generate, then it would be a very different story. Only when the British Horse Society is the National Governing Body for Riders in deed as well as in name will it be as influential, effective and helpful as it ought to be.

When I came to the end of my close involvement with the Society, stretching well over thirty years, I realised that although I liked to think that I had achieved a certain amount, my success was limited. The founding of the National Centre in 1967 was, I believe, the most important single event in the Society's history. I am still of the opinion that the new constitution introduced in the late seventies enabled the Society to progress and expand its responsibilities. Otherwise, looking back over my years as a member of the Council, as Chairman and as President, I have to admit that nothing of world-shaking importance was achieved, nothing particularly appreciated by the horse world as a whole or by the Society in particular – certainly nothing compared with the pioneering of dressage and horse trials by my father in the 1950s. This inability to make much of a ripple on the water, despite one's efforts, probably reflects the nature of the horse world. Basically conservative, it is not easy to introduce new ideas. Britain is the only country that lacks a generally accepted 'doctrine' in equitation similar to, say, the Germans, French or Americans. British riders and instructors are too independent, perhaps: one can only hope that ultimately they will see the wisdom of drawing as close together as possible, whatever their individual interests might be.

The generous presentation made to me when I retired as President in June 1984 persuaded me that my efforts over thirty years had not entirely been in vain.

Chapter 9

White City Revisited

In theory the official shop window of the British Horse Society is the Royal International Horse Show: but it never has been because, paradoxically, the main feature of the Royal International has always been the jumping, which is the one discipline with which the Society is in no way involved. In view of the somewhat traumatic experiences of the last few years, the changes of venue, it is worth looking at the show in its proper perspective.

Immediately after the war, Mike Ansell was elected Chairman of the British Show Jumping Association. He had, of course, been blinded at the time of Dunkirk, but what he lacked in physical sight he made up for with mental vision. In his prisoner-of-war camp he had spent much time envisaging the show jumping of the future. As soon as he had become Chairman of the BSJA, he planned a Victory Show Jumping Championship which would give him an oppor-tunity to put into practice some of the theories about the designing and building of show-jumping fences that he and others had discussed in Oflag IX A/H Spanenburg. As one of his Committee, Brigadier John Allen, knew Frank Gentle, who was then Chairman of the Greyhound Racing Association, it was arranged to hold the Victory Championship at the White City. So successful was it that it was immediately decided to hold another show there the following year, making it bigger, more comprehensive, by including show classes as well as jumping. This was called the National Show and was presented under the Chairmanship of my father on 20, 21 and 22 June 1946, Mike Ansell being responsible for the show jumping events. As I have already described, I was invited to be Public Address Commentator, or Announcer as it was then called.

Again, the show was so successful that it was decided to revive at the White City the old International Horse Show, which between 1907 and 1939 had been held at Olympia. A number of guarantors, including the Holland Martin brothers, Lord Cowdray, Lord

Margadale, Sir Ian Walker-Okeover, Sir Harold Wernher and Colonel Harry Llewellyn agreed to underwrite the show. As they were all members of the newly formed British Horse Society – an amalgamation between the Institute of the Horse and the National Horse Association of Great Britain – it was agreed that the show should nominally be presented by the British Horse Society, despite the fact that it was predominantly a jumping show. No one at the time seems to have remarked on the anomaly of a Society that had nothing to do with jumping putting on a jumping show. The pre-war International had, of course, been more involved with showing classes than with jumping, though by 1939 both the King George V Cup and the Prince of Wales Cup – the team championship – had become top international events, the former being considered the leading competition for individual riders in the world, the latter being comparable with the Aga Khan Cup in Dublin.

The revival of the International in 1947 by no means met with universal approval. There are many who felt that the elegance and smartness so associated with the exclusive Olympia had been lost: others felt that it was too large, too remote. 'Curlew', reporting in *Horse and Hound*, found it dirty, a barrack and totally lacking in atmosphere. Before long, however, it was to become a big success, due to two factors. The first was the holding of the Olympic Games in London in 1948. The final event was held at Wembley stadium on 14 August. The show at the White City opened two days later, on 16 August. Naturally the majority of the leading international riders who had taken part in the Olympic Games stayed on for the International, which meant that there was a greater gathering of leading riders assembled for a single show than ever before. They were all there: the Italians, the French, the Spaniards, the Belgians, the Swiss, the Argentines, the Irish and, of course, the Americans jumping in Britain for the first time and underlining their outstanding ability, incidentally, by winning the Prince of Wales Cup most convincingly.

Not surprisingly, crowds flocked to the White City that week, many of those attending never having seen show jumping before. The weather was kind, the evening performances under floodlights dramatic, the jumping exciting. When Colonel Harry Llewellyn won his first King George V Cup on Foxhunter the huge crowd stood and cheered for minutes. By the end of the week, when the dashing Chevalier d'Orgeix won the Daily Mail Cup, his brilliant, bouncing black stallion, Sucre de Pomme, had already become a firm favourite with the public, as had a little mare called Finality and her attractive young rider, Pat Smythe, who finished equal third. When Britain won the Gold medal for show jumping in the Helsinki Olympics in 1952 it set the seal on the sport's popularity. Our jumpers became household names: everyone wanted to see them. Here was a sport at which the British could succeed; more than that, it was a sport which could be understood and enjoyed by a large lay public. Even in 1956 the BBC was referring to the Horse of the Year Show as one of the year's most popular broadcasts, going so far as to liken its last night, with the famous Cavalcade and Tribute to the Horse, to the last night of the Proms. The other factor in popularising the International Horse Show at the White City was Mike Ansell himself. Not only had he a charismatic personality, not only was he naturally authoritative, respected, dominating, as his father had been, but everyone admired his enormous courage, in particular the way in which he had overcome the handicap of his blindness. His determination that this little-known sport which he had introduced to a new public should succeed, his determination, no less, that he personally should succeed in its promotion, allowed no interference, no opposition, no hint of defeatism. He expected and received universal support, from royalty downwards.

It must be remembered that as far as the general public, which included the horsey public, was concerned, show jumping was a novelty. It was making the same sort of impact that the invention of lawn tennis had made on the middle and upper classes a hundred years earlier – or snooker in 1982. Suddenly everybody wanted to be involved in the sport. Mike Ansell brilliantly exploited this. Anyone who was anyone wanted to boast an acquaintance with him, or with Harry Llewellyn, or with the young Pat Smythe. So they came to the White City: every entrance would have queues an hour before the gates opened; cars would be parked miles away; the members' enclosure would be crammed from end to end; the forecourt with its little brightly lit bars and umbrellas was as crowded as the Royal Enclosure at Ascot; everyone lucky enough to get a table in the glass-fronted restaurant was the envy of their friends. King George VI and Queen Elizabeth maintained the pre-war tradition of attending in person and, having arrived in an open landau, could be seen in the magnificent flower-bedecked royal box. It was glamorous, it was elegant, it was exciting. And when the Band of the Royal Marines School of Music brought the show to an end with its rendering of 'Sunset' as the great spotlights faded and the flags floated slowly down, it was extremely moving: an unforgettable experience for those fortunate enough to be present.

It is no exaggeration to suggest that the White City in the fifties and early sixties could be bracketed, socially, with Gold Cup Day at Ascot, Men's Final Day at Wimbledon, Ladies' Day at Henley. Being part of it, indeed at the very centre of it, one felt that it would go on for ever. But in 1966 the British Horse Society was notified that the following year would be the last for the Horse Show at the White City. An enormous flyover was being built connecting Western Avenue, the A40, with central London. Construction, estimated to last three years, made the holding of a horse show requiring collecting rings, stabling, car parks and so on, impossible. After much discussion, a decision was taken to move to the Cup Final Stadium at Wembley where, in the Empire Pool, the Horse of the Year show had already been successfully installed in 1959 after the closing of the Harringay arena. After twenty happy years at the now much-loved White City, the show felt lost in the great Wembley Cup Final Stadium: the 15,000 or so people that in those days one could count on to attend the Royal International – it had become Royal in 1957, just fifty years after the first International at Olympia in 1907 – looked but a handful in a stadium built to accommodate more than 80,000. Long before the simple logistics of the situation forced the Horse Show Committee to think again, the Football Association had decided that horses' hooves must never be allowed to damage the sacred Wembley turf. In fact, the footballers' reaction turned out to be more emotional than realistic.

But the Royal International Horse Show was once again without a home. Wembley suggested that the show be moved to the Empire Pool, but most people felt that, apart from it seeming wrong to have a summer show indoors, to have two shows in the same arena within three months might well prove counter-productive. The White City was not ready to have the show back; various other football stadiums were considered, but proved, for one reason or another, unsuitable. What about the Crystal Palace? The LCC, as it was then, was keen to have the show and was prepared to spend £100,000 on adapting the complex to our requirements.

In October that year the Horse of the Year Show was followed immediately by a visit to Wembley of the Spanish Riding School of Vienna. Mike Ansell and his wife, Victoria, stayed up for the first night, Mike having decided to go down next day to inspect the Crystal Palace, its possible use for the Royal International having been the main topic of conversation during the Show the previous week. I was up at Stoneleigh that week, then being Honorary Director of the National Centre. When I returned to my office from the school on the Monday morning there was a message for me from Mike Ansell at the Crystal Palace. He was convinced that it was the answer to our problems. We could hold the show there in 1970, but it would mean holding it one week later than the usual date. This he believed to be feasible, so would I pass the word round? He would get in touch with me after he had returned to his home in Devon later that week. But he never did: it all worked out tragically different. On his return to the Hyde Park Hotel that afternoon, he learned that Victoria had died in their room shortly after he had left for the Crystal Palace. It was a terrible shock. Not only had it been a wonderfully happy marriage, but since he had lost his sight she had been his devoted, unfailing help and support. The Crystal Palace was never once mentioned again: it was as though it must ever be associated with the death of Victoria – the very name hurt him, reminded him.

Thanks to the help of his family and friends he was not for long out of action. When at the end of the year he returned to his office in Belgrave Square his mind was made up. The Royal International Horse Show was to move indoors to the Empire Pool at Wembley, as Wembley itself had suggested. If there were any who objected to the idea, they had not the heart to protest: in any case there seemed to be no alternative. So it was that the Empire Pool, home of the very popular Horse of the Year Show, became the new home of the Royal International. And for the first few years it proved very successful. Knowing the place so well, a great help with his blindness, Mike Ansell was able to direct the show with all the skill and panache with which he had directed the Horse of the Year Show since its move to Wembley in 1959. A new venue might have presented difficulties.

When eventually, in 1975, after an innings lasting nearly thirty years, at the age of seventy he retired, he was succeeded by his assistant, John Stevens, who carried on the show and, indeed, the Horse of the Year Show, equally effectively. But the writing was on the wall. 1976 was one of the hottest summers of the century, certainly the hottest since the Second World War. As an indoor stadium did not seem the right place to be on a hot July afternoon, or even on a warm July evening, the riders not only complained that it was punishing on their horses to jump indoors in such weather but they started grumbling that it created all sorts of problems having to come inside between the Great Yorkshire with its splendid spacious arena – or, if they were riders from overseas, Aachen, which was even more spacious – and Hickstead and then Dublin, the techniques of riding in a small indoor arena being so different from riding outside. It was, in fact, remarkable that the show continued to be successful, and profitable, for another five years. That it did so was due to the first-class management under John Stevens, the exceptional prize money – almost £100,000 during the week – and the boost given to the show by television. In 1981, however, the show made a loss of £12,000, the first loss it had experienced since the second year in the outside stadium in 1969. It reflected a major fall in attendances, a pattern which was to continue the following year. Sadly, it reflected too the fall in television viewing figures, which suggested that the popularity of show jumping could be declining.

There was now increasing pressure to leave Wembley and find an outside stadium. At a meeting of the Royal International Horse Show Committee, Raymond Brooks-Ward, now Managing Director of British Equestrian Promotions, a company promoted jointly by the BHS and the BSJA to help in sponsorship for shows and their management, was instructed to re-examine the various possibilities, in particular the Crystal Palace and the White City. I do not deny that I was one of those most in favour of returning to the latter: indeed, at a meeting of the Show Committee in December 1982, after every possibility had been debated, I formally proposed that the 1983 show should be at the White City, having first ascertained that the move would have the approval of the BSJA, the show jumpers themselves and the show class enthusiasts. My proposition was carried unanimously. I still believe that at the time it was the right decision.

Hopes were high on the opening night when after a refreshing shower, the first for three weeks, an open landau from the Royal Mews, drawn by two bays, swept into the sun-drenched arena carrying Sir Michael Ansell, Sir Harry Llewellyn, Wilf White and Pat Koechlin-Smythe, all stalwarts of the original White City, to be greeted by the show Chairman, Sir John Mogg. When they had alighted, as President of the BHS and the show's original announcer thirty-seven years earlier, I introduced the Gala opening of the show, full of confidence that the success of the show twenty and thirty years ago would be repeated.

But it was not to be. By the end of the week we were to feel disappointed, dejected, even frustrated. We had hoped, firstly, that everyone would be delighted that the show was again being held out of doors, for it was for this that there had been the greatest demand. Secondly, we believed that many who had gradually given up coming since the show had left the White City in 1967, would flock back on a wave of nostalgia. But nostalgia is an elusive emotion. Because people look back on something with happy memories, it does not necessarily mean that they want to return to it, especially when they are fifteen or twenty years older, especially when they have an instinctive feeling that it is not going to be quite as good as it used to be. We liked to think that young people who had not been old enough to go to the White City in the fifties and sixties would seize the opportunity of going in the eighties, having heard how wonderful it was: they would want to see for themselves. With hindsight, I realise that there were some serious miscalculations – and errors.

Despite the fact that the show was promoted with the greatest possible determination and industry, the public stayed away: even fewer came to the White City in 1983 than came to Wembley in 1982, when the lower attendance had forced us to seek a new venue. But apart from people failing to be lured to the show by reasons of nostalgia or curiosity, there were other factors that were responsible for the show's failure. Whereas Wembley has its own staff, there is no permanent staff at the White City. Staff had to be specially engaged: obviously they were unfamiliar with the amenities, the result being that it was not as clean as it might have been. There were causes for complaint, too, in what one might describe as the menial administration. Used to the limitless car-parking facilities at Wembley, the public was reluctant to accept the virtually non-existent parking facilities at the White City. The arena itself was in poor condition, which led to complaints from the riders, who are usually ready enough to grumble – not surprisingly in view of the money now involved in show jumping – this time with justification. When eventually the arena was properly watered, the sprinklers were by mistake left on all night, the resulting soggy patches necessitating the re-siting of the fences. The food and the service in the restaurant, too, left much to be desired. Two other factors resulted in people staying away or leaving dissatisfied. The first, which, surprisingly perhaps, we had never foreseen, was the distance between the audience and the arena. Since last there had been jumping at the White City, spectators had become used to seeing jumping in indoor arenas where the action is extremely close, or watching it on television where it is for the most part in close-up, or even being in a stand or at the ring-side at a county or agricultural show where there is nothing between the audience and the arena. It is very different at the White City: first of all there is the forecourt, then there is the greyhound racing track, then there is the running track. Finally there is the ten yards or so left around the perimeter of the arena for the judging of the show classes, all of which makes the actual jumping, or a display, very remote. Even those in the front rows of the stands are separated from the horses by over thirty yards. People put up with it in the old days, partly because it was a novelty, partly because there was no alternative. But for an audience brought up on jumping on television or in a tight little arena like Wembley or Olympia, it was too impersonal.

Unwittingly, television did the show a disservice in another way – not helped by being a classic chicken and egg situation. Because of the crowded summer schedules, because, too, perhaps the BBC had, over the last two or three years, detected a waning interest in show jumping, the transmissions from the White City were extremely late at night. This inevitably resulted in a much-reduced viewing audience, which meant that with fewer people being stimulated by the show on television the previous evening, fewer people went through the turnstiles. Worse, with television coming on so late, viewers gained the impression that the show was running as late as it was shown, when in fact they were watching a recording, a point that was not always made clear. Hesitating to go to a show which did not finish until after midnight, they preferred to stay at home and watch it on television or, even more unfortunate, had gone to bed before the transmission started.

It would, however, be a mistake to think that the show's return to the White City in 1983 was all failure: far from it. A correspondent in *Riding* wrote to say how much she had enjoyed it, despite the criticisms: 'The only difficulty I found was having too much to watch and do.' She found, too, that far from having no atmosphere, the White City had 'a beautifully relaxed country atmosphere'. It was, in fact, attractively and imaginatively presented; it ran scrupulously to time; by halfway through the week the early teething troubles were for the most part ironed out; all tastes were catered for, especially with the morning 'teach-ins' and the walk-about areas where the audience could shop, visit the stables, watch horses being shod, examine old farm machinery and patronise the attractively set out Garden Centre. The attendances picked up through the week, the last night producing an atmosphere which could genuinely be compared with the old days. The weather was ideal: the jumping was world class, though unfortunately it seldom produced a nail-biting climax – not that that was the fault of the organisation. Although there was no shortage of grumbles, there were also many people who obviously enjoyed the show greatly.

But the damage had been done. The Press was not very kind, the advance bookings had been sluggish, suggesting lack of interest. Compared with the packed stands at Wembley or Olympia, the White City looked deserted, as was emphasised by the BBC cameras being so placed as to exaggerate the emptiness. The Members' Enclosure was in fact well-filled, even at the beginning of the week, and the restaurant sold out. To add to the troubles, during the show it was confirmed that the Greyhound Racing Association had sold the White City and that in all probability it was to be pulled down at the end of July 1984, which meant that at the most the show could only be held there for one further year, even if it were considered desirable. And I personally am not convinced that having learned from our mistakes and misfortunes we might not have been able, with determination and hard work, to establish the show once again at the White City, even restore it to its former glories: but such thoughts are now, of course, of only academic interest. The ultimate disaster, disclosed a few weeks after the show had ended, was that a loss of some £35,000 had been sustained, to add to the losses of the previous two years which amounted to £15,000. This, of course, was a totally unacceptable situation for the British Horse Society. Their reserves were in no position to stand such losses.

So once again, for the fourth time since the war in fact, it was a case of where do we go from here?

Where indeed?

Every possible venue, both inside and outside London, was discussed, visited and inspected. Finally, the choice was narrowed down to three: Hickstead, the East of England at Peterborough and the National Exhibition Centre at Birmingham. Inevitably financial viability was the deciding factor. The terms that we were able to negotiate with the National Exhibition Centre were too attractive to be ignored. In addition they offered unrivalled amenities with both indoor and outside arenas and ideal stabling accommodation. Further important factors were the suitability of the date which allowed the Royal International to be fitted into the international calendar, and the availability of the BBC to provide the vital television coverage. Without television, the all-important sponsors would not be forthcoming.

This was the fifth move for the Royal International. Up till 1939 it had been held indoors at Olympia; from 1947 to 1967 it was held out of doors at the White City; then for two years out of doors at Wembley. In 1969 it went indoors at Wembley. For just the one year, 1983, it was outside again at the White City. Now back indoors, but not completely, the showing classes being held outside in their own arenas, at the National Exhibition Centre: out of London for the first time.

On Sir John Mogg's retirement as Chairman of the show in October 1983, I was invited to succeed him. Not surprisingly, to do so gave me great pleasure, having been associated with the show as a steward or a member of the committee since 1946. But I fully appreciated that it was going to be a great challenge: a challenge which, however, I accepted confidently, knowing full well that I had a wonderful team with which to work. It was my dearest wish to see the Royal International restored to its former glory. Over the last few years it was, of all the London shows, the Olympia International that had stolen the thunder: but even Olympia was to have its problems.

My experience with the Olympia International, of which I had been Chairman since it was founded in 1972, had been nothing but happy and harmonious, until 1983. My role as Chairman had been to preside over an extremely experienced and hard working committee with Raymond Brooks-Ward as Show Director, and to devise, write, produce and act as narrator for what quickly became the traditional Christmas finale, ending so effectively – one could, I think, justifiably say magically – with snow falling gently from the roof on Father Christmas and his sleigh in the centre of the arena. (At one matinee some years ago the snow failed to fall. On enquiring what had happened, I was told by the Olympia management that the man responsible for arranging the snowfall had definitely gone up to the gantry, high up in the roof, half an hour before the finale. Someone was immediately despatched to find out what had happened, only to discover that the poor gentleman had fainted, due to the rising heat, on the eighteen-inch gantry. Miraculously, he had fallen against one of the widely spaced uprights which alone had prevented him crashing into the arena.)

The 1983 show started on the wrong leg when at the Annual

Dinner held at Olympia on the eve of the show, at which the British Show Jumping Association Awards were presented, Harvey Smith seized the microphone as he was being presented with his President's Cup memento from the BSJA Chairman, John Blakeway, and harangued the company, complaining that the top show jumpers' services were not properly appreciated or rewarded. 'We work bloody hard for our country and all we get is something in an envelope' – an inscribed silver armada dish in a leather case – 'David and me are not very pleased: not pleased at all.' Continuing in similar vein, he was particularly critical of the fact that top riders were expected to pay their entry fees and for their stabling. 'It's us who provide the entertainment,' he concluded. 'You couldn't do without us.' 'Typical Harvey,' one might say, tolerantly, but it was not the right occasion to raise such controversial matters, let alone in such an aggressive manner. Not surprisingly, most of the guests were shocked, some, including one or two sponsors, even walking out. John Blakeway briefly put the other side of the question, but the damage had been done. Two days later, half-way through the second day of the show, I was informed that the British show jumpers at Olympia wished to have a meeting with Raymond Brooks-Ward and myself. This was arranged, with some difficulty, during the afternoon performance. The show jumpers, represented by Lister Welch, David Broome's manager, a personable, articulate man chiefly connected with the theatre, came straight to the point. They wanted their expenses paid: accommodation, travel, stabling, entry fees, parking fees. They pointed out that they had originally raised the matter in the summer, but had received no satisfaction. Now they had made up their minds that they could put up with it no longer. Unless they got what they wanted, they might feel obliged to pull out of the show altogether.

Anxious to avoid a confrontation during what has always been the happiest show of the year, I promised that we would try to find time for the committee to discuss their demands: but I pointed out four facts. Firstly the committee had already discussed fully their requests at two meetings and had unanimously felt that it was impossible to agree to their request for what was virtually 'appearance' money, to which the BSJA was officially opposed: it could, therefore, be creating a difficult precedent. Secondly, our biggest problem as a committee had always been pacifying those riders, both from home and overseas, who were not fortunate enough to be invited to the show. Thirdly, it had already been agreed that all the jumpers should be allowed to pay a £10 blanket entry fee entitling them to enter any competition for which they were eligible throughout the show, a saving of some £140 for each rider. Fourthly, the Olympia International was the one major show at which show jumping was probably not the principal attraction. Many, perhaps the majority, went to Olympia for the wonderfully varied and entertaining programme, not least the famous finale – how often have people told me that they do not feel that Christmas has really started until they have seen the snow falling on Father Christmas at Olympia. The presence of top-class riders is a bonus.

I gathered together as many members of the committee as I could directly after the matinee and we discussed the matter for an hour. Finally we agreed that, as a gesture of goodwill, we would accept the show jumpers paying only half their stabling charges and waive the parking fees for their boxes and caravans, providing that the Earls Court Olympia management was agreeable – which it was. With the blanket entry fee this would save each rider rather more than £200. At least we had met them on three of their five demands. To pay their accommodation was out of the question, as on their own figures this would cost the show at least £10,000, which obviously had not been budgeted for.

It was understandable that the jumpers should imagine that the show made a handsome profit, boasting as it did a 95 per cent capacity audience. In fact, it is an immensely expensive show to put on, the difference between profit and loss depending almost entirely on the last two or three hundred seats sold at the box office on the day. Bad weather, rail strikes – let alone a bomb scare – can seriously affect those final sales with, possibly, resultant loss. It is, in fact, a very tight budget, as I explained to the jumpers. A pop concert that week before Christmas could well be very much more profitable. I accepted that at one time it had been the BSJA's policy to allow riders officially representing their country free stabling. But that, of course, did not apply at Olympia. It was out of our hands.

Our decision was communicated immediately to Lister Welch and David Broome, representing the show jumpers. Much to my disappointment, the offer was turned down as 'derisory' – where had one heard that word before? They would, however, like to meet us again the following day. Accordingly I called a committee meeting at 11 p.m., after the evening performance. It went on until 12.15 a.m., with a full attendance. The decision was unanimous: we did not want trouble, we had no desire to upset the riders, but we just could not offer any more – even should the jumpers 'withdraw their labour', in which unlikely event the show's President, David Westmorland, Master of the Horse, had said that he was quite sure that the Queen would agree to the finest of the carriages in the Royal Mews being brought down for a parade.

In the middle of the Saturday afternoon performance Raymond Brooks-Ward and I met the show jumpers again, all twenty-four of them – at the original meeting Ted Edgar's team had been absent as they did not wish to be involved in anything that sounded like a protest. In reply to Lister Welch asking if we had made any progress, I had to inform him that the committee was of the unanimous opinion that we could go no further than we had already offered: 50 per cent of their stabling charges and free parking in addition to the £10 blanket entry fee.

'Is that your last word?' he asked. Yes, I said, it had to be. I assured the riders that I had a certain sympathy for their attitude. Obviously they were aware of the vast payments made to the players in other sports. I could understand, too, that those not right at the top might well find it difficult to make ends meet – though surely Harvey's statement to the effect that half the riders present were on the bread-line was a little exaggerated. In fact, thanks to the way the sport had recently developed, the situation was inevitable. The best horses, which were now expensive, went, understandably, to the top riders: only by their horses winning – obviously more likely if ridden by the best riders – could the patrons see a return on their money. But facts had to be faced. Whatever the reasons might be, show jumping was not at present as popular as it used to be: the viewing figures were down by 50 per cent – 'because it is shown so late', I was told. 'A chicken and egg situation,' I replied: with the sport less popular it misses a peak viewing; without peak viewing it loses popularity. Today it is snooker and darts that get peak viewing. (With the arrival of cable television, incidentally, there will probably be a further reduction of show jumping on television.) I further warned them that by using Olympia as the occasion for their protest, they were, surely, chancing their arm. Should bad publicity or a loss force the Earls Court Olympia Ltd Directors to abandon the show they would forfeit over £60,000 prize money shared between thirty of them.

That was all that I had to say, other than to urge them to think very seriously before they decided to withdraw from the show: which I do not believe they ever seriously considered. Show jumpers not only have the reputation of being good sportsmen, but also of being cooperative, particularly in a crisis. In the end, only two withdrew: one because his horse was lame, the other was not happy about the bomb scares. It had not quite finished, however. After the show on the Saturday night, Jennifer drove me home as, having a number of things to do before Christmas, I had decided to give the Sunday matinee a miss, just returning to Olympia in time for the finale in the evening. However, at lunch-time the telephone rang. The riders were holding a press conference at 5 p.m. The press would like to meet me immediately afterwards. So back to Olympia I drove for what is graphically described as a grilling, though in this case conducted in the friendliest manner, but lasting over an hour. I could but repeat the points that I had made to the riders, finally telling the correspondents that as I saw it we were a committee that had been appointed to manage the show. Back in October we had produced, after proper consultation, our schedule and conditions. It was now our duty to manage the show according to the schedule and conditions: which we had done. We would be happy enough to hold further discussions with all concerned before the next show, but there was no way that we could change the conditions in mid-show, even if the top international riders, being a big draw, genuinely do deserve their expenses, as in other sports; even if, having withdrawn their demand for accommodation, the difference between the two sides was not all that big – some £1,600, according to the riders, rather more according to our calculations, depending, of course, on how far riders had to travel.

It was all very unfortunate. It could well be that the riders had a case, though it seems to me that the figures published the week after the show make it less convincing. With one horse of his considerable string of top-class horses, Harvey Smith won over £30,000 in 1983. Twelve different horses each, in fact, won over £15,000 for their owners in 1983. The total sponsored prize money for 1983 amounted to well over £1 million. But surely the claims that they were making were really the responsibility of their own ruling body, the British Show Jumping Association, not the Olympia International; though the basis of their protest was without doubt the fact that Olympia is a commercial show, any profits going back to the Company, whereas most shows are run by equestrian societies, through which any profits ultimately benefit the sport.

Perhaps it was all put into proper perspective a few weeks later in a letter which appeared in *Horse and Hound*:

If Harvey Smith and other top show jumpers are complaining about
the cost of stabling and entry fees at Olympia, I would suggest that
they look into the economics of unsponsored 'eventing', where the
top prize money does not even cover the cost of petrol on most
occasions. Having been forced out of the sport (for economic reasons)
I feel that it ill becomes the ambassadors of the horse world to make
such complaints – and then have side-bets of £200 on their third horse
winning [as was suggested on television during Olympia].

That show jumping can still be a great sport, holding its own with
any sport for nail-biting excitement, is undeniable, as in fact the
show jumping at Olympia in 1983 demonstrated, yet it would be
unfortunate if with the sport in an undeniably parlous state at present
the riders themselves were to rock the boat. The failure of the Royal
International Horse Show at the White City in 1983 necessitated its
move to the National Exhibition Centre at Birmingham, a move
only made possible by the abandoning of the Spring Show at the
National Exhibition Centre due to the plans to televise it being
cancelled. This cost the show jumpers some £40,000 in prize money.
They can ill afford to lose another show. By exploiting their
popularity in the right way, the show jumpers can, I am convinced,
ensure the survival of their sport: but it is a time for totally
disinterested realism.

Chapter 10

Pendley the Priority

Throughout the last forty years, all through my involvement with the British Horse Society, my commentating for the BBC, my Mastership of the Whaddon Chase, it was Pendley that had been my priority. More than that, it had been my only permanent involvement: employment is not the right word, for I never received a salary; occupation implies something full-time, which Pendley never was; nor is hobby correct, as Pendley had always been something much more serious to me than any hobby. Looking back, it is, I suppose, surprising that I doggedly devoted so much of my life to Pendley, knowing that many, even close friends, even relations, have wondered whether it was all worth it. It can only say that I believe it was.

Even more surprising now is the considerable stir that the founding of Pendley created back in 1945. Today, short residential courses on every subject, every interest and activity, are held all over the country in hotels, adult centres, country clubs, even private houses. In 1945 a short course of an educational nature, as opposed to a conference, held in comfortable surroundings where the atmosphere was more that of a club than a classroom, was something completely novel. An experience that I had a few weeks before Pendley was officially opened confirms this. Only derequisitioned on 1 July, it was a case of everyone taking his coat off if we were to open at the end of October. On this particular day at the beginning of that October I was up a ladder in what is now known as the Verney Room, the old drawing room, painting the dado – the fact that I cannot possibly be described as a handyman emphasises the urgency of the situation. Suddenly I was aware of the presence of a stranger. I called down to him, asking him what he wanted. He informed me that he had come from the Ministry of Education to find out what was going on at Pendley Manor. Coming down from my ladder, wiping my paint-covered hands on my overalls, I did my best to explain our plans to him.

For some minutes he listened, an increasingly incredulous expression on his face.

'How many people do you expect on these courses?' he asked eventually.

'Forty to start with,' I told him, 'but once we have redecorated and equipped the top floor we hope to accommodate fifty.'

'Fifty!' he echoed in astonishment. 'Fifty! But this room is not big enough for fifty!'

'Not big enough?' I replied. 'I remember dances here in my youth when there were two hundred and fifty.'

'Ah, yes,' he said, 'but by the time that you have your desks and benches, your lockers and blackboards there won't be room for more than twenty.'

Desks and benches and lockers! He could not envisage 'education' without desks and benches and lockers. Nor could most people, while I, of course, had had first-hand experience of this relaxed, informal type of 'education', first at Llangedwyn in the school holidays, later at the Nuffield Services Centre and the Gordon Services Club in wartime London. Moreover it had all been envisaged in the famous Butler Education Act of 1944, though his proposals for residential education had up to this time been ignored. The whole of the Ministry's pamphlet (No. 8) which accompanied publication of the Act cannot be quoted in full. Certain paragraphs, however, seem relevant:

> The need for leisure-time occupations in such organised creative and recreative activities as are suited to people over compulsory school age who are able and willing to profit by the facilities provided is paramount.
>
> Further education is a community effort, requiring qualities of inspiration and encouragement which can transform the least likely premises into a place of enlightenment and culture.
>
> Residential courses have in the past been an outstanding success. This suggests that there is considerable scope for and value in the short course as a permanent part of adult education.
>
> The importance of environment cannot be overstressed. Roomy and comfortable buildings suggesting a cultivated mind, provide an atmosphere in which, under enlightened leadership, can develop with an astonishing rapidity a vigorous and inspiring educational life.
>
> Experience in the forces confirms that education is a social process, often flourishing best in an atmosphere that is free and informal.
>
> There is a great scope for informal activities which, besides having an educational value of their own, may serve to arouse a more lasting interest.
>
> Opportunities for residential education have special values which

make it very desirable that they should be included in schemes for
further education. In particular there is the opportunity in the short
residential course to create an atmosphere and engender an enthusiasm
for learning that is possible no other way.

I might well have written the pamphlet myself. Yet there was no
sign whatever, in 1945, of anyone doing anything about it. Today it
is all accepted, even taken for granted. Then, only forty years ago, it
was considered revolutionary – so much so that it had to be spelt out
in the simple, straightforward sentences quoted above. Why did
Local Authorities not act immediately following the recommend-
ations that Lord Butler had so clearly defined? The answer, of
course, was shortage of money. There was little money to spare at
the end of the war. Local Authorities' Education Officers had plenty
far more pressing schemes on which to spend their money: they were
reluctant to risk expenditure on anything so new, so experimental,
so untried as short-term residential adult education.

With one exception: John Newsom, Director of Education of the
Hertfordshire County Council, was, fortunately for Pendley, a very
unusual person. The story goes that one day during the war
Newsom walked into County Hall as a representative of the Board
of Trade to discuss with the Chairman some mundane matter,
walking out two hours later as Director of Education! He was
certainly a remarkable man, with a brilliant brain and a wit to match.
He was also an opportunist. When on 3 November 1944 I went to see
him about my scheme for Pendley, he immediately saw the
opportunity to implement this provision for short-term residential
education in the Butler Act without it costing his authority a penny.
By so doing, Hertfordshire would be first in the field, thus enabling
him to be one up on his colleagues, the sort of situation that John
Newsom relished. This is not intended to be cynical: it so happened
that he was, by nature, a man with an eye for the main chance,
indeed, a man after my own heart. Not only did his help and support
enable Pendley to be launched in 1945, but I am confident that had
not Pendley been able to prove so convincingly, with his guidance,
that such an educational establishment was both viable and valuable,
then similar places might never have come into being at all, other
Local Authorities needing the nudge that John Newsom, held in such
high esteem in educational circles, had given them.

That there was an appreciation of the need for places like Pendley
is shown by the names of some of those who were happy to serve on

Pendley's Council in those early days: Edwin Barker, Education Secretary of the YMCA; Miss K.T. Butler, Head of Girton College, Cambridge; Harold Clay, General Secretary of the Transport and General Workers Union; Mrs Walter Elliot, President of the National Association of Girls Clubs; M.L. Jacks, Director, Department of Education, Oxford University; Professor Mottram, Robert Speaight, Viscountess Davidson, our local M.P., the Chairmen of the Education Committees and the Directors of Education of Hertfordshire, Buckinghamshire and Bedfordshire.

Impressive and gratifying as this was, I personally was even more convinced of Pendley's useful contribution to society by the unsolicited comments made by people who had attended courses there in the first few months. Douglas Cook, Chief Education Officer of Bucks County Council, one of our first speakers, wrote: 'It would hardly matter what the lectures were like, because for the average man or woman so much is to be gained by spending a few days in surroundings such as these in this sort of atmosphere,' which showed clearly that he understood what Pendley was attempting to achieve. R.R. Hopkins, Personnel Director of Vauxhall Motors, which sent many employees to Pendley in the forties and fifties, a speaker at our first course for workers from industry in 1946, wrote: 'Pendley is doing exactly what it set out to do – providing an educational "cocktail" for folk who left school at an early age and who had never taken part in much if any adult education: nor would normally be persuaded to do so. The atmosphere which arises partly from the surroundings and setting, and partly from the democratic and skilful way in which the project is organised, contributes much to its total success. Industry should study Pendley, take advantage of it, learn its lesson.'

'Hoppy', too, obviously understood, as was demonstrated even more effectively when later he became a Governor of Pendley.

Two of his employees also wrote rewardingly, one in a personal letter to me, one in the *Vauxhall Mirror*. Mr W.H. Evans wrote:

> Summing up, Pendley is made attractive through its surroundings and provision of warmth, comfort, excellent food, together with the informal, happy atmosphere. Pendley has proved that we all have a responsibility. We have learnt at Pendley that growth is accomplished by slow changes, rather than by drastic upheavals. Pendley, I am sure, can tap the great reservoir of energy that is locked inside the human being. What an opportunity! Thank you, Pendley.

11a. The Royal International Horse Show has a gala opening for its brief return to the White City in 1983. Flanked (left to right) by General Sir John Mogg, Wilf White, Colonel Sir Michael Ansell and Sir Harry Llewellyn, I introduce Pat Koechlin Smythe to open the show.

11b. The popular Christmas finale at the Olympia International.

12a. Pendley Manor, the family home since 1870.

12b. Foscote Manor, our own home since 1964.

13a.
Formally receiving
the Queen and
Prince Philip
at the Olympia
International
in 1979.

13b.
Informally
accompanying
Princess Anne to
a film theatre
in Piccadilly
in 1980.

14a.
With some of the
All-Party
Parliamentary
Adult Education
Committee at the
House of Commons
in 1983,
hoping to drum up
support for
Pendley.
From left to right:
Harry Greenway,
Chairman,
Don Concannon,
Stephen Dorrell,
Frank Haynes,
Iain Mills.

14b.
The Pendley
Shakespeare
Festival,
founded in 1949
and never lacking
support:
the climax of
Romeo and Juliet
in 1983.

From the *Vauxhall Mirror*:

> I had been primed about Pendley, and though reports were all good
> for some reason they got my hackles up. Reflecting on this strange
> emotional bias I can now analyse my feelings fairly accurately. To
> begin with my education was of the usual utility kind, an initiation
> ceremony into the harsh world which awaits youth: it has to be dull to
> be good. And here were these Pendley people taking the sting out of it
> all and doing away with the austerity. My innate conservatism was
> shocked. Pendley is such a comfortable place: you can lounge in an
> armchair while listening to a talk . . . . Is it of permanent value? Let's
> not argue about that: let's adopt Pendleys up and down the country
> where we can recapture the pastoral, the spacious atmosphere that
> makes our countryside unique . . . . I believe Pendley has started a
> new and worthwhile idea about Adult Education: an idea that could
> grow – like football – into part of our culture. It was suggested that
> Adult Education Centre was too cold a title and it should be changed.
> I suggest that Pendley keeps the name and changes ideas about Adult
> Education.

Oddly enough Sir John Maude, then Permanent Secretary at the
Ministry of Education, told me some time later that he always
referred to 'Pendleys' rather than Short-Term Centres of Adult
Education, adding that the only analogy that he could think of was
'Borstal'. People invariably referred to Borstals rather than the full
official title of these centres of correction, unaware probably that
Borstal just happened to be the name of the village in Kent where the
first one was founded. It could, suggested Sir John, be the same with
Pendley: but it never was.

One of the many police officers sent to Pendley on a course in the
early fifties wrote in the *Police Magazine*: 'I am sure that anyone lucky
enough to visit Pendley will want to go again. Some students were
even discussing the possibility of spending part of their annual leave
at Pendley, paying their own expenses. The Pendley course may be
short, but it is more than worthwhile.' Another police officer
stopped me in a London street some ten years after he had been to
Pendley and told me that later that same day he was conducting the
Police Male Voice Choir at the Albert Hall in a composition of his
own: 'And until I went to Pendley I did not even know that I had any
interest in music.' Could one ask for anything more gratifying?

The letter that I have valued most, however, came from a
complete stranger a few weeks after we had opened Pendley: 'I
thought that you might like to know that when I asked a friend of

mine if she had enjoyed her weekend at Pendley she told me quite simply that she believed that she now understood what was really meant by the post-war world.'

It was an exciting and encouraging beginning to this new venture, though there were plenty of vicissitudes – mostly financial – which somehow we managed to overcome. One might have assumed that the whole idea would have taken wing, reflecting not only some of the idealism of the post-war world, but being so obviously in tune with people's more leisurely, informal approach to life after the strictures of war. While there was no lessening in the demand for scholarship, there was an increasing demand from ordinary people, especially those returning from the services or wartime jobs, for what Hoppy described as an educational cocktail. This was exactly what Pendley provided: whether individuals chose, in the words of the Ministry of Education pamphlet, to allow a short course to arouse a more lasting interest in some subject was up to them. The truth is, of course, that the idea did take wing – up to a point. There are now forty or more such places like Pendley. All over the country short-term residential courses are held in one guise or another, for one purpose or another, yet down the years the powers that be have only accepted this kind of 'dilettante education', as it was once described, with reservation: it is tolerated rather than encouraged. Never, for instance, has it in any way gained the reputation of the Scandinavian Peoples' Colleges which had so inspired the great Sir Richard Livingstone, Vice Chancellor of Oxford University, who became Pendley's first President, to develop his absorbing interest in residential adult education, becoming, of course, its greatest authority. Talking of the Danish People's High Schools, he said: 'It has transformed the country economically, giving it spiritual unity, and producing, perhaps, the only educational democracy in the world.' Karl Manheim in his book *Diagnosis of Our Times* wrote that before the Peoples' Colleges were established, Denmark was a poverty-stricken country, lacking in energy or enterprise. 'Its transformation into one of the most progressive and prosperous democracies in Europe was largely the work of the education provided in these colleges.'

Someone who had been to Pendley wrote to me from Norway: 'Here I am living not only in a great democracy, but in a civilised and educated democracy. The happiness and outlook of these people is greater than anything that I have ever met, and there is no doubt that it is due to the Folk High School. Would that we could one day see something like this in Britain.'

Naturally one hoped that 'Pendleys' might achieve the same for Britain: but for a variety of reasons it did not, sadly, work out that way. That it did not never deterred me from continuing my efforts to make Pendley itself a success, hoping that one day, however far in the future, the value of this type of education would be properly appreciated, as up to a point it has been, even if its acceptance has always been somewhat low-key, largely due to the fact that it had to develop in a continuously unsympathetic economic climate. I have never felt that my efforts were in vain. Far from it. Despite all my other interests and involvements, Pendley was always my priority. How is it, then, that while the general public associates me with show jumping on television, a more limited public associates me with foxhunting, or the British Horse Society, few people associate me with Pendley and education?

There are, of course, three simple answers: firstly, thanks to television, I am, or was, almost exclusively associated with the horse: secondly, it has to be admitted, most people have little interest in education and therefore limited contact with it; thirdly, there has never been the money available properly to promote Pendley. For forty years we have quietly carried on as best we could, by no means unsuccessfully, as the figures show. Since 1945 over 5,000 different courses have been held at Pendley, attended by over 200,000 people, at virtually no cost to the community. Apart from two small grants received from the LCC, as it then was, such grants as have been received from local authorities have always been used to subsidise local students. The Shakespeare Festival, founded in 1949, now attracts audiences of 15,000 annually. In 1978 the Arts Centre was founded providing various cultural activities for anything up to 10,000 local people each year. In addition the Sports Centre, which was founded in 1967 when my family leased twenty-eight acres of land for sixty years at a peppercorn rent to a specially formed Sports Centre Management Committee, provides amenities for soccer, hockey, squash and bowls.

Pendley, it could be said, was a thriving complex of education, culture and recreation: probably it was unique – certainly as a private enterprise project. How is it, then, that it has received comparatively limited recognition? The first answer must be similar to the previous one: there has always been insufficient money for a well-orchestrated promotion. Pendley is used – more often than not it is full: there is no need, therefore, to spend exorbitant sums of money on advertising. It is well enough known to people who patronise it, not so well known beyond.

A second answer must be that, rightly or wrongly, people especially those in positions of authority, invariably harbour a certain suspicion of amateurs – and I, of course, was an amateur. People find it hard to take seriously one who, as they see it, dabbles. Is he really sufficiently dedicated? Can he really give it his full time? Might it not be just a hobby? A gimmick even? The *Concise Oxford Dictionary* defines an amateur as 'one who is fond of – ; one who cultivates something as a patron'. Not a definition of which to be ashamed. But having no degree was definitely a handicap: to break into education without a degree, to be accepted in scholastic circles unqualified, is almost asking the impossible. The world of education in the 1940s was very tightly knit and suspicious of anything unconventional. There is a further explanation for the apparent reluctance fully to accept Pendley, one that has probably been the most difficult to overcome. I owned Pendley or, more accurately, my family owned Pendley. Nepotism was inevitably suspected: just something for him to do, or, more damaging, just a scheme to prevent the old family home having to be sold. In the early days John Christie suffered similarly at Glyndebourne. I have no doubt that there were times when he felt hurt, as I did, that one's efforts to utilise one's home for the benefit of the community were misinterpreted. That life ought to have taught one to expect cynicism does not make it any easier: it is never easy to accept something one knows to be false. What is he getting out of it, was the constant cry? And it was not easy to combat it.

My conscience could scarcely have been clearer. During the first five years I was seldom away from Pendley. Apart from those few days off each year from 1947 onwards for the Royal International Horse Show, I only had one proper holiday, and then under rather sad circumstances. I was present at every course, almost invariably introducing it, frequently taking part. Being unmarried, I spent much of my time with the guests, eating with them, joining in their parties, visiting the local pubs with them (we had no bar at Pendley then). Guests very much felt that they were coming to my home. I was happy to be their host. Had I deployed my energy more sensibly, it might have continued like that indefinitely, but by 1950 I was exhausted. In January I had a slight breakdown, collapsing one morning when, ironically, there was no course in the house. In fact, Pendley was empty, apart from a young assistant secretary, who sensibly phoned a local family with whom she knew me to be friendly, even suggesting that as obviously as I could not look after myself perhaps they could put me up for a few days – which they did, with unforeseeable results.

Realising, belatedly, that no one can work unceasingly in one environment without ever taking a break, I decided, more or less on impulse, at the end of 1950 to take up hunting again. As I have already described, not only was I within a year hunting two or three days a week, but within eighteen months, as much to my own surprise as everybody else's, I had become Master. People naturally wondered how I ever found time for my work at Pendley, doubtless becoming even more sceptical when the following year I started broadcasting regularly for the BBC. In fact, blessed with more than my fair share of energy, I still managed, with careful planning and wasting no time getting from one place to another, to spend a great deal of time at Pendley, never failing to put in an appearance at any course held there. I was fortunate, of course, in having an experienced staff, several of whom had been there since the beginning. As far as broadcasting was concerned, I decided strictly to limit myself to commenting on equestrian events. In 1953 I had done one season fronting *The Smokey Club*, a programme about dogs which was transmitted from Glasgow: this and other programmes, such as panel games, I now turned down, a decision which was to prove to my advantage in that by concentrating solely on equestrian events I gradually came to be regarded as an 'expert', which led to invitations to write books and articles and give talks, in particular for the Foyles Lecture Agency. After a time I decided to give up my Grafton Mastership because of the distance from Pendley and the requirement to hunt four days most weeks. Instead I accepted an invitation to take on the Mastership of the Whaddon Chase, which was not only on my doorstep, but which only hunted two days a week. To continue hunting, as Master, may have been an error in that it still encouraged people in the belief that being so involved with hunting I had no time for Pendley, though nothing, in fact, could have been further from the truth: I certainly put in as many hours at Pendley as any other member of the staff. This, of course, was made possible by the fact that Pendley was in operation every evening and at weekends. Nevertheless, I have to admit that it was not in my nature ever to allow any one interest wholly to dominate me. Indeed, I do not believe that I could ever have retained my absorbing involvement with Pendley for so long had it not been for my other interests. If my conscience did not trouble me, however, where broadcasting or hunting were concerned – nor, later, when the British Horse Society demanded so much of my time – it certainly did when Karen came into my life.

The family with whom I stayed after my little collapse in 1950, and who had been great supporters of Pendley ever since its opening, consisted of the parents, three children in their late teens and an elder married sister. Karen was the youngest. Sixteen years old and attending a local drama school, she was extremely attractive. After I had stayed there I became a regular visitor to their home. At first I just enjoyed Karen's company because she was so lively and such fun, having a keen and mischievous sense of humour; but she was, of course, only a schoolgirl. That, unfortunately, did not prevent me a year later discovering that I was falling in love with her, despite the fact that I was seventeen years older. I was well enough aware of the problems, of the need for caution, but unfortunately the heart does not always heed the head. Convinced that she was unaware of my feelings, I believed that there were only two courses of action open to me. I could either break with the family altogether, which would not be easy as it was, ostensibly, the whole family with which I was friendly, or I could carry on for the time being, behaving as if there were no problem, hoping that eventually Karen might learn to feel for me as I felt for her. But deep down, certain that I could not for long conceal my feelings – I am inclined to wear my heart on my sleeve – I knew that this must be impossible, even were the age gap not an almost insuperable problem. Girls have, of course, married successfully at seventeen or eighteen, but it is doubtful if it can ever be right to ask a girl wholly to commit herself at that age, especially to someone much older. I was well aware of this, yet by now I was so infatuated that I was more or less incapable of thinking rationally. At length I decided that I must try and do the gentlemanly thing and confess everything frankly to her mother, hoping that she would understand, might even advise me in such a way that I could enjoy the best of both worlds.

Eventually I plucked up the courage to tackle the mother, chose a suitable moment and told her of my feelings. The result was shattering. Her reaction was completely, disastrously, different from anything I had ever expected. She was appalled, horrified, distraught even, finally tearful: apparently she thought that it was she with whom I was in love, she herself being in love with me! I was totally unprepared for such an unbelievable volte-face. What on earth should I do now? After a few tense weeks, however, the mother generously accepted the situation, even becoming something of an ally. Being realistic enough to appreciate that for me to have an affair with her, her husband living at home, would have been out of the question, she also knew that at present Karen was far too young: the solution, as she saw it, was for us all to continue for the time being in a happy family friendship, as she had sufficient confidence in me to know that I would not take advantage of the situation. Certainly I could be trusted never to abuse Karen, but having failed to make a clean break I now found that there was no way of preventing my feelings for Karen becoming stronger and stronger, the more I saw of her, the better I came to know her. Needless to say, as she grew older she became even prettier and more delightful company. Her father, away a good deal on business, seemed innocent of what was really happening, and appeared to assume that it was his daughter who had a crush on me. He decided, therefore, that it would be wise for her to board at school for a term, which inevitably only served to intensify my feelings, and, I hesitatingly believed, to awaken for the first time feelings in her.

For the next few months, during which I was shamefully neglecting Pendley, I lived in an agony of uncertainty and frustration, spending every moment that I could with Karen and her family, yet all the time unsure of her feelings, if any. On her eighteenth birthday, fully aware of how irrational my behaviour was, I proposed to her. With no embarrassment, simply and very sweetly, she said she was too young, as she was sure I realised. I felt neither resentment nor despair. I knew only too well that she was right – but hope springs eternal. We carried on as before, sometimes, I fancied, making progress, sometimes standing still.

Her schooldays came to an end. There was a brief, very happy holiday – with her mother – in the South of France; then she was offered employment in the theatre, which understandably she accepted. This meant her travelling with her company all over the country, occasionally appearing in London, frequently going overseas. Whenever it was practical I would dash to wherever she was appearing. Whenever she was in London I became nothing less than a stage-door johnny, yet our relationship, refreshingly natural and relaxed thanks to her totally unspoilt and happy personality, and despite my intensity, survived, even developed.

It was when, for a brief period, she was at home between tours that I became aware of her genuine love for me, a love tempered, that is, by her instinctive awareness of the unpredictability of the future. I was less able, so absorbing was my love for her, to accept this unpredictability. One New Year's Eve we were having our usual dance at Pendley when just before midnight I happened – fortunately, considering the noise – to hear the telephone. I answered it, overjoyed to find that it was Karen ringing to wish me a happy New Year: but it was more than that. I could tell by her voice that she wanted me. After a few moments, diffidently, she asked if there was any chance of my joining her at the New Year's party that she and her friends were attending in London. I did not hesitate, pausing only long enough to pick up my mother's diamond engagement ring which I had kept hidden in a secret drawer in my office ever since my father had given it to me. This, surely, was it. At last! My dream was no longer a dream, but a reality. I reached London in forty minutes, in a rather ancient, borrowed car, mine being out of action, to find her waiting for me at the entrance to the hall. She led me to the table where her friends were seated. Four pairs. Four pairs with, until my arrival, one extra girl: mine. I guessed the truth: without a partner she was the odd one out. That was why she wanted me so urgently that evening: a partner, not a lover. I think I knew then that it was never to be. Her friends and her career were what mattered to her: and at her age, why not? I fingered the ring in my pocket, but it stayed there. It was still there when I reached Pendley at about 4.00 a.m.

The tours seemed to get longer, taking her further and further afield, with longer trips overseas. Now playing leads, she was more than ever dedicated to her developing career. At Bolton, of all places, she told me, very sympathetically, that our affair must end – in fairness to me, she said. There could be no future in it, it was, even, ruining my life. I was sad for a time, very sad, but I accepted it, knowing in my heart of hearts that it was the truth. I missed her very much for a long time; even more, the emotions associated with her. For four years she had totally dominated my life, bringing me enormous happiness – and much anxiety. We were not to meet again for fifteen years, by which time we were both happily married. An easy, unembarrassed friendship developed between the four of us, resulting in our enjoying several holidays together. With hindsight I realise that my infatuation was the result of the almost complete suspension of my emotional existence since Moyra and I had parted company when Pendley was first opened, our parting being followed by six years of ceaseless creative activity. It was as though time had stood still for me until, able for the first time to relax, with Pendley satisfactorily launched, I was swept off my feet, as I might have been had I been ten years younger. Whatever the reasons, I have no regrets whatever, other than guilt for any damage that I might have inflicted on Pendley.

As if the Karen affair had not been disrupting enough, I was troubled, at about the same time, with a bizarre experience involving the police. One evening during a course for police officers from the Hertfordshire Constabulary I noticed a superintendent among my audience. As we walked out into the hall for coffee at the end of my talk, he asked me if he could have a word with me. I took him to my study where I offered him a drink, which he refused. While I was pouring myself one he told me that he had an embarrassing duty to perform. 'I regret to have to inform you that we have received a complaint concerning yourself and two boys who work here. Such is the nature of the complaint that we have no option but to carry out an investigation.'

I was staggered. It was true that when first Pendley was opened the housekeeper had suggested that as we were woefully short of staff we might offer employment to two boys from a local orphanage. Accordingly I called on the headmaster, who selected two fifteen-year-olds who appeared smart, well-mannered and obviously gratified at the prospect of working at Pendley. One was very musical, eventually finishing up as a tutor at a Further Education College in Hertfordshire; the other was an outstanding ball-games player, representing the county both at cricket and squash. Later he was to marry a Swedish girl who worked at Pendley. They settled down quickly and happily, getting on well with the entire staff, all of whom went out of their way to help them. Inevitably, after a short time they regarded me almost as their father, though favourite uncle might be more apposite. All in all we had an extremely happy staff relationship at that time, a totally integrated unit, I, in those early days, being very much regarded as part of the staff rather than as someone in any way superior.

By the time of the superintendent's visit the boys, now seventeen or eighteen, had left Pendley. The musical one had enlisted in the army and was in his regimental band; the games player had joined a firm in Watford run by another games enthusiast. The superintendent seemed taken aback when I told him that the boys had left, but he would not divulge who it was that had made this preposterous insinuation. He repeated, noticeably uncomfortable, that he had no option but to instigate an investigation. Was there anything that I would like to say? Obviously not, although I could not help feeling that had he been aware of all that I had been going through in my infatuation with Karen he would see how idiotic such allegations were. It was worrying, nevertheless, as entries in my diary of that year clearly show. As with rape incidents, it is often a case of one person's word against another's. Adolescents can be notoriously, and dangerously, unreliable, and however clear one's own conscience may be, it is not always easy to be convincing when one is defending onself against scurrilous accusations. In my more depressed moments I could imagine only too well the headlines, guess at the effect on Pendley. Indeed, a member of my staff felt impelled to inform me that there was a rumour circulating locally, how I could not imagine, for as far as I was concerned only the superintendent and I were aware of this unsavoury matter.

It was with a certain anxiety that some three or four weeks later I heard that the superintendent wished to speak to me. He quickly put me at my ease. A thorough investigation had shown the accusations to be entirely false, malicious and unprincipled, without a shred of evidence to support them. He even went so far as to say that he would now be happy to name the person who had made the complaint so that I could, if I wished, institute proceedings. But, of course, I did not: I only wanted the whole matter to be forgotten. I was sure that it could only be one of two people, neither of whom were worth suing. One was a singularly vindictive person who a few years later, while actually attending a dance at Pendley, telephoned the police to inform them that the bar was still open although it was after closing time. Fortunately we had always had the friendliest relations with the police: not surprisingly, therefore, when the sergeant arrived he first called at the kitchen for a cup of tea. By the time he came through to the bar it had, miraculously, all closed down. The other person was a mentally deranged lady who, professing a passion for me through 'our joint love of literature', had been troublesome for some years. Possibly her knowledge of my affection for Karen goaded her into this irresponsible, revengeful behaviour.

Whether all these distractions were either directly or indirectly responsible one cannot be certain, but for the first and only time since 1945 Pendley finished the year with a sizeable loss. As we had no reserves, the seriousness of the situation brought me to my senses. Not before time. Almost overnight I was the dedicated guardian of Pendley once again. Within two years we were back on course with Pendley busier and more successful than ever. I attribute this welcome return of stability to two important developments, the first concerning Pendley, the second concerning myself. In 1954 I decided to appoint a full-time manager, or Warden as we chose to call him. While I retained the overall responsibility, continuing as titular head and providing what one might call the flair, the Warden was responsible for the day-to-day running of the Centre. I was still fully involved at Pendley, but was no longer indispensable, therefore experienced no undue anxiety – or feelings of guilt – when I was absent.

In 1956 I married Jennifer. My marriage to Moyra had ended shortly after the opening of Pendley. Not surprisingly, perhaps, being granddaughter of the first Lord Avebury, one of the greatest scientists of his age, her leaning was towards the intellectual, in particular towards research concerning psychological behaviour, both in human beings and in animals. Indeed, in connection with the latter she has had published a number of successful books. A community existence such as at Hawtreys or at Pendley was not really her metier; nor was a normal humdrum family life. Our parting was civilised and amicable. We just went our own ways, each achieving a certain amount of success independently. I will always be grateful to her for sharing so courageously those early difficult days. Moyra never married again. I was more fortunate. Jennifer was nearly twenty years younger than me, but in many ways competent beyond her years. When, less than six months after our marriage, the housekeeper left, Jennifer, to my surprise and delight, volunteered to take over that department. Although she was only twenty-two she made an enormous success of it, not only exercising a strict control over expenditure but also achieving a most harmonious relationship with our cook, who was exceptionally able, liked and respected by everybody, but who did not always find it easy to suffer fools gladly – and in any large community one is bound to encounter a few fools. Jennifer and our cook, Mrs Moffatt, developed the happiest of partnerships with the result that for ten years the domestic side of Pendley was efficient, trouble-free and much appreciated by the guests.

This was a remarkable achievement by Jennifer, especially when one remembers her youth, her inexperience and the fact that within four years she had two small children, Piers and Carola. In addition, she found time to look after my hunters and start her pony stud which during the next twenty years was to achieve so much.

Naturally enough, when we married people said that our marriage would not last because of the difference of our backgrounds and the age gap. Thankfully they have been proved wrong. Though still fully stretched, I became increasingly fond of and more dependent upon my family and home, the first real home that I had had since Greens Norton nearly thirty years earlier. Our contrasting approaches to life – Jennifer's cautious, mine impulsive; Jennifer's single-minded, mine more expansive – were to prove complementary. No marriage is easy: ours, I like to think, has been less difficult than many. Certainly Jennifer has been tremendous support in quite a number of crises that we have experienced in nearly thirty years of marriage, which, of course, has more than made up for one or two little failings such as a certain obstinacy – which is made more aggravating by her so often being proved right – her not infrequent failure to observe the merits of punctuality and her seemingly inescapable dependence on the telephone. But I am assured by friends that these are faults with which most husbands are familiar. Certainly I am not complaining – much!

Chapter 11

Masques and Antique Pageantry

While Jennifer and I share, of course, a great love of horses, in many other respects our interests and ambitions lie in different directions. Although effective when lecturing on something dear to her heart, such as the producing of a show pony, it would take a great deal to persuade Jennifer to make a speech, let alone appear on a stage – though she always says that she would love to have been a dancer, like our daughter Carola – whereas a large part of my life has been taken up with speaking in public and in activities connected with the theatre. The date of my first ever speech is easily identified. At Greens Norton my father gave a little dinner party for all his employees and tenants. After the butler had proposed the health of my parents and my father had replied, the stud groom unexpectedly proposed the health of the children. 'You will have to say something,' my father whispered. So I did. 'I do hope you've all enjoyed your dinner,' I started, and then as if instinctively prompted I added: 'You must have done, as it all seems to have disappeared as completely as Agatha Christie.' That was 1928, at the height of the mystery which was filling all the papers.

I am often asked, firstly, whether I enjoy speaking in public, secondly, whether speakers are born or made. Most people, I am sure, enjoy impressing an audience, conscious of their reaction. Most speakers, on the other hand, however experienced they may be, are nervous before they start. This is because each audience that one faces is different, an unknown quantity: one cannot be certain beforehand what the reaction of an audience is likely to be. A speech or talk or lecture that has gone down well with one audience can misfire with another, each audience creating its own atmosphere, according to its make-up. In the early days of Pendley we carried out some simple research on audience reaction and lecture techniques. Apart from discovering that the average concentration time for a group of listeners is twelve to fifteen minutes, after which their attention begins to wander, only the more experienced speaker being able to restimulate their concentration, we also learned the importance of such mundane accessories as the temperature of the room, the lighting and the comfort of the seats. No speaker, therefore, is ever going to rise with complete confidence: the one that does is probably the overconfident bore who alienates people. There is so much that can affect the rapport between a speaker and his audience. Once launched, however, conscious of the audience's attention, his confidence is restored. He is encouraged, before long enjoying the experience, the temptation then, perhaps, being to continue speaking longer than the audience desires. S.H. Wood, a Permanent Secretary at the Ministry of Education many years ago, once told me that he found a genuinely therapeutic value in speaking: he might be exhausted at the end of a long, tiring day, might even be feeling unwell, yet within minutes of starting to speak he was his fittest, healthiest self. One has heard of similar experiences with actors. It suggests, of course, that determined mental concentration, conscious projection of oneself, can obliterate a worry that is nagging at one, can even enable one to forget physical pain.

It goes without saying that the more experienced a speaker is, the less he is going to be disturbed by nerves. Indeed, I believe that with sufficient experience anyone can become an adequate speaker. If someone is fortunate enough to be born with certain qualities such as love of language, a good voice, a sense of occasion, then the likelihood is that he or she is going to prove a more than adequate speaker. But with the exception, perhaps, of a few, who probably hail from Wales, I doubt if many speakers are born rather than made. To have the gift of the gab is very different from being a good speaker. To be effective one has to work hard. I personally always memorise my speeches or talks, partly because vanity, coupled with a dislike of anything clumsy, makes me keen to avoid picking up my glasses and putting them on every time that I want to refer to my notes; partly because I believe fluency to be vital if one is to hold an audience's attention. Memorising, of course, is not the same as learning by heart: the latter can make a speech sound stilted, insincere; the former enables one to proceed naturally and fluently from one point to the next. My own experience has been that in making a few notes, planning the sequence, one is automatically committing to memory whatever it is that one wants to say.

I have certainly found speaking stimulating, so long as I am properly familiar with my subject – and no one should speak unless he is – whatever the occasion, it making no difference, whether it is a professional engagement through Foyles Lecture Agency or Associated Speakers, or an Earthstoppers' Dinner. Occasionally there has been a less than happy situation such as when the Chairman neither knew my name nor my subject, making it quite clear that he personally could not be less interested, his boredom all too easily being communicated to the rest of the audience. There was the time, too, when shortly after Pendley opened I was invited to address a public meeting at a local village. As only eleven people turned up, the Chairman asked me to help him lift the table off the stage on to the floor. 'We only ask the speaker to address us from the stage if he has attracted more than twelve people,' he told me bluntly. Later I suggested to him that it would have been better psychology to start on the floor, then when thirteen people turned up to ask the speaker to help lift the table from the floor to the stage, in view of the good attendance. I remember, too, on more than one occasion being constantly interrupted by a very inebriated guest, the business of removing him proving even more distracting than his drunken comments, making it virtually impossible to carry on. Even worse was an occasion when, having given my talk, I was about to depart only to be stopped at the door of the hall and asked to wait for a few minutes as one of my audience had dropped down dead right in the path of my car: he could not be removed until an ambulance arrived. There has certainly been no shortage of occasions when people have fainted during one of my talks, due more, I like to think, to prevailing conditions rather than to anything I had said.

The highlight of speaking at a Save the Children function at the Albert Hall was the thought that I was entering through that little door at the back of the stage which had been used by so many of the most famous conductors and artists in the world. Apart from the Albert Hall, where I was only making a brief appeal in the interval of a charity concert, the largest audience to which I have ever spoken was the Inner Wheel's Annual Conference at the Empire Ballroom, Blackpool, in 1983, when I faced an audience of 3,600 people, only a handful of whom were men. As a result of a talk I gave on speaking in public at the Royal Air Force College at Bracknell, I was invited a few years later to address a conference in Manila. The theme of the conference was Air Safety. My talk, which was the first on the programme, was to be on communications. I was very conscious of the fact that the response to it had been rather restrained, but as the Conference developed it became obvious that most accidents involving aircraft were the result of bad communications. At the final session the Chairman, an American Admiral, was kind enough to suggest that, seen now in its proper perspective, my talk had been the most useful of all. It was the vital importance of being intelligible that I had been trying to emphasise, citing as an example the difficulty of hearing what was being said over the intercom on an airliner or at an airport – or railway station. To hear inaccurately can lead, at best, to inconvenience; at worst to disaster. As the last day of the Conference was taken up with technical matters I did not attend. Later, when I was asked where I had been, I teased my hosts by pretending that, having heard about so many crashes, invariably due, it seemed, to faulty communications, I had been looking for a travel agent who could exchange my air ticket for a passage home by boat.

I had an interesting and instructive experience when I was invited to give the principal address at an Equine Symposium at the University of Calgary in Canada. In addition to a talk on 'The Mind of the Horse', which I had given as part of the symposium itself, I was to deliver an address based on my book, *Great Riding Schools of the World*, after the banquet to be held at the end of the conference. Some 500 people who had had three very hard days were present; an excellent four-course meal was served, lavishly accompanied by wine, at the end of which the Chairman made a short speech. After this the guests were invited to move to another hall where I was to give my address, which, being illustrated with slides, necessitated darkness. Not surprisingly, guests either dozed off or chatted happily to each other at the back of the hall. The Chairman was apologetic, generously admitting that he had made a mistake in asking me to speak after the banquet: a light-hearted speech at the table would have been preferable. Alternatively, had my talk been part of the Conference proper it would probably have been acceptable, but at the end of a long day, after a heavy meal, people could not be expected to pay attention to a more or less serious lecture, a lesson that we had, in fact, learned at Pendley many years earlier.

After the Conference I had the pleasure of staying with its Chairman, Professor Ron Cole, at his stud some forty miles from Calgary. It was in open country stretching away to the Rockies at the foot of which nestled Banff. I was very much intrigued by Banff, as it had started in as small and simple a way as Pendley, a group of enthusiasts bringing together, under one roof, all the drama societies and classes functioning in Alberta. Such was their success that, supported by public funds, it grew quickly into a complex the size of a university with wonderful amenities. I was extremely envious, and full of admiration. Before returning home, the local Equestrian Federation kindly arranged for me to explore the Rockies and surrounding countryside from a four-seater aircraft.

It is interesting that, as at the brilliantly successful Banff, the first course at Pendley was connected with drama. Interesting but not necessarily surprising, the link between education and drama being very close: indeed in the earliest days of civilisation education and drama were one and the same. It is this link which may well have been responsible for my interest in pageants, for the pageant, as well as being spectacular and entertaining, is invariably of educational value. Indeed, most pageants are devised and produced to celebrate some local historic occasion. It was in 1951 that I was first invited, on the strength of our then young but increasingly successful Pendley Shakespeare Festival, to write and produce a pageant at Aylesbury in the attractive grounds of Prebendal House, at that time a girls' school. Fortunate enough to have good weather, the pageant was extremely successful, so much so that in Coronation Year, 1953, a further pageant was proposed, to be entitled 'The Pageant of the Queens'. This was an even greater success, with capacity audiences. From these two pageants I learned two important lessons. The first was that nothing gives spectators a greater thrill at an outdoor production than the sight of horses, something that is, of course, impossible on an indoor stage – though I remember as a child seeing *The Whip* at Drury Lane, in which the Derby was created with horses galloping their hearts out on conveyor belts. The second was the contribution made by flares or torches. As the light fades on a summer evening, nothing is more effective or exciting than flames from torches dancing dramatically in the night air. In the first pageant a scene was enacted in which, at a reception to welcome Disraeli, a rider leaped over a dinner table round which were seated a dozen people – an incident which had allegedly taken place at the old White Hart in 1854. This episode was immensely popular with the audience, never more so than when, at one performance, the horse, startled by some sudden movement, swerved, depositing its rider onto the table in the midst of the guests.

The importance of effective lighting was originally brought home to me when Pendley's very first Festival production, *Henry VIII*, was performed in the Priory Gardens at Dunstable. This was because of Dunstable's connection with Catherine of Aragon, whose divorce

from Henry was heard and proclaimed at the Priory. The performances at Dunstable were to be held in September. In July it is light
until ten o'clock; in September it is dark soon after eight o'clock,
which means, of course, that for a play to be performed out of doors
in September there has to be floodlighting. That floodlighting could
make quite such a difference surprised me. The lighting that year at
Dunstable was very primitive, crude by modern standards, but I
learned the important part lighting could play in a production out of
doors if it is properly and imaginatively used. From that year
onwards the plays at Pendley have always been performed during the
last week of August and the first week of September, with the
lighting invariably an outstanding feature. When, in 1963, I was
invited to produce a pageant at Dunstable, I had great difficulty in
persuading the council to have it as late in the summer as possible,
thus benefiting from the lighting. The thought of the floodlit Priory
as a backcloth for the pageant was challenging, with changes of
lighting reflecting the different mood and emphasis in each episode,
rather like *son et lumière*. The Priory provided a fine setting which,
combined with the participation of nearly a thousand people,
ensured the pageant's success. The weather, too, was kind, rain only
falling during the finale of the last performance, which was attended
by Princess Alice, Duchess of Gloucester, who despite the rain
insisted on descending from the 'royal box' to meet the cast.

The weather was less cooperative when some years later I was
asked to produce a pageant to be attended by the Queen Mother at
South Mimms, the beautiful home of General Sir George Burns,
Lord Lieutenant of Hertfordshire, to celebrate the centenary of the
Red Cross. As I was very busy that summer, and because there
seemed to be insuperable rehearsal difficulties with those taking part
coming from every corner of one of the longest counties in Britain, I
suggested that instead of a pageant we should present a series of
tableaux vivants, something that I had done with considerable success
to celebrate the centenary of a wing of the Royal Bucks Hospital at
Aylesbury. A giant picture frame, with curtains behind, is placed in
front of the stage, and when the curtains part a living picture is
disclosed. With not a movement from anyone for up to five minutes,
against a background of suitable music, a narrator describes the scene
and its relevance. Well lit, with good costumes and properties, it can,
simple as it sounds, prove very effective. The Royal Bucks Hospital
tableaux in 1962 with Florence Nightingale as the centrepiece, are
talked of to this day. So might have been the Red Cross *tableaux*,

again featuring Florence Nightingale, had it not been for the weather. The dress-rehearsal took place on a perfect summer day: the small, invited audience was ecstatic, profuse in their praise. The players enjoyed it enormously, conscious of providing a most impressive performance without ever having had to learn a line. On the official day, however, the weather looked ominous from mid-morning. Most uncharacteristically, the Queen Mother was about twenty minutes late. Had she been punctual, we might just have been all right. As it was, at the commencement of the third *tableau* huge drops of rain began to fall. During the fourth *tableau* someone thoughtfully produced for the Queen Mother a rug and one of those umbrellas that look like an inverted cellophane pot. As the fifth *tableau* was introduced, the heavens opened. I had no option but to announce that the performance was to be suspended. I felt it right that I should first inform the Queen Mother, so dashing out in the rain I fell on my knees by her side, pushing my head up under her umbrella, and told her that we were abandoning the performance. With a charming smile and a little chuckle she remarked: 'I think that is the nicest thing that anybody has said to me all day.'

Years later, when I met her staying at Badminton, she was to make another rather disconcerting remark to me. Dressing for dinner, I discovered to my horror that my dress shirt was missing the middle button. With remarkable ingenuity, as I thought, I cut a gold thread from a Waterloo banner which was acting as a fireguard in my bedroom, pierced a hole with a pair of scissors where the button should have been and threaded through the two ends of the gold thread, tieing them in a neat little bow. As the other visible button then looked somewhat lacking in style, I repeated the exercise with another piece of gold thread from the Waterloo banner. I was really pleased with my initiative, but have to admit to being a little taken aback when later in the evening the Queen Mother suddenly told me, with what seemed a tell-tale twinkle in her eye, that she thought my shirt studs the most unusual that she had ever seen!

We were amused, too, that evening when at dinner the Duchess of Beaufort, wishing to catch the Duke's attention at the other end of the enormously long table, had to ring a little silver bell. What a pageant might one day be devised on Badminton, recording its centuries of history right back to John of Gaunt, a part of whose surcoat is always, for me, one of the most exciting of the Badminton treasures.

That Dunstable pageant was particularly valuable to me in that I first experienced a technique which I was to use to great advantage on a number of later occasions. The sound and effects were in charge of a certain J.D. Baxter, who was then employed by A.C. Delco. When I was first introduced to him, he made the suggestion, remarkable to me at the time, that the entire sound – music, dialogue and fanfares – should all be pre-recorded. After some discussion it was agreed that we should try this method, the advantages, as one quickly appreciated, being considerable. The most important, of course, was that, like the *tableaux*, no one had to learn any lines, which not only meant that the actors could perform with much more confidence, but should an actor with the required stature and presence – or one who, for political reasons, it had seemed wise to employ – lack a suitable voice, it was possible to use for the recording someone whose voice was more suited. It meant, too, greater mobility in the arena, as there was no necessity for the actor speaking to be near a microphone, which can often appear contrived: indeed, microphones were not required at all, saving much trouble and expense. Fanfares or incidental music needing to appear 'live' – accompanying a dance, for instance – could be recorded by expert musicians, the 'musicians' on the stage merely miming. The principal value of all this was that far more time and attention could be given to the actual production, no time being taken up with rehearsals when people were struggling with their lines. Today such a technique is taken for granted – it seems incredible now that it was ever done any other way – but in 1963 it was considered very novel, some people, incredibly, even suggested that it was cheating and were quite resentful.

I was certainly glad that such a technique was used when in 1966 I produced the charter pageant at Bedford. As the idea had come from the town council, the community tended to resist it, feeling that it had been imposed upon them. Such combined efforts must, if they are going to be successful, be generic, coming from the citizens themselves, which was very far from the case at Bedford, though a handful of councillors and colleagues did all that they could to create a harmonious production. While internal squabblings were being sorted out, with episodes tossed about like shuttlecocks from one group to another, while political issues were being argued behind closed doors and resignations hurled back and forth, I pre-recorded the whole pageant, finding my own 'voices' and effects. When, eventually, all the problems were resolved, there was only time for three full rehearsals. But thanks to the pre-recording, three rehearsals proved sufficient, the first of the six performances going without a hitch. The only disappointment that first night was the size of the audience, the town seeming uninterested in the project right up to the opening. Word of mouth, however, is the surest publicity of all. By the end of the week it was standing-room only, the pageant, finally, being hailed as a triumph.

The Berkhamsted pageant, by contrast, had the whole town behind it from the start. Devised by one Winston Moss, a member of the local Rotary Club, every organisation of any importance in the town was involved. The only anxiety for the organising committee was, not surprisingly perhaps, my rehearsal technique. They found it difficult to believe that to have only three full rehearsals in the castle grounds would be adequate. My plan, which I had explained, but which still caused serious doubts, was to take the first rehearsal of each episode myself, then leave it to the episode's own producer for, say, a month, before taking one rehearsal – of each group separately – in the castle grounds. The first full rehearsal, lasting all one Sunday, was like fitting all the pieces of a jigsaw together. The second full rehearsal was to coordinate the technical effects and communications. To bring the performers from the assembly points to the arena, a special Bailey bridge had to be built over the moat, as an army exercise. The third full rehearsal was the first dress rehearsal which, to everyone's astonishment, went as well as any performance. With amateurs it is so easy for a production to lose its edge by over-rehearsing. Amateurs soon get bored, but with no lines to learn there is no necessity for protracted rehearsals, which in any case are seldom attended by everyone required.

The pageant was pre-recorded by my old friend J.D. Baxter, one of my staff at Pendley, Margaretta Bennett, providing some excellent dialogue. (Margaretta's niece, Susan, had played Rosalind in *As You Like It* at Pendley in 1955 before turning professional, later marrying Peter Bowles, famous for his performances in *Only When I Laugh, The Bounder, To the Manor Born* and other television successes.) I adopted an unusual device in this particular pageant, playing it backwards. As it was to celebrate 900 years since William the Conqueror was offered the Crown of England in Berkhamsted Castle on his way to Westminster, it seemed appropriate that the 1066 episode should be the climax. We started, therefore, with the 1914 episode, the forming of the Inns of Court Regiment at Berkhamsted, working back through the centuries, a ploy which turned out to be very effective. There was never an empty seat in the stands for any of the ten rain-free performances. There were 2,000 in the cast, every one of whom felt, I believe, that they were privileged to be part of an historic occasion. Certainly I did, still considering it to be one of the pinnacles of my dramatic career.

As long as I live I shall recall with excitement the overwhelming finale: the arena packed with 2,000 performers, some hundred of them carrying flares; William the Conqueror with his entourage in scarlet and gold spotlit over 100 feet up at the top of the Castle Keep; the full company, led by pre-recorded organ and choir, singing words specially written for the great refrain from Elgar's 'Pomp and Circumstance' No. 2; then, as the last line 'Land of Liberty' ended and the music died away, the spots cut, the arena plunged into darkness by the simultaneous thrusting of the flares into the ground. For a few moments there was an absolute, almost eerie silence before the huge audience, 2,000 strong, burst into applause, sometimes cheering, on the last night standing. How could anyone ever forget such an experience? As a performer wrote to me a week or two later, paraphrasing the Crispin speech from *Henry V*: 'From this day to the ending of the world, but we in it shall be remembered, and gentlemen in Berkhamsted now a-bed shall think themselves accursed they were not here.'

Producing *Julius Caesar* in the Roman Theatre of Verulamium in 1977 was another stimulating experience, rather more than the pageant in the vast Leisure Centre at Bletchley to celebrate the inauguration of Milton Keynes, though the production itself was enjoyable enough. Achieving effects by the use of space and large numbers always gave me a tremendous satisfaction: a satisfaction similar, I assume, to that of a General planning his strategy, then seeing it effectively exploited.

These successful pageants in the years between 1950 and 1966 led to my receiving a number of invitations to produce pageants all over the country, even as far afield as South Wales. It was tempting to accept, but with so many irons in so many fires already I did not want to become a professional pageant-producer, like Gwen Lally who I remembered so well from my youth. Her productions were indeed outstanding. I can vividly recall at Warwick, for instance, a crippled leper ringing her little bell to part the crowd – 'Unclean! Unclean!' – and the magnificent tournament and the charge of Prince Rupert of the Rhine's Cavalry at Edge Hill. Imitation being a form of flattery, I make no apology for having adopted many of her brilliant ideas in my own productions. Most important of all, I learnt the value of the broad, sweeping visual effect. It is not without interest that the original production in the Pendley Shakespeare Festival in 1949 was advertised as Shakespeare's great Pageant Play, *Henry VIII*.

While my busy life made it impossible for me ever to consider pursuing an additional career as a Pageant Master, I was not for a moment prepared to allow it to prevent my directing the Pendley Shakespeare Festival. From 1949 to 1960 the plays were performed by local actors and actresses who rehearsed regularly for perhaps three months throughout the summer. Obviously the number of local performers sufficiently talented to mount each year two Shakespeare plays was limited, but it was impractical for people further afield to take part as it was unrealistic to expect them to travel to Pendley every weekend to rehearse. In 1960, therefore, I decided on an entirely different policy: everyone taking part would stay at Pendley for a week before the Festival, thus being available for concentrated rehearsals, twenty-four hours a day if necessary. In fact, assuming that people had, as requested, taken the trouble to learn their lines in advance, a week was more than enough to prepare a play with no more than a reasonable amount of rehearsing. After all, a professional weekly rep has only a week of rehearsals – with no evenings as they are already performing.

There was something of the old country-house cricket match weeks about Pendley during the Festival fortnight: everyone there shared the same interests; all enjoyed the hard work; success at the end was stimulating and gratifying. But there was time for fun, too, especially once the Festival was launched, with the rehearsals all completed. Most nights saw a private party or an informal disco; golf, tennis and cricket matches between the two casts were organised; there was 'The Party', organised by a small group of volunteers who provided a lavish buffet and first-class entertainment, the highlight of which was always the 'Western Brothers' turn – 'bad show chaps! bad show!' – when for many years Michael Charlesworth, a Repton School Housemaster, together with another member of the Company, took the mickey out of just about everything and everybody, not forgetting the Director and Pendley itself. The 'Party' evenings were hilarious, producing each year some astonishing individual talent.

The Festival was a happy experience with, fortunately, very rare exhibitions of temperament: there was no time for them. It was also successful, for those taking part, being leading members of their own companies, were often extremely talented. Because they were amateurs it did not mean that they were incompetent; far from it: not every good actor wants to earn his living professionally. There was keen competition, too. In 1983, for instance, no less than sixty-four Juliets were auditioned. To be offered any part, however small, one had to possess ability. Producers, too, were very talented, often having had long experience of production with top-class amateur societies or at schools. Even performers with less immediately obvious ability could impress at Pendley, acting in the open air being a very different technique from acting in a theatre. In the open air, with the audience yards rather than feet away, subtleties are out of the question: a carefully judged inflection, a suggestive raising of an eyebrow goes for nothing. An actor, in the open air, has to be larger than life, sometimes little more than an exaggeration of his own personality. There can be intimate scenes, of course, by usage of the lower stage, which is connected to the main stage by a flight of steps. Here, isolated from the rest of the set, the actors are very close to the audience. But such intimate scenes are used sparingly, the priority in an open-air production, as with a pageant, being the large-scale effect made possible by the spacious stage – and naturalism. How can three-ply cardboard flats and painted canvas compete with real trees, real grass, real rain even? Actors surrounded by reality rather than artifice become more real: the audience finds itself watching the behaviour of real people, thus more easily identifying with them and their emotions. On an indoor stage one is, as it were, in close-up. A high degree of technique is required if an audience is to be convinced, involved. In the open air those taking part appear as living as the trees, part of a natural environment. The producer's role is to exploit that environment. At the back of one stage at Pendley there is a glade running over 100 yards through to the park: how effective for an impressive entrance, even mounted, or by a carriage and pair, as in the 1972 production of *Love's Labour's Lost*. Also on this stage is a dell which for one production of *The Tempest*, in 1965, became a pool into which, nightly, fell Trinculo, to the delight of the audience. The other stage is backed by a ten-foot-high ornamental yew hedge with half a dozen openings, ideal for a play such as *Twelfth Night* or *The Two Gentlemen of Verona*, or for one of the more formal histories. Both stages are flanked by towering Wellingtonias, which gives any producer of *A Midsummer Night's Dream* unique opportunities for his Puck and fairies. At the back of the glade stage there is a wood: where else could Birnham Wood come to Dunsinane more effectively? Or could any stage, forty yards wide, twenty yards deep, better contain the smouldering camp fires between the waiting French and English armies on the eve of Agincourt?

I will not deny that when I started plotting a play at Pendley my first thoughts were as to how I could utilise the setting, employing large numbers, which sometimes led to my being dubbed a de Mille or a Rheinhardt (and later a Hitchcock, due to my occasionally taking a small cameo part in my own productions, preferably unrecognisable). Although I worked on all the movements and the characterisation as well as the interpretation of the play that I was producing, I could never interest myself very deeply in 'business', which was why I never enjoyed producing plays indoors. It was the broad sweep of a production that appealed to me, as with a pageant. I was, for the most part, happy to leave my more experienced and talented actors to work out the minutiae of their own performances, though I was only too happy to help a young actor playing a Juliet or an Ariel or a Puck. One outstanding Juliet, Penny Casdagli, who was also a delightful Desdemona, has achieved great success on the professional stage especially with the Arts Theatre. An Ariel, Roberta Iger, became the exquisite second Mrs Onedin in *The Onedin Line*. A Puck, Lynda Bellingham, daughter of a local farmer, has been extremely successful both on stage and television. Martin Weedon, son of a factory worker at Cowley – he used to arrive for rehearsals on the pillion of his father's motorbike – having been a most intelligent Romeo at Pendley, became a professional, landing the juvenile lead in *The Mousetrap* amongst other rewarding jobs. I like to think that I may have helped them a little with their first major roles.

It was, I suggest, as a splendid, well presented, more than adequately performed spectacle, that the Pendley Shakespeare Festival achieved its fame. Of all the many and varied experiences that I have enjoyed at Pendley, the one that has never ceased to give me pleasure is the sight of those hundreds of people on the lawns during the Festival. They come from considerable distances, from any age group, from any background, from any country even. In the late sixties, a Swiss couple from Basle happened to be spending a holiday at Rickmansworth with English friends who brought them to one of the plays, since when they have visited their friends at Rickmansworth the same week every year, so that they can come to Pendley. In 1982 I met a couple from Melbourne, Australia, who told me that they deliberately timed their visit to England every three years to coincide with the Festival, having originally, quite by chance, been brought to the Festival to see *A Midsummer Night's Dream* in 1973. Watching those crowds – more than 1,000 people every evening of the Festival – I know that my efforts have not been entirely in vain. My decision in 1945 to make my home available to ordinary men and women has surely been justified. For some, I hope, I have enhanced their love of Shakespeare; for many, I like to think, I have brought Shakespeare into their lives for the first time, enabling them, perhaps, to enjoy him for the rest of their lives. Without Pendley he might, sadly, have eluded them. I cannot help feeling a little proud during the Festival: just as I sometimes used to feel proud during, say, the Horse of the Year Show knowing that I had helped many people to be more interested in horses.

In 1972 we decided to accept the ultimate challenge for any amateur society – and most professional companies – and produce *Hamlet* the following year. We had had to wait until we had someone with the necessary talent. In 1971 a young schoolmaster from Hemel Hempstead had given a very fine performance as *Richard II*. Here, we thought, was our Hamlet. The two characters have much in common: both are dominated by a stronger relative, cousin Bolingbroke and uncle Claudius respectively; both are indecisive; both are romantic and poetic. Douglas Verrall, as well as teaching, gave illustrated talks on Shakespeare and wrote plays. (In 1983 his play about the Brontës was successfully produced by the Youth Theatre.) This was the sort of dedication required if Hamlet produced in the Pendley style with limited rehearsing was to be successful.

Fortunately, as soon as we had reached our decision in the autumn of 1972 I started planning my production and had a number of useful sessions with Douglas, for at the end of that year it was discovered that I was suffering from cancer, which to all intents and purposes put me out of action until rehearsals began in the middle of August. Not surprisingly, the possibility of abandoning the production was considered and a reserve producer was appointed. *Hamlet*, however, had been one of the targets in my recovery and the opportunity of realising a lifetime's ambition to produce *Hamlet* undoubtedly helped me. In the event the production was, to my relief, extremely successful, thanks to some very strong performances, effective music from Sibelius's First and Second Symphonies and one or two striking effects, the most impressive of which was the appearance of an ancient authentic horsedrawn hearse carrying the body of Ophelia.

It had a profound effect on the audience each evening, heightened by the extraordinarily moving performance that Barbara Latham had given as Ophelia. Luckily the audience was unaware of the unexpected, almost profanely comic situation that had arisen at the dress rehearsal when the glass sides of the hearse fugged up thanks to the corpse's breathing in the confined space! The solution was to leave ajar the glass panel at the back which was raised to slide in the corpse.

Not surprisingly, I was very tired at the end of *Hamlet*, although I had enormously enjoyed the experience of directing it, which had been of real therapeutic help to me. Now approaching sixty, I began to think it might be time for me to retire as Director of the Festival: it had grown into something very important and required a great deal of organisation. My decision was partly influenced by the fact that I had just become Chairman of the British Horse Society and was determined to make a success of it after all that had happened two years earlier, and this again would demand much of my time. There was, however, another factor which influenced me. I had a feeling that some of the company were beginning to query my methods of production. While accepting that they were effective, they believed that they were at the expense of detail. My own feeling was that if one spent too much attention to detail there was a risk, with such a limited time for rehearsal, of not achieving a wholly effective performance. Having had such a wonderful innings lasting over twenty-five years, I decided that I would definitely retire two years later with my fiftieth production. I had no wish whatever to spoil what had been such a happy and harmonious relationship ever since the beginning of the Festival. It seemed only right that others should now be given the opportunity of imposing their influence on the Festival. I was still convinced that the type of audience that Pendley attracted – coach parties of Women's Institutes, Rotary Clubs, youth parties, ordinary people who seldom went to the live theatre – required a straightforward, unsophisticated production which was visually satisfying and not too long. (I seldom cut a play by removing a whole scene, but I pruned it, sometimes even dropping well-known lines, the loss of which was probably resented by the purist, but seldom by the general public.) I was always anxious lest what had happened at Stratford-upon-Avon might happen at Pendley. At Stratford they had built their reputation on straightforward productions acceptable to their tourist audiences; now, in a kind of self-indulgence they seemed to think that their productions must be gimmicky, *avant-garde* or downright provocative, seemingly forgetting that their audiences were still made up of tourists, both from home and from overseas, the latter probably having only a rudimentary knowledge of the language. The number of people from overseas in a Pendley audience is, obviously, very limited, but it is still basically an audience of ordinary people out to be entertained rather than to have their intellects tested. My direction of the Festival had throughout been based on this belief. I appreciated, however, that it could well be that my ideas were now out-dated or at least were ready to be looked at afresh. A change, therefore, seemed desirable.

For my final production I chose *Henry V*, probably Shakespeare's best historical play, with many good parts, some fine language and some of the best comedy scenes in Shakespeare. Being in the open air, it was possible to create a memorable effect with the King wandering amongst his followers huddled round their braziers, the smoke from which drifted eerily across the stage in the breeze. Nature, too, played its part by providing on the final night a wonderful full moon rising behind the trees. I reckoned it to be one of my most successful productions, to be compared with *Twelfth Night* (1957) in a remarkable Japanese-lantern setting designed by Roger Bryson, now a member of the Glyndbourne Opera Company, *Macbeth* (1962), when Birnham Wood really did come to Dunsinane, *The Tempest* with Penny Casdagli as Miranda and Roberta Iger as Ariel, both of whom went on to achieve success professionally, and haunting music from Sibelius's 'Swan of Tuonela', and *Hamlet*. The rightness of my decision to retire was underlined by the success of Andrew Boxer's brilliant production of *The Two Gentlemen of Verona* in 1981. Produced in Edwardian costume as an English country-house party, even including a cricket match and, inevitably, croquet, it was certainly the best comedy ever seen at Pendley and was something that I could never possibly have devised myself.

I was, nevertheless, delighted when to celebrate the 35th anniversary Festival in 1983 I was invited to produce *Romeo and Juliet*. That it was such an outstanding success – 'easily the best production of all those that I have seen since 1954,' wrote one dedicated patron – was entirely due to two factors. The first was that we had an exquisite and very intelligent Juliet in Helen Mackenzie and a very physical and exciting Romeo in Michael Brazier, both of whom will surely go far. Secondly, we were fortunate in recruiting a number of young

men as the supporting Capulets and Montagues any one of whom was
capable of playing Romeo himself. With this talent we were able to
accomplish an interpretation of the play which I had always envisaged
but, although our Juliets and Romeos were invariably outstanding,
had never been able to achieve. If the first half of the play can be lively,
light-hearted and entertaining, then the tragedy of the second half is
going to be that much more effective. And if the young people who
dominate the first part of the play are sufficiently talented, it is possible
through them to develop a real hope that, despite the historic enmity
between the two families, tragedy is not inevitable – though, of
course, in reality the great majority of the audience knows perfectly
well that it is: as a local reviewer was kind enough to say, 'One found
oneself waiting expectantly and in suspense for the dramatic ending,
which is all too well known.' After all, 'three civil brawls,' complains
the Prince, have disturbed the quiet of Verona's streets – but only
three. Capulet himself shows a willingness to let byegones be
byegones by welcoming the young Montagues to his party.
Montague's nephew, Benvolio, is constantly trying to keep the peace,
while his own son, Romeo, even before he meets Juliet, makes it quite
clear that he is anxious to avoid trouble with the Capulets. There is
every likelihood of romantic young love uniting the two families.
Mercutio, related to the Prince himself, only wants everyone to be
happy: indeed he is his fellow students' ringleader, influencing them
with his happy-go-lucky approach to life. For him all strong
emotions are nothing more substantial than dreams. There is no place
for conflict in his philosophy – hence the 'plague on *both* your houses';
everyone can enjoy life together, have fun together, as is demonstrated by the teasing of the nurse, the mocking, but not unkindly, of
Romeo, the gate-crashing of the Capulet's party. True, Capulet's
nephew, Tybalt, is a firebrand, but he can be contained, or so it seems,
with a little goodwill on both sides. Conflict is not inevitable, surely.
Tragically, however, in one mad moment Tybalt goes too far, his
action is inflammatory: conflict *is* inevitable. Within a minute two
young men are dead – and the whole mood of the play is changed.
One quick, isolated incident has affected completely the lives of
everyone concerned. As we know it can. This is something with
which most people in an audience can identify: the sudden change
from the uncomplicated, well-trodden routine to abject horror
brought about by one disastrous moment – a wholly carefree driver
knocking down a pedestrian, with subsequent inquest and, possibly,
prosecution; a cigarette thoughtlessly tossed away and one's home

burnt down; an innocent child disappearing and found murdered. Life can be changed in a split second. In *Romeo and Juliet* it was the result of a stupid quarrel. If this disastrous moment can come as a shock, then the tragedy of the 'star-crossed lovers' can have as great an impact as the sudden traumatic experience in the life of ordinary people.

It was very gratifying as a producer to see this somewhat different interpretation of the play realised. That it was possible was entirely due to the natural, vigorous, infectiously cheerful performances by the young men playing these vital roles. In the first half they swept the play along at enormous speed, and the audience with it. One member of the audience with a number of years' professional experience behind her described it as the 'most moving and energised production' of *Romeo and Juliet* that she had ever seen. Another wrote that 'It was the design of the production that was so superb', by design implying interpretation, for the only scenic design, apart from the façade of the Capulet's house at one corner of the stage, was the superb natural setting.

Interestingly, someone who was present on the only wet night of the Festival wrote: 'In a strange way I had the feeling that the appalling weather, with the rain pouring down and the wind howling, somehow added to the pathos and the passion at the end of the play after its beginning, before the weather really broke, had been so lively.' Words which could never have described an indoor performance! Basil Ashmore, a writer and critic himself and producer of a number of West End successes, after referring in his review to the great challenge of *Romeo and Juliet* 'boldly and successfully tackled', and 'the magnificent area of lawns, trees and avenues used with great skill and taste', then added something which gave me particular pleasure, summing up, as it seemed to me, the natural, realistic production that I had attempted. 'The fact that Dorian Williams is a famous horse-lover would, in itself, have justified the use of a horse in his production: but he not only allowed us to enjoy the sight of a beautiful animal, but it seemed absolutely natural for Romeo to flee into exile on horseback and to rush back to Juliet's tomb in the same way. It so enhanced the excitement without in any way being gimmicky.'

Shakespeare needs no gimmicks. His language, his dramatic instinct, his genius for characterisation are sufficient. My only wish was to utilise the magnificent Pendley settings to the advantage of Shakespeare and to the benefit of those who enjoy his plays. Over the years one of my most rewarding experiences has been the opportunity to interpret some twenty-five of his plays – which is why, perhaps, I have dwelt at length on this less-known aspect of my life.

At the end of the 1983 Festival I felt quite content to allow my reputation as a producer to rest on my production of *Romeo and Juliet*. Thanks to my cast and the setting, I believed it to have been my most effective in over thirty years. The great irony, however, known only to myself and one or two others, was that when at the end of 1982 I was invited to produce *Romeo and Juliet* I had had serious doubts as to whether there would be a Festival at all, for Pendley was enveloped in a desperate crisis. My acceptance, therefore, had been very much a matter of faith – and hope.

Chapter 12

The Battle for Pendley

When I had eventually recovered from my frozen shoulder in February 1981, I decided to take a brief holiday in Malta. On my return I was met at the airport by John Holifield, who was our agent at Pendley and Secretary of our family company, Pierdor. I could tell by the expression on his face that there was some sort of trouble about which he was anxious to tell me, but I had no idea how serious it was. Pendley, it seemed, was encountering a financial crisis more serious than any in its existence. Before I was laid up in October I had regularly held each Monday morning a meeting with senior staff, once a month receiving a financial report. At no time during those first nine months of the year had there been any cause whatever for anxiety: each month had shown us exactly on target. Now, some four months later, it seemed that for the whole year expenditure had exceeded income by a quite frightening amount: probably as much as £70,000. Shades of the British Horse Society only two years earlier – and apparently exactly the same amount involved.

It appeared that our Manager had had personal problems and allowed them to deflect him from his day-to-day duties. To conceal his dereliction he had, for our monthly meetings, produced the budget figures – again as had been the case at Stoneleigh, and again we had accepted them too trustingly. Before my return from Malta he had departed from Pendley, admitting his shortcomings and very contrite, which was of little help to us. When on my arrival at Pendley I had studied the figures and read our accountants' report, I appreciated even more the severity of the situation. We had occasionally made losses at Pendley, but never of this order. On one occasion, in the early years, I had had to persuade the Pendley Estate to bail us out, but that was a matter of £4,000. There was no way the Estate, or Pierdor, could be expected to find £70,000: indeed, it would never occur to me to approach them. But where else could I expect to find the money? I certainly could not provide it personally,

15. My father, Colonel V.D.S., aged 86,
with his Appaloosa stallion, Speckled Hawk.

16. With Jennifer and the dogs – Miss Piggy, Lucky and Piaf – at Foscote.

nor did I believe that I could ever borrow it, only owning my home at Foscote. In any event there was too big a risk that I could never pay it back.

'What, then, do you suggest that we do?' I asked John Holifield.

'I am afraid,' he said, obviously embarrassed and upset at the thought of distressing me, 'I am afraid that there is absolutely no option but for Pendley to go into liquidation. There is no longer the money to pay the wages or the monthly bills.'

'Liquidation!' I repeated. 'Go bankrupt, you mean?'

'If you put it that way, yes.'

'When? How soon?'

'At the end of this week.'

'But that's not possible,' I expostulated.

'I am afraid that it is inevitable,' he replied.

It was also unthinkable. In fact, the whole situation was far more complicated than it appeared on the surface. Before arriving at such a calamitous conclusion, some very hard thinking was demanded.

Our problems really dated back to Britain's entry into the Common Market, which had a quite unforeseen effect on Pendley. Ever since Pendley had first been opened, the domestic staff had consisted of five or six girls from different countries in Europe. To work for us – in fact, they only worked for their board and a few pounds pocket money – they required a work permit, which meant that they could not leave for another job (not that they seemed ever to want to after the first few weeks). Now no longer requiring a work permit they could, if they so wished, leave at a moment's notice: in fact, they need not even turn up, as happened when a girl met a young man on the train from Dover to Victoria and was persuaded to go to a job that he was in a position to recommend. More than that, due to new labour regulations we were not entitled to employ an *au pair* unless we could prove it was impossible to find a suitable girl in Britain who, of course, had to be paid the minimum domestic wage. After a series of excellent housekeepers had been driven to distraction in their attempts to find staff – on one occasion when a weekend course arrived the staff consisted of Mrs Moffatt, our faithful cook for more than twenty years, and one girl from Newcastle! – we decided to engage a reputable firm of outside caterers who, having a pool of labour, were able to ensure that we would never be entirely without staff. This having worked well for two or three years, it seemed a logical step, in 1978, to arrange for this organisation to take over all the domestic administration at

Pendley, leaving only the running of the courses to the resident Pendley staff, a plan which seemed to develop satisfactorily.

This, of course, meant that the defaulter was, in fact, an employee of the caterers and presumably, therefore, their responsibility. If that were so, then was not the loss their responsibility? I suggested this to John Holifield, who pointed out that while this might appear to be the case there was nothing in their contract to the effect that they accepted responsibilities for losses. With his clear thinking he quickly summarised the situation as follows: we could go at once into liquidation, then refuse to pay our debts, the majority of which were in favour of the caterers who had acted as our agents. This could entail their suing us for the money, but the likelihood of their doing so was slender as our defence might well bring their organisation into disrepute. Alternatively we could sue them for negligence and mismanagement; but if we did this we must realise that when a sprat takes on a whale the cost of litigation, even for the winner, is astronomical. As a character in a Frederick Forsyth story says: 'Only the rich can sue the rich.' The other possibility, of course, was to attempt to do a deal with them. Obviously it was the latter that appealed to me. In the first place, while appreciating that it should not be the priority in my thinking, I was well aware that if we either allowed the caterers to sue us for the money or if we sued them for mismanagement then the first casualty would be Pendley. We would have no option but to close, 'at the end of this week', because we had no money either to pay the debt or to continue in operation. A 'deal' must somehow be arranged: but how?

I called an immediate meeting of the Directors of the company that had been created in 1974 and called Pierdor Enterprises Ltd which now, to all intents and purposes, owned Pendley. A typical will (of my great-uncle) had entailed Pendley to the third generation. In other words, everything had to be left intact to my son. To avoid double crippling death duties, both my father and I had, by a rather complicated process, disclaimed the income from the estate, to ensure, ironically, that Pendley survived as the family home. It was on the coming of age of my son that this company was formed to control the capital, a Trust then being set up within the company to look after my son's interests. The result of all this was that it was virtually the Trustees of this Settlement who had the ultimate control of Pendley. Understandably enough, they were reluctant to provide any more money for a scheme which, however successful on paper, had since 1945 cost both the Estate, and indeed myself, a considerable amount of money, either to pay for maintenance and refurbishing or, occasionally, to underwrite the Centre's losses. Only the previous year assets worth £50,000 had been realised to pay for repairing the roof and eliminating dry rot. The company could not be expected to advance any more. They were, however, prepared to support us for a week or two while we attempted to negotiate with the caterers.

A meeting was accordingly set up, by which time the caterers were suggesting that our debt was now in the region of £100,000. Fortunately our relations with the caterers' staff and management had always been excellent, which meant that although there was hard bargaining and indeed tough language, with no holds barred, on both sides, we were able after a series of meetings to persuade the caterers to agree to accept a Colt house, which had been built at Pendley for the Manager and which had recently been valued at approximately £70,000, in lieu of the debt. At the same time they agreed to run Pendley for a two further years, accepting full responsibility for any losses that might, during this time, be incurred. All this, with a certain amount of additional detail, was eventually coordinated in to a heads of agreement to be presented to the Board of Directors. The great advantage in this agreement, as I saw it, was, firstly, that Pendley could continue to operate, at no cost to the Governors, Trustees or anyone. Secondly that we would gain two years' breathing space, within which time we would surely be able to work out a solution which would satisfy everyone and, we hoped, ensure Pendley's survival.

The Directors, however – unfortunately, from my point of view, but understandably from their own – saw it rather differently. They were not happy at the thought of disposing of this valuable little house within the property. Such a proposal impressed neither the legal, financial nor property experts. But what was the alternative? A long meeting ended with no agreement. The three 'family' members of the Board – my wife, my son and myself – with little expert knowledge, were in favour of the plan. The three 'independent' members, all experts, were opposed to it. Was this an occasion when the heart should rule the head? Or should we accept the cautious orthodox advice, knowing that it could only mean the end of Pendley? The stark, basic fact was that either we raised £70,000, by one means or another, or Pendley would be closed. It was as simple as that. It could be thought that had I been less personally involved I might have thought differently, been less determined somehow to save Pendley. I am not sure. I had run Pendley for thirty-five years; I knew its value and example, not just because of its early pioneering days, but because of what it was offering today when, it could be said, that with early retirement and unemployment it was more needed than ever before. Had not Margaret Thatcher when Secretary of State at the Department of Education and Science written to me on the occasion of our thirtieth anniversary: 'I know something of the great variety of work and your extensive and valuable contribution to adult education. It gives me particular satisfaction to know that in your work you have regard to the whole purpose of education, industrial and cultural, for leisure and for work.' It had always been thus, but surely more vital today than ever before. Pendley had still, I believed, a very special contribution to make, from every point of view. I have written earlier of the rewarding comments from people who had attended our courses, but even those who had been employed at Pendley had frequently told me how much Pendley meant to them, often writing many years after they had left to say that they still regarded their time at Pendley as the happiest part of their lives. 'Looking back,' Solveig, a Swedish girl, wrote to me just twenty-five years after she had left, 'I realise that although I was at Pendley only one year, that year was the most important year of my life.' Roully, from Holland, who some years after she had been employed at Pendley used to bring the whole of her class from the college at which she worked at the Hague, once wrote. 'I used to feel part of a big happy family. I wanted my students to experience this feeling. It is something unique and wonderful.' I genuinely believed that such a place as Pendley, with its record, its reputation, its relevance in a modern world, should not be allowed just to disappear.

I still feel a certain guilt at the decision that I finally took. It was uncharacteristic of me, perhaps unethical, but desperate situations always demand desperate actions, and, as I saw it, the situation was indeed desperate. I called another meeting of the Board, reiterated all the arguments both for and against the proposition, then called for a vote. Three in favour, three against. As Chairman I had the casting vote. By my casting vote Pendley was saved – provisionally. We could breathe again. But it was not for very long.

In fact, sale of land which had been used as an overflow for Jennifer's stud, but which being ten miles from Foscote had proved inconvenient, provided the money with which to pay the debt, reduced after further negotiation to £60,000. In due course the caterers agreed to extend their administration at Pendley from two to three years; but this still, unfortunately, and unexpectedly, proved insufficient time to find a satisfactory way of making it viable. Moreover, not altogether surprisingly, in 1982 the Trustees had reached the conclusion that something considerably more than making Pendley viable was now required. While sympathising with my situation and understanding a certain resentment that I harboured, having been passed over, due to the terms of the original will and its entail clauses, they insisted, nevertheless, that as Trustees their prior responsibility must be in favour of the beneficiary, my son. They pointed out that a large amount of capital was tied up in Pendley, but that it was not realising an appropriate income: in fact, it was not only producing no income at all, but maintenance and repairs was causing a steady eroding of the capital. Inevitably, after a lengthy meeting with Piers, my son, the Trustees decided, regretfully, that there really was now no alternative but to sell Pendley. Accordingly they instructed me to arrange with leading London estate agents to put it on the market – immediately.

First, however, I consulted John Wilkinson, our local estate agent, who had for some years handled Pendley affairs. I remembered that a few years earlier he had approached me with a proposition from a leading tobacco company who were looking for a large property for training purposes. In fact, nothing came of it, but I thought John Wilkinson might have another customer up his sleeve. He kindly made a number of enquiries while I contacted all my acquaintances who had influential industrial connections. In the back of my mind I had the idea that we might find some large organisation to take over Pendley as a going concern. Even now I was still reluctant to admit defeat.

Before inviting a major estate agent to market Pendley, glossy brochure and all, we decided, with the agreement of the Trustees, to have an advertisement inserted in *The Times* and the *Financial Times* in the hope that it might arouse interest, even attract a sponsor prepared to put up between £50,000 and £100,000 *per annum* – not a fortune in the context of international commerce and industry. It did not mention Pendley by name, though anyone living locally would have little difficulty in identifying it from the description: 'Conference Centre of National Repute and Architectural Distinction; overlooking superb parkland and amidst woodland and grounds' – and so on. To our delight it produced some twenty requests for particulars, seven of which pursued the matter further. Meanwhile,

John Wilkinson had been approached by someone who had, oddly enough, taken part on several occasions in the Pendley Shakespeare Festival and was now a senior representative of a well-known multinational company. Although when John had originally contacted him he had shown no interest, now, after further reflection, he had come to believe that Pendley might be exactly what his company was looking for. Talks, visits, fairly detailed discussions were soon taking place. Twice we were informed that a firm decision would be taken the following week, giving us the impression that there was every chance that a deal would be concluded. It seemed too good to be true. However, we were, sadly, to be disappointed. While the company was extremely interested, we were informed, it felt unable to reach a decision until 1983 at the earliest, by which time, of course, we were hopeful that all would have been settled with one of the other interested parties. The representative of an even better known multinational company, for instance, told us that he had looked at at least thirty properties, but that Pendley was 'far and away the most suitable'. More talks, visits, detailed discussions, but with exactly the same outcome: they were extremely interested but could not make a decision until 1983 or even 1984. One was tempted to wonder whether some of the world's industrial problems might not be due to the fact that managements seemed unable to reach major decisions in under a year.

We turned to some of the other organisations that had answered our advertisement, embarking upon exploratory talks with three or four of them: for one the price either to lease or to buy was too high; for another the distance from their offices and headquarters in Essex was a little too great. At one stage we felt that we were near achieving an agreement with an organisation that provided comprehensive, factual and useful information for companies considering opening up trade relations overseas. After a number of visits, each one more positive than the last, there was a sudden silence, which was never broken. That left us with just one other organisation that had shown serious interest: a world-wide religious body which was looking for an estate where they could open a mini-university. As it would be essential for them greatly to increase the accommodation, planning permission would be required, Pendley being in the green belt. An informal approach was made to the authorities, from whom we understood that an application would be considered sympathetically so long as it was connected with education. Eventually, however, the prospective purchasers decided that to buy Pendley and then to build accommodation for 150 students would stretch their resources too far. They withdrew. One private individual had, at some time during all these negotiations, made an offer for the whole estate with the intention of living there himself, but his offer was very much less than half what we were asking.

While, surprisingly, few people seemed to have been alerted by the advertisement, a 'leak' from the planning committee virtually spelt out our intentions. Local papers carried banner headlines and reports to the effect that Pendley was for sale, which was exactly what we had hoped would not happen. If it was once suggested that Pendley was closing, then obviously we would lose much of our business. A rumour that Pendley was for sale would very quickly become a fact; it would be all over the country; to all intents and purposes Pendley, as a Centre of Adult Education, would be finished. Firm denials had to be issued, though one felt that most people who read them would be suspecting that there was no smoke without fire. I was annoyed about all this at the time, though ultimately it turned out that it might have proved to have been more of a help than a hindrance. Meanwhile, the Trustees, understandably enough again, felt that I had been dragging my heels long enough which, of course, I could not deny. My only excuse was that I sincerely feared that were we to close down Pendley and, having offered it for sale had no immediate response, it would quickly deteriorate. As things were, it was inhabited and well maintained. Lived in, its value must be enhanced, especially as an institution which, we believed, was its only possible use. Empty, its value could only diminish. I had to admit, however, that, almost subconsciously, I was delaying putting Pendley on the market, so sure was I that, given time, an organisation would be found to take it over as a going concern. Some such organisation must surely exist: but where? If only we could hang on long enough, I felt sure that we could find a solution: or so I hoped and prayed, but pious hopes do not greatly impress professional people. Pendley, I was told, must definitely be advertised for sale – at once.

By chance, just at this moment when I was attempting to come to terms with the almost inevitable closure of Pendley, I was invited to address an All-Party Committee on Further Education at the House of Commons. Naturally, I accepted with alacrity, hoping that this might possibly lead to help from the Department of Education and Science. At the meeting, held in one of the many committee rooms, I spoke factually and with what I felt to be a permissible amount of passion, but with little fluency: every ten minutes or so my talk was interrupted by a division bell and my small, select audience dashed off to vote, returning a few moments later, usually one or two fewer. I outlined the history of residential short-term courses since the founding of Pendley in 1945. I divulged, with statistical support, the approximate cost to local authorities – peanuts compared with the expenditure on any other form of education. I tried to convince the committee, which made an attentive and appreciative audience, of the value of such education: I quoted part of Mrs Thatcher's letter to me about my 'valuable contribution to adult education'. I was able also to quote from a recent letter in the *Daily Telegraph* which commenced by stating, 'Our weekend courses are the envy of the world' – though, sadly, it did not mention the fact that Pendley was the pioneer. The article concluded by suggesting that it was impossible to calculate the value provided for ordinary people, especially in these times of increased leisure, by the short-term residential colleges. As a result of my talk, the committee's chairman, Frank Haynes, a charming and genuine Labour Member of Parliament for Ashfield and a Whip, arranged for a small group including Jack Dornand, Chairman of the Labour Parliamentary Party, and Harry Greenway, himself a teacher by profession and Conservative MP for Ealing North, to visit Pendley. This they did a month later, but although they were obviously impressed and sympathetic – 'Your marvellous record at Pendley speaks for itself' Harry Greenway wrote after their visit – their efforts to interest the Department of Education were unsuccessful. There was no option but to proceed with the sale of Pendley.

The proofs of the brochure arrived, and with them a sense of finality. It was defeat at last and very sad. The sale of Pendley would not only mean the end of a scheme that I had started with such enthusiasm and faith nearly forty years earlier, it would also mean the end of the connection between Pendley and my family that had commenced in 1835. This was no sentimental platitude. It was a fact: surely a little sentiment was permissible.

By a curious coincidence exactly two years to a day since John Holifield had so shocked me with the news of the defection of our Manager at Pendley, from which all the subsequent problems stemmed, John Wilkinson, our agent, received a telephone call from someone representing a local organisation which, having heard a rumour that Pendley was for sale, wanted to know more about it. Could there possibly be an eleventh-hour rescue? John Wilkinson told them briefly about the situation and suggested a meeting. He was sufficiently impressed by his first contact with the principals of this local organisation to arrange an immediate meeting at Pendley. John Holifield and I were no less impressed and immediately began to talk business. Grass Roots, as this firm was called, specialised in organising and running training courses, assessing the potential of employees for promotion, promoting new products: to use their own phrase, 'motivation solutions to business problems'. Having expanded very quickly, they were looking for a place where all their activities could be coordinated. With their local connections, Pendley seemed ideal. Equally, their approach and their requirements suggested that they might be ideal as far as Pendley was concerned. David Evans, their Managing Director, was the kind of go-ahead, enthusiastic type of man who immediately appeals to me, one of the new generation of thrusting executives, single-minded, a little ruthless, and although he was the antithesis to myself, I felt that I could speak frankly to him, thus avoiding much of the shadow-boxing that can so delay negotiations. From the beginning I put him honestly in the picture. The Trustees of the Estate were responsible for the administration of a large capital sum tied up in Pendley. It was their duty to ensure that it generated the proper amount of income. The Estate had either to be sold, therefore, and the purchase money invested, or, alternatively, it could be leased, so long as the rent produced an equivalent income. They were looking for 10 per cent on the capital.

David Evans now knew exactly where he stood: there could virtually be no bargaining, only adjustments or variations. The property could be bought at the price demanded by the Trustees or it could be leased at a figure which amounted to 10 per cent of the purchase price. The Trustees would thus be satisfied in that either way they would now be receiving the amount of income that they believed the Estate should generate.

No time was wasted, thanks to the efforts of John Holifield, John Wilkinson, Nigel Freeth, the Grass Roots' surveyor, and Chris Matthews, their Company Secretary, in exploring the possible lines of development. In less than two months we had hammered out provisional heads of agreement which seemed mutually satisfactory. Grass Roots would lease Pendley for three years, at the agreed rent. At the end of three years they would have the option either to purchase at the prevailing valuation or to extend the lease for a further twenty years. Immediately they were in possession they would carry out extensive improvements and modernisation in the interior. After three years they would be responsible for all maintenance inside and out. They would continue the best of the existing Pendley courses and, most important of all from my point of view, the Shakespeare Festival. It seemed almost too good to be true. At the earliest possible moment I called a meeting of the Trustees and Board of Directors. Confidently, even proudly, I produced copies of the heads of agreement which John Holifield passed round the table, allowing them a few minutes to read and digest the paper. In that few minutes I felt my confidence evaporate: somehow the atmosphere – or was it the expression on their faces? – told me that for some reason they were not as impressed as I was.

I was right. Their reaction was cautious, even suspicious. Did we really think that today 10 per cent was enough? How much did we know about Grass Roots? Should we not be able to exploit such an Estate more effectively? I suggested that, unless one was prepared to speculate, 10 per cent could surely be considered a very satisfactory return, particularly in view of the fact that one was retaining the capital. Our accountant had checked on Grass Roots' bona-fides; their record gave no cause for concern. But when it came to their third point I realised that we had serious opposition. The Trustees, one of whom had a property company, had seen the possibilities of a big development at Pendley. He had even gone so far as to produce an illustrated and comprehensively explanatory brochure. This carried a proposition that the Manor House could be the nucleus of a modern training centre with a number of two- or three-storey extensions to be used for accommodation and offices. In addition, there would be dining and administrative blocks, in all nearly 200,000 square feet. It was estimated that the cost would be approximately £8 million, to be raised by a finance house or development company, or possibly raised by private borrowing, at 12½ per cent. Provisional figures suggested that the value of the new complex would be £10 million, leaving a profit of £2 million. Total rent could amount to £700,000 p.a. Additional usage and activities, with interest on capital, could increase this to £1 million.

I was quite stunned. I just had not envisaged a scheme on such an enormous scale. I could not but be impressed, but surely it was too ambitious: and how long would it take to develop? Planning permission would be required: but would it be forthcoming? Could such a scheme, even if it were entitled International Training Centre, as proposed, really be regarded as educational? Borrowing at that level, what would happen if the scheme failed? Was it not a highly speculative gamble? I could see, of course, that the end situation might indeed be highly profitable: but when?

It was all just too large for someone like myself who had had no experience of commerce, property, big dealing, to comprehend. I felt quite lost. I suggested that perhaps, as we had not been prepared for such an ambitious project, we could have time to consider it; meanwhile, they might like further to peruse the heads of agreement that we had worked out with Grass Roots who, I could not help feeling, might well think that we had let them down if having gone so far we now switched to something entirely different, though we had always warned them that the Trustees would insist on the most advantageous deal.

The more I thought about this huge plan, the more frightened I became. I could understand a company with limitless resources proceeding with such a scheme. I could understand, therefore, the Trustees taking the line that if big profits were there for the picking, why should they be allowed to benefit someone else? Why should not the family be the ones to gain? But for me, cautious by nature when it comes to finance, and never a gambler, it seemed dauntingly speculative: to raise £8 million – the mind boggled! Surely the Grass Roots scheme was much safer: indeed, virtually risk-free. If the worst happened and they failed, we still had Pendley – indeed, an improved Pendley: we had lost nothing. If at the end of three years they neither took up their option to buy nor extended the lease, the Estate was that much better off, having received 10 per cent of the capital value three years running and, again, still possessing Pendley. To my simple mind it seemed to be a case of the bird in the hand compared with pie in the sky. It was not, however, for me to make the decision: in the last resort it was the Trustees who decided, and I was not even a Trustee. This I accepted, but felt nevertheless that I was entitled to set down my personal feelings on the matter, which, after very careful consideration and discussion with the two Johns, Holifield and Wilkinson, I did. To my great relief their reaction – generous and wise, I believe – was that their own plan should be shelved while the Grass Roots scheme was more fully investigated, which meant, amongst other things, having an independent assessment of their offer, as set out in the heads of agreement, by a leading London estate agent. This being satisfactory, negotiations proceeded all through the summer with the production of schedules, surveyors' reports, draft contracts and endless meetings at all levels. Though by now I had learned to take nothing for granted, constantly reminding myself not to count my chickens until they were hatched, it did seem to me as June became July, and I entered my seventieth year, that I was entitled to a certain cautious optimism. But as the weeks crept by with more delays and further argument I felt as though the agreement would never be finalised. Finally, however, in the last week of August, typically – or symbolically? – when I was in the midst of the *Romeo and Juliet* rehearsals, a meeting was arranged at Pendley between all parties for the final problems to be ironed out: it was one of those locked doors, a plentiful supply of black coffee and no leaving the table until everything is settled meetings. Three hours sufficed; a brief adjournment for the two parties to have separate discussions, final agreement and, at last, a drink – before hurrying back to my rehearsals. 'They stumble that run fast,' says Friar Lawrence in *Romeo and Juliet*. To me it seemed as though our negotiations had been anything but fast, despite which there had been many stumbles; but I suppose that for such a deal nine months is not excessive.

It still took another six weeks for the solicitors to produce the final agreement for the Pierdor Directors' ratification – and signing. As soon as this was ready – in the middle of the Horse of the Year Show! Typical again? – a meeting was convened at Wembley and the document was signed, the exchanging taking place at Pendley a few days later. It was, however, the Annexe to the main agreement that understandably afforded me the greatest pleasure. This affirmed that Grass Roots undertook to continue the 'weekend liberal studies courses traditionally associated with Pendley'; further, to continue the Pendley Shakespeare Festival for a period of ten years 'subject to the interest and desire of those associated with the event'. As there had never been any evidence of a decline in the interest or desire of those associated, could one possibly ask for more? David Evans insisted moreover, that I should continue to be involved and 'very much to the fore in our artistic, creative and social activities'.

The battle for Pendley was won.

Four months earlier a lawyer friend had written to another friend of mine: 'I hear that Dorian is locked in a fight to the death with his Trustees over the fate of Pendley. I make Dorian a certain winner since under the cloak of apparent helplessness he is as good an infighter as a mongoose with a snake.' Apart from certain inaccuracies in his interpretation of the situation, I did not look at the situation in that light at all. I accepted absolutely the logic of the

Trustees in wanting to realise a valuable asset that was producing no income, while I hoped, if it were possible, to preserve the work that for so long had been carried on at Pendley. This had been achieved.

Perhaps I only fully appreciated what we had done when the moment came for me to leave the rooms which had been mine for so long: indeed, before I married in 1956 I had actually lived in them, though now they were my office and dressing room. The office being the most attractive room in the house it was, not surprisingly, required as Grass Roots' board room – and required immediately. Turning out those rooms after so many years, coming across photographs, cuttings, books, letters, was like having my life spread out before me in some great scrap book. But if, of necessity, all that had happened had resulted in my saying goodbye to a way of life that had spanned almost forty years, at least Pendley had survived its many vicissitudes, and in so doing had more than justified its existence.

Chapter 13

Half-a-Has-Been

In three short years, in my sixties, I had relinquished my responsibilities in the four activities that had most dominated the last thirty years of my life: Pendley, the British Horse Society, the BBC and the Whaddon Chase Hunt. It did not, however, noticeably affect my lifestyle. I have always believed that it is far better to retire early rather than late. If one stays too long, people are thankful to be rid of you and happy to forget you, whereas if you go when you are still of some use then those concerned usually find interesting and often rewarding roles for you still to occupy. This has certainly been my own experience. As Honorary President of Pendley I am still loosely involved in the cultural activities there, in particular the Shakespeare Festival. As Past President of the British Horse Society, and a coopted member of the Council, I am still associated with the Society's development and expansion, in addition to carrying out a certain amount of what one might call public relations work. As President of the Hunt I am sufficiently in touch still to feel a part of the Hunt, especially the political side, as it were, attending committee meetings, helping in appointments, generally being an elder statesman. Though I no longer commentate on television, I still broadcast occasionally both on radio and television, and am now free, of course, to work for either channel. In addition to all this, my responsibilities as Chairman both of the Royal International Horse Show and the Olympia International are by no means negligible, the former offering a real challenge, the latter demanding a certain amount of diplomacy. I am a regular speaker for Foyles Lecture Agency and Associated Speakers and continue to be invited to speak on numerous social occasions, not all of them by any means confined, I am thankful to say, to equestrian activities. Recently I was invited to stand in at short notice for Eric Sykes at the Men of the Year Lunch, the other speaker being Lord Tonypandy, one of the warmest and wittiest speakers – pardon the pun – whom one could wish to listen to: in fact, it turned out to be an enjoyable experience, especially after I had sat down. I am still Chairman of Hawtreys, in which I take the closest interest, while as President of the Pendley Sports Centre I like to keep abreast of the various developments there. I take conscientiously my responsibility as a Court member of the Worshipful Company of Farriers, of which I was Master in 1977. I also follow keenly the activities of the Milton Keynes Amateur Operatic Society, of which I have been President for nearly twenty years. Finally, I find extremely interesting the discussions of the working party on training qualifications for working with horses, a body set up under the Department of Education and Science by the National Consultative Group for the Consideration of Validation Arrangements in Agriculture and Related Subjects, of which in 1983 I was appointed Chairman. (The titles they think up in the Civil Service!) This committee interestingly and for the first time represents the whole spectrum of the horse world.

And, of course, there is still my hunting. I am out cubhunting as often as possible, mounted or on foot, on those beautiful early autumn mornings in September. The woodlands are as fascinating to me as ever: the thrill of seeing a cub stealthily crossing a ride, caring not a damn for the hounds that it hears behind it crashing through the undergrowth, is still indefinably and indescribably exciting. When the season proper starts at the end of October or beginning of November, I usually hunt two days a week. Feeling a little frailer now, thanks to the interferences of one sort or another that my body has experienced, I do not, as a rule, stay out to the end. Nor do I ride quite as hard as I used to, unless by some stroke of luck I find myself on my own or with only a handful of riders, when for a few minutes it seems just like the old days. I have to confess that being now just an ordinary member of the field – which can number a hundred and more – I do not always relish the apparent determination of everyone to be first through a gate or over a tiger trap or hunt jump. Whether, if I were still privileged to ride in front as Master, I would enjoy it more I cannot honestly say. I rather doubt it. David Barker, who now hunts the Whaddon Chase hounds, is fearless, frequently jumping what appear to me singularly uninviting obstacles, particularly iron gates, of which two or three a day are more than enough for me. I am thankful that I am not now obliged always to follow him. I am more than content to ride a little independently, trying always to keep hounds in sight, or within earshot, often with Albert Buckle, my old Huntsman and friend. Occasionally, if there is a good scent and hounds are really racing, the adrenalin starts running and I find myself trying just as hard as ever to keep in front. Whatever the situation, I am happy to be out there, on a good horse, watching the hounds, enjoying the company of my friends and the opportunity to appreciate the sights and sounds of the winter countryside. I shall continue to do so for as long as I still enjoy it, and am fit enough.

It is as well, perhaps, that writing is something from which one need never retire – Dr Margaret Murray wrote two books at the age of ninety-nine! – for I have probably derived as much pleasure from writing as from any of my other activities. It is surely an indication of how well occupied I am that I still do most of my writing between 6.00 a.m. and 8.00 a.m., when there are few interruptions or distractions, only correcting my work in the evenings. If ever I want to escape for a few days to do some really concentrated writing, then I am fortunate in being able to fly down to the Dordogne in south-west France where our great friends Igor Nares, who before his retirement hunted for some thirty years with the Whaddon Chase, and Lolita, his wife, now live. We often think of them as a mini United Nations. Igor is Russian-born, Lolita is Spanish, Peter, their son, is married to a Peruvian and Sonia, their daughter, to a German. Their home, Laroque, is so beautiful, so peaceful, and they are such stimulating and understanding hosts that it provides the ideal retreat. Fortunately, but not perhaps remarkably, I am almost invariably lucky with the weather. As I frequently tell them, if one cannot find inspiration at Laroque then one could not find it anywhere. It is possible to follow there the routine that I have always imagined one should be able to indulge in as a professional writer: two or three hours of uninterrupted work in the morning, a walk through one of the beautiful valleys in the afternoon, an hour's correcting in the evening, all accompanied by first-class food, wine and friendship. I have never been able to stay at Laroque for more than four or five days, but in that brief period I am often able to achieve more than I can in a month at home. Obviously the pressures in my life are less than they were ten yeas ago, but at three score years and ten I feel anything but a has-been – hardly half-a-has-been, though I fully accept the fact that this is probably how the majority of people now think of me, especially those who for so many years used to listen to my commentating on all the major equestrian events. If a has-been can still be as fully occupied as I am, then I am not complaining.

Attending a Hunt Dinner in the Midlands recently, I was amused when the Chairman, introducing me, told how he had had to admit to a friend that he had no idea what to say as, not being horsey, he really knew very little about me. 'But that's easy,' said his friend. 'Just ring up *Horse and Hound*: they're bound to have his obituary in their files.' Unfortunately the Chairman feared that to do so might be considered bad taste, so instead he borrowed a copy of *Master of One*. I was quite disappointed. Not many people are fortunate enough to learn in advance what will appear in their obituary notice!

I was amused too – though some people, to my surprise, were shocked – when a Chairman at another dinner introduced me as 'the poor man's celebrity'! It seemed to sum me up fairly accurately. I could never be regarded, in television for instance, in the same category as a David Coleman or a Frank Bough, or even specialists such as Peter O'Sullevan or John Oaksey. In the world of education my name is totally unknown compared with that of A.S. Neill, pioneer of the 'free', 'no inhibitions' method, or centenarian Bradley, founder of Bedales, the first co-educational school. In hunting circles I was always small fry, even in my own time, compared with the great 'hound' men, the late Duke of Beaufort, Sir Peter Farquhar, Captain Ronnie Wallace, Captain Charlie Barclay, or amongst the younger generation Captain Brian Fanshawe or Captain Ian Farquhar, Sir Peter's son. My only claim to fame was, perhaps, my record partnership of twenty-six years as Master and Huntsman with Albert Buckle, which could suggest a certain administrative ability. I presided over a good team, which provided consistent sport.

Truth to tell, I have to confess that I am better suited temperamentally to a less then 100 per cent involvement in any of the interests which have principally occupied me during my adult life. I would never have wished to hunt five days a week, let alone six. Even if the BBC had decided fully to exploit me, as they did David Coleman in the sixties or more recently Terry Wogan, I would never have enjoyed being a full-blown television personality. I was more than happy just to have a recognisable voice and to do my job in an adequately professional manner. As far as education is concerned, I had, in fact, abandoned the stereotyped three twelve-week terms of a prep school, with its more or less stabilised routine, for the much more varied and variable adult education, but I doubt if I could ever have committed myself totally to adult education had the type of education that I had pioneered in 1945 become wholly acceptable as a vital part of our education system, as the Peoples' Colleges had in

Scandinavia. I always preferred experimenting, throwing up ideas for others to develop rather than to be totally involved and responsible myself. Similarly, I was happier producing plays and pageants as a part-time hobby than being associated full time with the professional theatre and its attendant hassle and insecurity. I have been fortunate in that I have throughout my adult life been able to earn sufficient from one source or another to enable me to enjoy what to many must seem a somewhat dilettante life. My being an energetic and fairly well-organised person has, of course, helped.

One advantage of such a way of life is that it is never too great a wrench giving up something, as must be the case if all one's eggs are in one basket. Obviously with one's interests so diffuse, one's 'image' is diluted, but as far as one's private life is concerned, that may well be an advantage. One need never become public property. Not surprisingly, people who are aware of only one side of my life frequently ask me what on earth I do with myself now that I have retired. Usually it is too complicated to explain that my life is not all that different because of all my other interests. Probably in the limited world of the horse my name is not much less well-known than ever it was, but it *is* a limited world and therefore 'poor-man's celebrity' seems a not inappropriate description. I sometimes feel, moreover, that this reflects my social standing. My family was fortunate enough to be born into a background of considerable privilege, but it was very far from being part of the old English aristocracy. I like to think, however, that we more or less epitomise an English country family, aware of our responsibilities, never taking our position for granted, active in local affairs. I personally would get little satisfaction as no more than a comfortably well-off country squire with nothing to do but manage his modest estate. Everyone, I feel, should have a positive occupation – possibly two or three; which I suppose sounds a somewhat adaptable philosophy.

I have frequently been asked why, having lived almost all my life in the same part of the world and having proved that I am capable of expressing myself fairly adequately and fluently in public – which is often what initially wins votes – I have never considered standing for Parliament. Nothing could ever have been further from my thoughts. To begin with, being by nature uncommitted I would find it difficult to toe a party line or support an issue with which I was not in complete sympathy. Secondly, being a not very political person I fear that I would soon become bored with politics, even with attending debates in the House, except on the big occasion when, obviously, one would be aware of the privilege of having a front-row seat at the unfolding of history. I have always imagined, however, that the level of debate in the Upper House would be far more to my liking than the party-biassed cut and thrust of the Commons, with its over-emphasis and plentiful supply of moral indignation.

Only on one political matter do I feel strongly, worrying about it increasingly. On 26 July 1945, at the time of the election of the first post-war Labour government – there was a delay of three weeks after the election on 5 July to enable the service votes to be collected and counted – I wrote in my diary: 'Nothing will ever be quite the same again. I am sure that the policies of these people will encourage a lowering of standards and a steady infiltration of fifth columnists' – a war-time expression – 'the opportunities were seized, during the last year or two of the war, in factories and through the TUC organisations, to propagate a specious "lefty" doctrine that obviously appeared very attractive to the electorate, especially the services, after four years of war.' I doubt, however, if at that time I appreciated how serious it would become. Why, over the last two decades, do both Labour and Conservative governments appear to have ignored the extreme left-wing infiltration into all sections of the community, especially the unions? Perhaps they have been more alert than we appreciate, but it is difficult to believe so. In the late seventies I even wrote to my then MP, Labour Robin Corbett, begging him to use his influence to prevent the Labour Party 'leaving on the table' their National Agent Underhill's report on Trotskyist infiltration, which had been contemptuously dismissed as 'reds under the bed' nonsense. Eventually having been created a Life Peer, in 1980, Lord Underhill published the report himself – and alarming reading it made. My fear has always been that in time extremists will have so ingratiated themselves into positions of influence that we will suddenly wake up to find that the vital qualities of tradition, order and discipline, on which a stable society depends, have been totally eroded. It is then, surely, that there could be the real threat of a dictatorship, either from left or right. We have seen it happen elsewhere. Might it not happen here? Have not developments in education over the last few years made it easier to happen here? Over sixty years ago, Lenin in his writings spelt out exactly how Communism was going to dominate the world. General Sejna, Chief of Staff in the Czech Defence Ministry, who defected in 1968, reveals in his book, *We Will Bury You*, the extent to which militant

left-wing penetration of British trade unions is an integral part of
Moscow's long-term plan for Communism to take over the West:
the first step, he explains, is to make the trade unions so strong that
they become accepted as part of government. Trade union influence,
dominated by Communists, is ultimately to be as influential as any
political party. Eventually it will achieve complete control. Perhaps
this is an exaggerated exposition of the situation. Who is to say? But
we cannot pretend that we have not been warned. Even while
enjoying the lifestyle of a modern, sophisticated, industrial society, it
is not impossible to envisage a change so sudden, so complete, that,
to quote from my diary written nearly forty years ago, nothing
would ever be quite the same again.

As a boy and a young man I used to get very impatient when my
father appeared as a prophet of gloom, bewailing first the certainty of
a financial crisis in the thirties, then foreseeing the imminence of war.
I just did not want to know. Years later I used to resent it when, as an
old man, he would say that he would not, thank Heaven, be alive to
witness the terrible results arising from the permissive society or the
development of nuclear weapons. It was, I would tell him, an
ostrich-like, head-in-the-sand attitude. 'You wait,' he would reply,
'you'll be just the same.' And sure enough I do frequently find
myself tempted to take exactly the same attitude.

But only tempted, I hope, because I know that I have no right
whatever to do so. At the very beginning of this book I asserted that
I did not really feel any different from the boy that I was sixty years
ago. How then, despite my reaching three score years and ten, can I
admit to feeling an old man? The fact of the matter is that I do not,
because one is only as old as one feels. Recently re-reading Diana
Cooper's autobiography I came across two passages which astonished me. The first was an extract from Duff Cooper's diary: 'She
hates old age and fears death. She is distressed that she cannot do
everything that she used to. She fights old age by taking greater pains
to preserve her beauty.' She was fifty-six! The second was a
comment by Diana Cooper on Duff: 'The fact that he so obviously
welcomed old age did much to soothe him. He was entirely without
regret at lost consequences, enjoying his writing, relishing his
liberty, a model of elderly contentment . . . though he would often
lose track of general conversation and then join in with an
irrelevance: but Duff did not seem to care a scrap.' He was sixty!

Lady Diana, of course, sailed into her nineties: Duff never reached
seventy. So there it is! The joy of life, surely, is, like hunting, its total

unpredictability. General Hackett, Commander-in-Chief of the British Army on the Rhine from 1966 to 1968, later Principal of King's College, London, once wrote: 'After you've reached three score years and ten officially you've had your lot and every day after that is one free to be used and enjoyed to the full. Retirement doesn't exist, there is only a withdrawal to a flank and regrouping in some other direction.' I am fortunate, of course, in that I can always 'withdraw' to Foscote Manor, the lovely Cotswold-type manor house near Buckingham which we bought in 1963. It was built in the twelfth century and originally lived in by the de la Haye family, who were succeeded for a short time by the Purefoys, a family with which we were friendly as children and who still live in the neighbourhood. The present house was built in 1656 by Earl Grenville, a kinsman of the Duke of Buckingham who lived, of course, at nearby Stowe. It had been valued at that time at 33 shillings 4d, a large part of the manor 'alienated to certain persons' – whatever that might imply. In 1557, a hundred years earlier, it had been valued at £13 5s. Much, inevitably, has been changed since then, but the original front and hall remain, and the magnificent staircase, though according to William Page's *History of the County of Buckinghamshire* this apparently has been moved from its original position. The twelfth-century church at the foot of the drive is now used as a house, cleverly converted by an architect, Patrick Lorimer, who specialises in making redundant churches into dwelling houses. The fine east window and priest's staircase have been retained and it is doubtless worth very much more today than the £10 at which it was valued in 1535.

Sometimes looking up at Foscote as I turn in the drive by the side of the church, after exercising a horse, or walking the dogs, I am overwhelmed with that sense of contentment that only beauty can produce. It does not matter whether it is the glowing colours of autumn; or the freshness of spring and early summer with the daffodils, the smell of new-mown grass, the cowslips in the paddock, and the foals; or even the solemn stillness of winter, Foscote is still beautiful, even in the snow. We love it. Particularly I love our little lake round which, when time allows, I like to stroll once or twice a week with the dogs. In the summer there are the Canada geese. Whether they are the same pairs each year or not I do not know, but their behaviour never varies. We are first aware of their presence in March, six or eight of them. After a lot of honking and mating-play, two are left in residence. Almost immediately one disappears, the other stalking around or swimming up and down, never very far from the little island where the female is hatching her eggs. Suddenly in May the female reappears, proudly leading six little yellow balls across the lake and back. After a few days they venture up into the park, pecking happily away at the grass, while the old gander never neglects his role of watchdog and lookout, seldom lowering his own long neck, rather stretching it up, turning his head sharply from side to side, constantly watchful: an exemplary parent. Occasionally they have visitors – last year's family? – who are treated with considerable suspicion though, it would appear, appropriate courtesy. By mid-July, when the young ones are already fully grown, the whole family disappears, leaving us deprived and looking forward to the following March.

Occasionally a kingfisher flashes down the lake. More frequently a great heron, sometimes a pair, stand sentinel at the edge of the water, quickly launching themselves into the air, furtive as ever at the sight of a human, and winging away in their laboured, cumbersome flight to the reservoir or down to the gravel pits at Hyde Lane. We had hopes once that they might breed, but so far they never have. A heronry down at the lake would be exciting, though the anglers might not think so. Not infrequently when the hounds come to Foscote they put up a fox in the undergrowth surrounding the lake, but all too rarely do we see one. Mallard, of course, and other water birds are on the lake constantly. Long ago a local doctor used to have a hide there, reputedly seeing many interesting and unusual birds that had strayed presumably from the nearby nature reserve. How often I have wished that I had so organised my life that I had found time to study ornithology or become a naturalist. However, down at the lake, while enjoying the peace and beauty and observing the wildlife, I can at least think and plan and reflect, even ponder on my faith and beliefs, which I know to be inadequate. Complete faith has so far eluded me, though I believe in some power greater than man, but listening to music or hearing the English language perfectly spoken, or in the beauty of the countryside, indeed down at the lake or riding round the quiet, undisturbed roads of north Buckinghamshire, I have often felt near to understanding. I hope there is still time, as I like to think that my mind is far from closed. Unless, however, one has been fortunate enough to experience some dramatic conversion, like St Paul, religion is too personal a matter, too complex a subject, for an autobiography. Not that I regard these reminiscences as such; which is as well, perhaps, for reviewing

J.P.W. Mallalieu's autobiography, *Larkhill*, in the *Sunday Telegraph*, Christopher Booker wrote: 'How often do you hear anyone say "I like a good biography?" How many people can one think of whose reputations have actually been enhanced by writing an autobiography?' Fortunately he finished his review by reflecting that 'the best sort of autobiographical books are by those who have never been tempted to think of themselves as very important in the first place'. My conscience is clear. I have no delusions of grandeur: indeed, I am more than content to accept myself as totally unimportant compared with those who hob-nob with the great and are involved in the making of history. My hope, nevertheless, is that there are still people who are also interested in the experiences and adventures of more ordinary mortals: I hope, too, that it will have become clear, reading between the lines, that despite the various problems which inevitably 'flesh is heir to', I have enjoyed a happy, satisfying and in many ways rewarding life. This, of course, is due to the support, friendship and love of Jennifer and my family, which includes my in-laws, to such as John Holifield, my help at Pendley, Albert Buckle, my partner in the Whaddon Chase, Wendy Anglis, my secretary, who came to us straight from school in 1960, and to many others whose names have appeared in these reminiscences. It is appropriate that Shakespeare should have the last word:

> I count myself in nothing else so happy
> As in a soul remembering my good friends.

Index